CRIME AT WORK:

INCREASING THE RISK
FOR OFFENDERS

Volume II

Edited by

Martin Gill

Perpetuity Press

First Published 1998
by Perpetuity Press Ltd
PO Box 376 Leicester LE2 3ZZ
Telephone: +44 (0) 116 270 4186
Fax: +44 (0) 116 270 7742
Email: info@perpetuitypress.co.uk
Website: http://www.perpetuitypress.co.uk/securitybooks/

British Library Cataloguing in Publication Data.
A catalogue record for this book is available from the British Library.

ISBN 1 899287 51 5

Perpetuity Press

Contents

Foreword

We take great pleasure in being associated with this second volume of *Crime at Work*. Dr Martin Gill is to be congratulated in bringing together such a distinguished group of authors who have produced what we at Reliance consider to be a unique work of practical value and relevance in countering the threats faced by businesses today. This second volume builds impressively on the pioneering of the earlier work and provides a unique and original body of knowledge on some areas of crime which have been shrouded in darkness.

Business Crime is poorly researched and there is an understandable reluctance for individual businesses to publicise their losses, yet crime against businesses costs well over £5 billion a year and some estimates put it at over £10 billion - equivalent to 6p on everyone's income tax or more than a quarter of the budget of the Health Service. A recent survey in the Midlands from the leading crime prevention charity Crime Concern showed 75% of businesses surveyed had experienced crime in the year under review. It showed the risks are much higher for businesses than for individuals or their households. Crime can affect the very survival of business, whether through a single act such as product contamination in the food or drugs industry, or through an accumulation of smaller thefts, frauds and acts of criminal damage.

The latest volume is published at what may prove to be an historic moment. The new Crime and Disorder Act makes a profound change in government strategy towards crime. The partnership approach envisaged which broadens responsibility for combating crime promises to give life to a powerful new era of partnership between all those in our society who can make life for criminals less tenable. Martin Gill in his subtitle for this volume, 'increasing the risk for offenders', surely exhibits great prescience.

Ken Allison
Managing Director
Reliance Security Services Ltd

5

Acknowledgements

I am grateful to a wide range of people who have both encouraged a follow-up book, and helped to make it possible. To my colleagues at the Scarman Centre, and my students on taught and distance learning programmes who have made me think through my ideas and then rethink them again, I owe a big debt.

I would like to thank all the authors for their help, I must be one of the few editors who can say that all the papers arrived before the final deadline, none were late. This helped my task enormously, and that they all arrived in such a good state was satisfying and an encouragement to me. I am grateful to Reliance Security for sponsoring this book, Brian Kingham is an enthusiast and I appreciate his support and that of his staff.

Finally, thanks to those at Perpetuity Press, to Neil Christie, and especially Sarah Hollyman who has been an excellent co-ordinator. And to Karen, we did it again! At least Emily and Karis were there to help this time, I think!

Contributors

Professor Joshua Bamfield is Director of the Centre for Retail Research, Nottingham. He has published studies on the impact and costs of retail crime, electronic article surveillance, and civil recovery, in addition to making a long-term appraisal of the impact of information technology upon retail competitiveness.

Adrian Beck is a lecturer in Security Management and Information Technology at the Scarman Centre for the Study of Public Order, University of Leicester and is Director of the MSc in Security Management and Information Technology. He has researched and published widely on different aspects of crime and its prevention in the retail sector. He has also studied the potential impact of a national identity card scheme on the relationship between the police and ethnic minority groups. He is currently working on a comparative analysis of gun control legislation in the European Union. He is co-author (with Andrew Willis) of *Crime and Security: Managing the Risk to Safe Shopping,* and assistant editor of the *Security Journal.*

Kate Bowers is a research student at the University of Liverpool. Her research is sponsored by the Safer Merseyside Partnership; a nine-year initiative aimed at reducing crime and fear of crime on Merseyside. The aim of her thesis is to discover more about the manifestation of crimes against businesses. She is also involved with the implementation of the Partnership's Small Business Strategy.

Mark Button graduated from the University of Exeter in 1991 with a degree in Politics. After spending a year working in the private security industry he returned to academia and obtained an MA in Industrial Relations at the University of Warwick. He then became a Research Assistant to Labour MP Bruce George and researched home affairs issues, specialising in the private security industry and the privatisation of criminal justice. In March 1997 he joined the Institute of Police and Criminological Studies at the University of Portsmouth as a lecturer. He has published widely on private policing issues and is in the final stages of completing a book on the private security industry with Bruce George.

Bonnie S. Fisher is an associate professor in the Department of Political Science at the University of Cincinnati. Her published research examines issues concerning college student victimisation, crimes against and within small businesses, and violence in the workplace. She is currently the principal investigator on two grants from the National Institute of Justice and the Bureau of Justice Statistics, examining the nature and extent of sexual victimisation among female college students and victimisation among female college students both on and off campus. *Crime and Delinquency, Public Administration Review*, and the *ANNALS* have published her most recent work.

Bruce George has been the Labour Member of Parliament for Walsall South since February 1974 and is currently Chairman of the House of Commons Defence Committee. He has been campaigning for statutory regulation of the private security industry since 1977 and has introduced private member's bills in 1977, 1988, 1990, 1992 and 1994. He has written and lectured extensively on the private security industry and is in the final stages of completing a book on the private security industry with his former assistant, Mark Button.

Dr Martin Gill is Deputy Director of the Scarman Centre at Leicester University and a Senior Lecturer in Crime and Security Management. He has published articles on the victimisation of businesses, the effectiveness of CCTV, private security and different aspects of policing in a wide range of refereed journals. He has authored and edited several books including *Crime at Work: Studies in Security and Crime Prevention* in 1994. He is presently completing a book on commercial robbery and is an editor of the *Security Journal*.

Justine Harris is a researcher at the Midlands Centre for Criminology and Criminal Justice at Loughborough University. She is currently working with Dr Jon Vagg on a project on product counterfeiting, funded by the Leverhulme Trust.

Dr Alex Hirschfield is Research Co-ordinator of the Urban Research and Policy Evaluation Regional Research Laboratory (URPERRL) at the University of Liverpool. He recently completed a two-year study into relationships between crime and disadvantage on Merseyside, funded by the Economic and Social Research Council. He is currently evaluating the Safer Merseyside Partnership initiative, which includes consideration of crimes committed against the business sector.

Matt Hopkins is a researcher in the Crime Social Research Unit, Nottingham Trent University. He has worked particularly in the area of crime prevention and crime against small business. He is currently working with Professor Nick Tilley on an evaluation of a Small Business and Crime Initiative project and he is writing a PhD thesis on abuse and violence in the workplace.

Lynn Jenkins earned her BA degree in Psychology from West Virginia University (WVU) in 1987 and her MA in Applied Social Research, also from WVU, in 1988. Ms Jenkins has been with the National Institute for Occupational Safety and Health (NIOSH) since 1990. She served for four years as the Chief of the Injury Surveillance Section, guiding the collection and analysis of data on all kinds of workplace injuries. Since February 1996, she has been in the NIOSH Office of the Director as a Senior Scientist. Ms Jenkins has published research on the topics of workplace violence, occupational injuries among women, and the use of various coding systems in the analysis of workplace injuries.

Michael Levi is Professor of Criminology at Cardiff University of Wales. He has published widely on organised crime, asset confiscation, jury trials for fraud, violent crime, and police-public relationships, and his books include *The Phantom Capitalists, Regulating Fraud: White-Collar Crime* and, forthcoming, *White-Collar Crime and its Victims*. Professor Levi is currently Scientific Expert on Organised Crime to the Council of Europe, is conducting research on organised crime and corruption, and is participating in a review of the abuse of offshore financial centres for the United Nations. He is also a member of the Institute of Chartered Accountants' Fraud Advisory Panel.

Sheridan Morris was, at the time of writing this paper, a Home Office PRG Research Officer, specialising in organised crime and police intelligence gathering and analysis. Home Office publications include work on tackling organised benefit fraud and policing problem housing estates. His other publications have included IT security and European police co-operation. He has since moved to Cable & Wireless Communications.

Ken Pease is currently Professor of Criminology at Huddersfield University, having formerly held chairs at the Universities of Manchester and Saskatchewan. He has published widely and was awarded an OBE in 1997 for services to crime prevention. His current interests include strategic crime prevention, ie the anticipation of crime patterns for prevention purposes.

Gavin Sugden is a senior provost officer serving with the Royal Air Force. From 1994-6 he was Station Security Officer at the Tri-national Tornado Training Establishment at RAF Cottesmore in Rutland, England. During this period he served as a member of the Leicestershire Crime Prevention panel and was appointed Chair of the Rutland Panel in 1995. He has been involved in a wide range of police and security issues, both in the UK and overseas, and has completed tours of duty in Germany, Cyprus, the Gulf states and the Falklands. He is a Fellow of the International Institute of Security.

Nick Tilley is Professor of Sociology at Nottingham Trent University. He has research experience in a number of areas, including the prevention of crime against small businesses, problem-oriented policing and scientific realist evaluation methodology. His research has led to numerous publications in journals and short works for the Home Office Police Research Group. He is co-author (with Ray Pawson) of *Realistic Evaluation*.

Michele Tonglet is a PhD student at Nene College, Northampton, researching shoplifting as aberrant consumer behaviour, and investigating the application of this approach to the prevention of customer theft from shops. She obtained a first class honours degree in Marketing with Accounting from De Montfort University, Leicester in 1995. Prior to taking her degree, she worked in the insurance industry and ran her own retail business.

Vicky Turbin completed an MSc in Security Management and Information Technology at The Scarman Centre, Leicester University, and has subsequently been employed as a research officer working on various security/crime prevention projects, including insurance and security, CCTV and shop theft, and data integrity. She has published in a range of journals.

Dr Jon Vagg lectures and researches in criminology at Loughborough University. His previous work and publications cover topics as diverse as prison regimes and management, armed robbery, juvenile delinquency, and piracy on the high seas.

Nicolas Williams is an Associate Professor in the Department of Economics at the University of Cincinnati. His research areas include labour economics, the economics of crime, and applied econometrics. His publications have appeared in the *Review of Economics and Statistics, Applied Economics, Crime and Delinquency, Social Pathology*, and *Criminal Justice Policy Review*.

Andrew Willis is Senior Lecturer in Criminology at the Scarman Centre for the Study of Public Order, University of Leicester and lectures on the International Commanders' Programme at the Police Staff College, Bramshill, which leads to the Postgraduate Certificate/MSc in Criminal Justice and Police Management. His research interests include police co-operation in Europe, various aspects of retail crime and its prevention, probation and criminal justice and the changing balance between public policing and private security. He is co-author (with Adrian Beck) of *Crime and Security: Managing the Risk to Safe Shopping*.

Chapter 1

Introduction

Martin Gill[1]

This book is about crime risk management, that is identifying who is at risk from workplace crime and why, and using the information generated to formulate effective strategies to reduce the risks of victimisation or to prevent it.[2] More specifically, the book seeks to highlight issues on one aspect of crime risk management, indeed an aim of it, that is increasing the risk to offenders.[3] This means making situations less conducive to crime by increasing the risk of offenders being identified and apprehended and reducing their belief that they will 'get away with it', thereby making them think more carefully about the wisdom of carrying out an offence. In practice, there are a variety of ways of increasing the risks for offenders, and in this book papers have been included which examine different aspects of crime risk management in the context of the workplace, and a variety of ways in which offenders' risks have been and can be increased. Moreover, and most importantly, it seeks to provide a framework for understanding the practice of crime risk management.

One of the aims of the book had been to bridge the gap between academics and practitioners and to ensure that the findings generated by scholarly research could be used to influence practice. Another aim of the book had been to generate interest in the subject area, and to show that for the development of both theory and practice the study of crime at work is important. It was argued that too often criminologists had been concerned with the business as an offender and were somewhat dismissive of the importance of organisations, and the people in them, as victims. Moreover, crime and its aftermath and crime prevention cost money, and there is evidence that smaller firms are disproportionately affected,[4] with consequences for their survival. This can result in lost jobs and a loss of services for the local community and/or it may mean higher prices for consumers, affecting the poor more. Indeed, one commentator has argued that business crime should be tackled as part of the process of economic development.[5] Precisely because the business is a part of the community it will be affected by its problems but, by the same token, it is one of the resources (and arguably one of the most underused) that the community can draw upon to solve problems. And, in a different way, the workplace is a community, or part of it, in microcosm.[6] If prevention and security ideas work well in the confines of the workplace, then lessons can be learned for wider society benefit.[7]

In the last few years, and quite independently, others have been taking an interest in workplace crime and its prevention (or containment) both in the UK[8] and overseas.[9]

Alongside these studies a range of surveys have been conducted which are in broad agreement in showing that crime levels against the commercial sector are proportionately higher for comparable offences than against households.[10] This finding has emerged from surveys conducted in Australia,[11] the Netherlands,[12] Spain,[13] England and Wales,[14] and South Africa.[15] Moreover, a number of studies have considered the concentration of crime and found that certain businesses are more likely to be victims and repeat victims.[16] The variables that render some more vulnerable have yet to be fully explored, although, in addition to size and the predictable factor of area characteristics (including the proximity of residences), the type of business (in terms of its product, market and the way it is organised) plays a part in determining both the level and the type of victimisation suffered. A recent survey found that retailers were more at risk from robbery, theft, and verbal abuse; customer fraud was most common in the retail and hotel and catering sectors, and the latter was also most at risk from assault; and that arson was most common within the agricultural sector.[17] It is very important to get a better insight into who is at risk, and to find better ways of managing the response. As will be clear, this can take a variety of forms and this book aims to highlight at least one aspect to it: to inform both the theory and practice of how to increase the risk to offenders.

The theory and practice of increasing the risk to offenders

It is only on the back of better research — and in the wake of better explanations for the causes of different crimes and by identifying patterns in the behaviour of offenders — that we can begin the process of implementing improved crime risk management strategies. It is especially helpful when those explanations can be applied to specific situations.[18] There is still a stark gap in our knowledge of what works. Since the 1970s scepticism about the effectiveness of schemes that attempt to change, treat or help offenders to stop them committing crimes, has resulted in an increased focus on situational measures. This marked a shift of emphasis away from consideration of the causes of crime to the commission of the offence.

Situational crime prevention draws on the tradition of the Classical School and derives its theory from rational choice. This postulates that the offender makes a choice when committing a crime: he/she will weigh up the chances of success and if he/she believes that the chances of success are greater than the chances of failure then the crime will be committed. The situational approach sparked a great deal of research in the ensuing years, and it attracted the attention of criminologists and others from diverse backgrounds, including geographers, environmentalists, architects, sociologists and psychologists, to name a few. Theorists sought to show the extent to which offenders were able to and did make rational or semi-rational decisions (bounded rationality), and feasible ways in which the situation could be manipulated to make crime less likely.[19] There were those who argued that situational measures merely displace or deflect crime elsewhere, not reducing it at all, although more recent research suggests that displacement is only partial at worst, and that it may even be benign.[20]

It became evident that there are lots of ways to reduce opportunities at the situation, that is the scene where crime has taken or could take place. Early fears that support for situational crime prevention was tantamount to support for a fortress society waned as an expanding security industry, and imaginative architects and environmental designers found new ways of reducing opportunities for crime while retaining an aesthetically pleasing context. In its most basic form, as Clarke has acknowledged, situational prevention is common-sense security precautions, installing and using locks, not leaving open windows and doors. But over time more techniques have evolved. Indeed, Clarke has devoted a considerable amount of thinking to developing a set of techniques for crime prevention. Originally, in 1980, there were eight; there are sixteen today, and these are shown in Table 1. While there is not the space to discuss each of these in turn, it is important to understand the four key objectives upon which Clarke considers situational crime prevention should be based: these are increasing the effort, increasing the risks, reducing the reward and inducing shame or guilt.[21]

Table I. The sixteen techniques of situational crime prevention

Increasing perceived effort	Increasing perceived risks	Reducing anticipated rewards	Inducing guilt or shame
1 Target hardening	5 Entry/exit screening	9 Target removal	13 Rule setting
2 Access control	6 Formal surveillance	10 Identifying property	14 Strengthening moral condemnation
3 Deflecting offenders	7 Surveillance by employees	11 Reducing temptation	15 Controlling disinhibitors
4 Controlling facilitators	8 Natural surveillance	12 Denying benefits	16 Facilitating compliance

Taken from Clarke (1997)[22]

Clarke has provided a classification of opportunity reduction techniques based on rational choice theory, and this takes us a part of the way to formulating a framework for developing a response to the risk of crime. However, there are problems with Clarke's model if it is used as a guide to policy: a major limitation is the overlap between the classifications and the consequent difficulty in differentiating between them, as well as the lack of recognition of the broader context in which crime (and its prevention) takes place.[23] There is much more to crime risk management in the workplace, although it could draw heavily on Clarke's work. In fact, risk management, which begins with a risk assessment, is a broad topic. It can be defined as:

> The process whereby decisions are made to accept a known or assessed risk and/or the implementation of actions to reduce the consequences or probability of occurrence.[24]

Risk management is thus relevant to a wide range of subjects and activities (eg finance, medicine, politics) and this includes crime and security. Indeed, crime risk management is a part of security management, although they differ, not least because the latter may include activities not directly related to crime such as safety and other hazards.[25] Yet, these two areas of management activities share the need to identify crime problems, understand them, tackle them and improve the response over time, and both aim to make things more risky (that is difficult and/or dangerous) for offenders. It is perhaps surprising therefore that, to date, criminologists and researchers of security management have operated completely independently; there has been remarkably little cross-fertilisation of ideas between the subject areas. Figure 1 is an attempt to stimulate thinking on what a crime risk management framework might include, presented in the form of a *Process*, and draws upon lessons from those who have studied criminology and those who have written about security management.

The *Process* begins with an *Assessment* of the situation; the better the assessment, the more chance that what follows will have the desired effect. Many of the papers in this volume will highlight problems that can occur at this point. On the basis of an *Assessment*, a *Decision* is made: either to *tolerate* the risk and not act, perhaps because the costs of action outweigh the risks involved; or to transfer it, typically by taking out insurance or contracting work to a third party; or by developing a more *specific strategy* to deal with the risk in-house.[26] This last is invariably the more complex decision and can include a variety of risk strategies. One option is to *avoid* the risk, which can be achieved by removing it altogether — thieves cannot steal radios from cars that do not have radios; another is to *reduce* the risk by, for example, minimising cash levels at tills so that there is a limit to what can be stolen; another method is to *spread* the risk, which can involve a variety of approaches including measures to achieve the four Ds; Deterrence of potential incidents, Denying access, Delaying offenders, and Detecting unsafe situations.[27]

The response can have at least three different *Foci*; this stage is important for understanding the various points or levels at which *Actions* can be taken, and the variety of *techniques* available to policy makers at the level of the *organisation, situation* or *society*. In the context of the workplace situational measures are usually implemented within an organisational structure; *management techniques* can be used to solve some (situational) problems and they will certainly influence the effective management and workability of different situational approaches. *Situational techniques* are derived from the work of Clarke. Some situational problems can be tackled by using *social/political/economic techniques*.

The *Process* is not designed to be comprehensive; it is questionable whether all the range of techniques could ever be fully included in any meaningful diagram. Rather it indicates the main stages that those involved in crime risk management may go through when thinking about a response to crime, while the techniques are designed to identify the key actions that could be taken. Thus in the top box of each set of techniques are the objectives, and beneath them some key (but not all-encompassing) examples. Thus, the objectives of management techniques include *improving staff, changing or establishing a culture in the organisation, implementing and modifying systems, adjusting leadership* and *developing policies*.

On a situational level I have been greatly influenced by Ron Clarke's work. Indeed, I have

Figure 1: The crime risk management process: in the context of the workplace

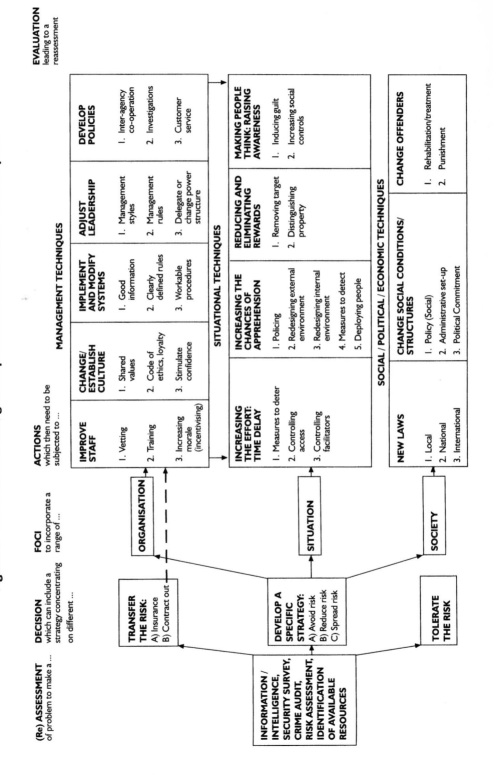

adapted his objectives and techniques; they have been modified for the different purpose they are being used for here. For example, target hardening has been subdivided into measures to deter and measures to detect. I have specifically linked *increasing the effort* with *time delay* and I have renamed the second set of objectives to more accurately describe what the techniques seek to do. Indeed, as will be shown, all of Clarke's objectives increase the risks (hence the subtitle of the book), whereas the objectives described here are much more specifically about *increasing the chances of apprehension*. Moreover, as part of the process of modifying this objective I have moved away from Clarke's heavy reliance on surveillance and invited attention to the key areas where action may be focused. Thus, to change a situational response one could introduce *policing* (of any type), or become involved in *redesigning the environment, redesigning the interior* (which Clarke's model misses altogether), *introducing measures to detect*, and *deploying people* (and here there is overlap with management techniques).[28]

Crime can be prevented or made less likely by *reducing or eliminating the rewards*, property can be distinguished (eg property marking) to render it less attractive to offenders, or removed altogether. And there is much to be gained from measures which make people think about their actions at the point at which they are about to commit offences. This is Clarke's most recent addition to the model and it is a very important one in that it offers a new set of techniques aimed at making situations more risky for offenders. It has still to be subjected to evaluation and there is still some overlap between the various techniques here. In a very helpful review, Wortley contends that the classification is not exhaustive and postulates two columns, one with the objective of *inducing guilt* and the other of *increasing social controls*.[29] While I am persuaded that Wortley's analysis offers an improvement in the classification, I am not yet convinced that they are out of place as techniques under a revised objective of *making people think: raising awareness*, and this is where I have included them.

Where the *Focus* is *society*, one can introduce *new legislation, change social conditions* and *society structures* or *change offenders*, and in any comprehensive model these would need developing beyond what is possible here. And whatever strategy evolves needs to be subject to *Evaluation* — this is crucial. One of the main limits to developing effective strategies and to improving what presently exists is a lack of independent and properly conducted research on security and crime prevention initiatives.[30] Analysing the findings of the *Evaluation* should lead to a *Reassessment*, and the whole *Process* starts again.

There is at least one other point that needs to be mentioned here, and it too has received little attention: that is the principles on which *Decisions* need to be based. Hamilton evolved 21 'principles of defence' which he considered should be the basis for a security system.[31] There is not the space to print them all here but they are helpful, and it ought to be recognised that good crime risk management (and security management) strategies benefit from awareness of principles such as: security should be commensurate with the threat; security must have a good image; no single measure gives security, but the sum of several; security is as strong as its weakest link; quality is more important that quantity; security can be increased by co-operation with others; security measures must ultimately defer to the concept of human freedom. There may be others that could usefully be included: eg initiatives should include a criterion for 'success'; all measures become dated and so on-going evaluation and reassessment are crucial. Indeed, crime risk management may be greatly enhanced by greater consideration and knowledge of these (and other) principles.

Crime risk management (and indeed security management) in organisations entails think-ing of more effective ways of making situations less conducive to crime. This involves manipulating environments to make a potential offender believe that the disadvantages outweigh the advantages of committing a criminal act; in short, to make individuals be-lieve that the risks are too great. The *Crime Risk Management Process* provides a way of thinking about and analysing the response to the threat of crime. It begins with the *Assess-ment* of a problem, and involves a *Decision* to formulate a response which can take several forms. Where a specific strategy evolves it will include *Actions* using a variety of *tech-niques*, invariably with different *Foci*. The outcome can then be subject to *Evaluation* leading to a *Reassessment*.

Crime risk management is a complex issue and any diagram runs the risk of being seen as an oversimplification. Similarly, it is doubtful whether any book could cover all the rel-evant issues, even when applied to a specific locale such as the workplace. Thus, this book is an attempt to stimulate thinking, and authors were asked to focus on the ways in which their findings can help inform the aim of 'increasing the risk for offenders' (rather than 'crime risk management', which was felt to be a rather more abstract concept).

The book outline

Whereas *Crime at Work*, Volume I included papers more generally covering the themes of security and crime prevention, Volume II is more focused on crime risk management and authors have been asked to discuss the ways in which the risk of crime can be managed by increasing the risks for offenders. This perhaps merits a comment. In an ideal world it would have been preferable to prepare a book which systematically evaluates each part of the *Crime Risk Management Process*. But this book is about crime at work, and here research is especially sparse. Nevertheless, good studies do exist, and they can be found in this book, and the papers do collectively (although perhaps not systematically) further understanding on how different parts of the *Crime Risk Management Process* might work or be improved; indeed, all the papers have a message about risk.[32]

A variety of approaches are adopted. Papers discuss the problems of obtaining good data (vital for introducing effective policies which present risks to offenders); look at the scale and patterns of crime and its impact in different businesses, with lessons for management, not least on how to target resources; evaluate issues in some of the more serious offences that modern organisations suffer from; and consider a range of policing and regulation issues. All the papers are based around original research.

A theme running through many papers in this volume is the need for good information on which to calculate a risk assessment. This issue is tackled directly by Vicky Turbin in Chapter 2, where she reports on a study of data corruption. She identifies the weak points where corruption can occur, showing that it can take several forms, including clerical error, theft, wastage, and variation in counting. The causes include human error as well as the limits of technology and company procedures. In developing ideas for good practice Turbin notes that accurate data is as important for quality control as it is for effective security.

The next three chapters consider the impact of crime on business. In Chapter 3 Kate Bowers and Alex Hirschfield report on their study of commercial properties in Mersey-side. Their discussion of how they identified the businesses most at risk, and the subsequent development of a security strategy is enlightening. In Chapter 4 Matt Hopkins and Nick Tilley continue the discussion on the levels and impact of crime against business by describing their findings of a survey of businesses on three streets. They note the difficulty of getting small businesses interested in crime prevention, and the reasons include a preoccupation with ensuring their survival, a suspicion of local people (most lived in a place separated from where they worked), and a belief that others, not least the police and local council ought to be assuming greater responsibility. They found crime problems to be highly localised and therefore suggest that a uniform approach to security and crime prevention is unlikely to work.

These findings are not just pertinent to three streets in London: they also emerge in Chapter 5, a report on violent crime at work in the USA. Bonnie Fisher, Lynn Jenkins and Nicolas Williams provide an insight into some of the problems in evaluating survey findings, not least in making comparisons between them, and synthesise the data from a variety of reports to show disturbingly high levels of violence, some resulting in death at work. As they note, no one is free from risk but some are in greater danger than others, and their discussion helps to untangle the web of factors that influences who becomes a victim. Their findings leave us in no doubt that collecting good data is crucial to the delivery of effective policy which, if faulty, can cost lives.

In Chapter 6 Gavin Sugden illustrates some of the problems that result from the absence of a good risk assessment. He reports on a crime prevention audit he carried out on a type of business that regularly escapes academic attention: farms. The countryside is more accessible today and, with growing concern about the drift in crime away from urban areas, his study is timely. Farmers, it seems, are not especially security conscious although a change in attitude is being driven by insurance companies. A major concern that emerges from this chapter is the preparedness of farmers to use guns for protection; here the risks for offenders may be considerable, but for farmers too.

In Chapter 7 Adrian Beck and Andrew Willis discuss prevention from a different perspective in a different context. They focus on the theft of small portable goods from an electrical retailer, using 'repeated systematic counting' to show how product location can affect offender decision-making. They found, predictably, that theft varied by store and by product and that the most vulnerable point for theft, the sales counter, was also the best point for sales. Thus they place the debate about how to increase risks for offenders in a broader context, examining the needs of security requirements against the demand for sales which drives business.

The link with shop theft is continued in Chapter 8, where Michelle Tonglet starts a series of chapters discussing different types of offences. Tonglet uses a theory of planned behaviour and reports on her survey of shoppers about shop theft. She found that 7 % admitted shop-lifting in the previous 12 months and 30 % at some point in their lives. The principal reasons given for offending were that shop theft was easy and carried few risks, and they were influenced by others and did not see it as wrong. Penalties were viewed as soft and most felt that they would not get caught. Tonglet's paper offers important data on issues that need to be included when considering the best approach to increasing risks for shop thieves.

Chapter 9 also concentrates on another major concern to retailers: staff dishonesty with the assistance of customer thieves. Joshua Bamfield, throwing some light on the hidden figure, suggests that levels of staff theft in collusion may be high. In discussing the vari-ous types of collusion Bamfield shows that offences are easy to commit. In the latter part of the paper Bamfield, building on the work of Gerald Mars, presents a new model to reflect levels of commitment to, and the impact of, theft. For Bamfield the solution to the staff dishonesty rests on businesses taking the issue seriously: he advocates highlighting punishments and introducing civil recovery as possible ways forward.

In Chapter 10 Ken Pease and I examine repeat victimisation and commercial robbery. We start by introducing 'flag' (risk heterogeneity) and 'boost' (event dependence) explana-tions as to why some businesses are repeat victims, and then move on to discuss the accounts of 341 commercial robbers. In all, a fifth admitted robbing the same premises more than once; only slightly fewer admitted to raiding a premises known to have been robbed by someone else; and about a sixth claimed that the last target they robbed had been victimised in the same way previously. There was support for both flag and boost accounts. Repeat robbers tended to be more organised, and knowledge of a successful prior raid was an indication that it was easy and/or less risky. The findings suggest that increasing the risk for robbers will be helped by installing effective measures after an initial raid.

Mike Levi examines fraud, or more specifically the perspective of the long-firm fraudster in Chapter 11. Levi shows how frauds are conducted and the considerable efforts that are taken to create a legitimate front to a business to facilitate a fraud. He shows that long-firm fraudsters are skilled offenders and not easy to identify and apprehend. In any event Levi notes that some businesses will tolerate fraud where other priorities linked to profit-ability take precedence. Thus, increasing the risks for offenders requires more than iden-tifying a problem: it is a matter of being committed to take action and devoting the re-sources necessary to make actions effective.

Drug dealing is the subject of Chapter 12, where the focus is on pubs and clubs. Sheridan Morris found that door staff could facilitate crime, by turning a blind eye; by receiving payment from dealers in return for being allowed to trade; or by dealing themselves. Some managers condone such behaviour. Morris discusses the organisation of drug deal-ing in two cities and moves on to consider initiatives to tackle the problem. For Morris, increasing the risks to offenders includes a major role for the police and local authorities, not least in introducing regulation of door staff.

Regulation and policing are themes of the final two chapters. In Chapter 13 Jon Vagg and Justine Harris examine an offence which has received scant attention: product counterfeiting. Their figures suggest that the costs of this offence to legitimate businesses are high. The way that counterfeiting takes place varies with the product and the response differs with the industry. They show that in the motion picture industry, where companies are used to collaborating with each other, a jointly funded agency was set up to prevent counterfeiters from having an impact; while in the fashion industry, where no such collaboration has been in evidence, the response has been more individual. They conclude that better information and collective action are crucial.

In the final chapter, Mark Button and Bruce George examine private sector policing provision where they consider the advantages of contract security over in-house security (in Volume I they discussed the advantages of in-house). According to most estimates, contract security is more common than in-house and the advantages include its cost, flexibility, standards and prestige. This is not to suggest there are not problems — there are, which is why the authors advocate statutory regulation, which they seek to show will have a positive effect on standards and help to make things difficult for offenders.

Summary

Increasing the risk for offenders may take a variety of forms and it will invariably involve applying situational measures (often with other types of techniques). Indeed, all the objectives of Clarke's model — and my modification for the purpose described in this chapter — may increase risks to a potential offender: via the time delay in increasing the effort; by increasing the chances of apprehension the risks are self-evident; by distinguishing property it reduces the rewards and may render goods more traceable; and by inducing shame or guilt it may increase general awareness and make crime more risky. This is one reason why the book has been subtitled 'increasing the risk for offenders'. Another is that it is an objective of those involved in crime risk management and those involved in security management where crime management is an issue.

It is hoped this book will raise some new questions and help to answer others. An additional aim is to throw light on an area which has for some time escaped academic attention. Collectively, the papers provide an insight into who is at risk and develop some thoughts on how best to respond to a range of offences that affect workers and the workplace.

Notes

1   Dr Martin Gill is based at the Scarman Centre, University of Leicester, The Friars, 154 Upper New Walk, Leicester, LE1 7QA (email: mg26@le.ac.uk). Helpful comments on earlier drafts of this chapter were received from Adrian Beck, Dr Tony Burns-Howell, Adam Edwards, Dr Anthea Hucklesby, Roger Hopkins Burke, Dr Claire Lawrence and Vicky Turbin.

2   'Crime risk management' is a more complete term than 'crime prevention' or 'crime re-
        duction' and it can incorporate the aim of either the prevention of crime or the reduction of
        it. These issues are discussed more fully later in the paper in the context of the *Crime Risk
        Management Process*. See also: Bridgeman, C. (1996) *Crime Risk Management: Making
        it Work*. Crime Detection and Prevention Series, Paper 70. London: Home Office Police
        Research Group; Ekblom, P. (1997) Gearing up Against Crime: A Dynamic Framework to
        Help Designers Keep up with the Adaptive Criminal in a Changing World. *International
        Journal of Risk, Security and Crime Prevention*. Vol. 2, No. 4, pp 249-266; Hough, M. and
        Tilley, N. (1998) *Getting the Grease to Squeak: Research Lessons for Crime Prevention*.
        Crime Detection and Prevention Series, Paper 85. London: Home Office Police Research
        Group

3   'Crime risk management' is an unfamiliar term to many (although the University of Leicester
        now offers a MSc in Security and Crime Risk Management and some consultants are
        promoting crime risk management as their specialist area of expertise). To avoid definitional
        issues and confusion, contributors to this Volume were asked to focus papers around the
        more specific (and familiar) theme of 'increasing the risk to offenders'. In so doing, and as
        was intended, papers touch on many issues of crime risk management.

4   Gill, M. (1999) The Victimisation of Business: Indicators of Risk and the Direction of
        Future Research. *International Review of Victimology*. Forthcoming.

5   Graham, P. (1997) *The Role of Local Government*. Presentation to Crime Concern Confer-
        ence on Business Crime. 30 September, Leicester.

6   Hotels are an example, where everything from living accommodation to restaurants to
        shops and leisure facilities are being located on one site. In a different way, the workplace
        is a community or set of communities, given that people spend a large part of their lives
        there (as do many customers). Much more can be learned about crime prevention, and
        issues such as security awareness by studying and understanding what goes on here and
        applying lessons learned to wider community problems.

7   Similarly, as Button and George show in Chapter 13 of this book, the workplace provides
        a forum for evaluating the role of private policing, a much under-researched topic.

8   Beck, A. and Willis, A. (1995) *Crime and Security: Managing the Risk to Safe Shopping*.
        Leicester: Perpetuity Press.

9   Felson, M. and Clarke, R. (1997) *Business and Crime Prevention*. New Jersey: Criminal
        Justice Press.

10   Bamfield, (1994) *National Survey of Retail Theft and Security, 1994*. Northampton: Nene
        College, School of Business; Brooks, C. and Cross, C. (1995) *Retail Crime Costs, 1994/5
        Survey*. London: British Retail Consortium; Burrows, J. and Speed, M. (1994) Retail Crime
        Costs, 1992/3 Survey. London: British Retail Consortium; Mirrlees-Black, C. and Ross,
        A. (1995a) *Crime Against Retail Premises in 1993*. Home Office Research and Statistics
        Department, Research Findings No. 26. London: Home Office; Mirrlees-Black, C. and
        Ross, A. (1995b) *Crime Against Manufacturing Premises in 1993*. Home Office Research
        and Statistics Department, Research Findings No. 27. London: Home Office; Speed, M.,
        Burrows, J. and Bamfield, J. (1995) *Retail Crime Costs 1993/94 Survey: The Impact of
        Crime and the Retail Response*. London: British Retail Consortium; see also Gill, M. (1993)
        Crime on Holiday: Abuse, Damage and Theft in Small Holiday Accommodation Units.
        Research Paper 1. Crime, Order and Policing Research paper Series. Leicester: Scarman
        Centre for the Study of Public Order, University of Leicester; Johnson, V., Leitner, M.,

Shapland, J. and Wiles, P. (1994) Crime, Policing and Business on Industrial Estates. In Gill, M (ed.) *Crime at Work: Studies in Security and Crime Prevention.* Leicester: Perpetuity Press.

11   Walker, J. (1996) Crime Prevention by Businesses in Australia. *International Journal of Risk, Security and Crime Prevention.* Vol. 1, No. 4, pp 279-293.

12   van Dijk, J. (forthcoming) Crimes Against Business in the Netherlands. *International Journal of Risk, Security and Crime Prevention.*

13   Barberet, R. and Strangeland, P. (forthcoming) Crimes Against Businesses in Spain. *International Journal of Risk, Security and Crime Prevention.*

14   Mirrlees-Black and Ross (1995a,b), op cit.

15   Naudé, B. (1995) *South African Businesses as Victims of Crime.* Paper presented to the British Criminology Conference, July 18-21, Loughborough University. Loughborough.

16   See Gill (forthcoming), op cit; Walker, op cit; Wood, J., Wheelwright, G., Burrows, J. (1997) *Crime Against Small Business: Facing the Challenge.* Leicester: Small Business and Crime Initiative.

17   Gill (forthcoming), op cit.

18   There has been a tendency across disciplines to move away from the broad application of theory to a more specific level of analysis. For example, see Lawrence, C. (1998) *Forming Impressions of Public House Violence: Stereotypes, Attributions and Perceptions.* Unpublished PhD thesis, University of Nottingham.

19   See Clarke, R.V.G. (1997) *Situational Crime Prevention: Successful Case Studies.* Second edition. New York: Harrow and Heston.

20   Ibid.

21   There is not the space to engage in a full discussion of the techniques here, although this task is undertaken by Clarke; see ibid.

22   Clarke (1997), op cit.

23   Gill, M. (forthcoming) *Robbers and Robbery: Offenders' Perspectives on Security and Crime Prevention.*

24   The Royal Society (1992) Risk, Analysis, Perception and Management. London: The Royal Society, p 5.

25   Wilson, J. and Slater, T. (1988) *Practical Security in Commerce and Industry.* Aldershot: Gower.

26   There is some overlap between the various decisions shown separately in the diagram. Insurance, a way of transferring the risk, may be a method which is used to spread the risk. The main point of the division discussed here is to identify situations where no actions are taken (Tolerate the risk), actions involve the risk be taken by others (Transfer the risk), or where a policy and response is initiated which is dependent on specific actions being taken by the company involving the *techniques* shown.

27   For further discussion see Hayes, R. (1991) *Retail Security and Loss Prevention.* Stoneham, MA: Butterworth-Heinemann.

28   Thus I have not been able to avoid overlap, although it is doubtful this will ever be possible; it is more a question of degree. I have tried to develop a framework which will assist those preventing crime and thus my aims are different from those of Clarke.

29   Wortley, P. (1997) Guilt, Shame and Situational Crime Prevention. In Homel, R. (ed.) *Crime Prevention Studies 5*. New York: Willow Tree Press.

30   For a discussion of problems, please see Ekblom, P. and Pease, K. (1995) Evaluating Crime Prevention. In Tonry, M. and Farrington, D. (eds) *Building a Safer Society: Crime and Justice: A Review of Research*. Vol. 19. Chicago: University of Chicago Press; Gill, M. and Turbin, V. (1998) CCTV and Shop Theft: Towards a Realistic Evaluation. In Norris, C., Armstrong, G. and Moran, J. (eds) *Surveillance, CCTV and Social Control*. Aldershot, Gower; Gill, M. and Turbin, V. (1998) Evaluating 'Realistic Evaluation': Evidence from a Study of CCTV. In Tilley, N. (ed.) *Crime Prevention Studies*. Monsey, N.Y: Criminal Justice Press; Pawson, R. and Tilley, N. (1992) Re-evaluation: Rethinking Research on Corrections and Crime. *Yearbook of Correctional Education*; Pawson, R. and Tilley, N. (1997) *Realistic Evaluation*. London: Sage; Tilley, N. (1993) *Understanding Car Parks, Crime and CCTV*. Crime Prevention Unit Paper No. 42. London: HMSO; Tilley, N. (1997) Whys and Wherefores in Evaluating the Effectiveness of CCTV. *International Journal of Risk, Security and Crime Prevention*. Vol. 2, No. 3, pp 175-186.

31   Hamilton, P. (1979) *Espionage, Terrorism and Subversion in an Industrial Society: an Examination and Philosophy of Defence Management*. Leatherhead: Peter A. Heims Ltd; see also *Klewers Handbook of Security*. London: Croner.

32   A new journal is about to be launched (by the publishers of this book): *Risk Management: an International Journal*, which seeks to evaluate the different ways in which Risk can be defined and used between practitioner groups and across academic disciplines.

Chapter 2

Shrinkage Figures and Data Corruption: Lies, Damned Lies and Statistics?

Vicky Turbin[1]

Effective security requires accurate data about losses. In retailing, estimates of loss known as 'shrinkage' are commonly used to indicate problems within a store. However, shrinkage not only includes theft by staff and customers but also some degree of unidentified 'clerical' error. Understanding how data is created and corrupted, is a vital part of understanding estimates of risk. By reducing data corruption, more reliable loss figures are produced on which to base security decisions. This is a vital component of any security strategy designed to increase the risk for offenders. This paper presents results from a twelve-month study of data corruption within a medium-sized jeans and casual clothing retailer. Using both hypothetical examples and case studies of real stock figures, the paper demonstrates how data is corrupted and how corruption impacts on stocktakes, loss figures, merchandising and sales.

Introduction

Spending on security hardware has risen dramatically over the past few years and cost around £525 million in 1994/95.[2] At the same time, losses due to theft in the retail sector are also high, with customer theft alone estimated at £664 million in 1994/95.[3] Loss prevention is quite simply an expensive business. In the battle against shop theft, accurate information about where and when losses occur is vital. Loss data provides the basis for security strategies designed to reduce or manage a particular crime problem. If the data used to make such decisions is inaccurate, then the security response may be inappropriate and ineffective. Increasing the risk for offenders is more likely to be achieved when security is both responsive and appropriate, and the key issue here is to accurately identify what problem is faced. It may be staff theft, customer theft or burglary, or theft may not really be a problem at all. A knee-jerk reaction of installing security hardware without proper consideration of this issue, could be the security equivalent of 'sticking a plaster on a headache'.[4] So how do retailers identify if they have a problem with theft?

Traditionally, retailers use a figure known as 'shrinkage' to indicate loss,[5] which can be defined as any 'unexplained loss of physical inventory'.[6] Shrinkage figures are constructed from two types of inventory data: first, the (computer) records of stock and second, the result of a physical count or stocktake. When these two figures are compared there is usually some difference. This difference will include losses due to theft (by customers, staff or suppliers), wastage, and data error. However, as the British Retail Consortium (BRC) survey found, retailers could only attribute 13% of losses to known crime, while an estimated 25% of losses were believed to be due to non-crime causes such as wastage or clerical error.[7] Clearly there is a lack of knowledge about what these loss figures incorporate. The diagram below summarises how both known and unknown factors in data collection combine to create the traditional shrinkage figure.

Figure 1: The known and unknown impact of data corruption on stock data

STOCK LEVEL DATA

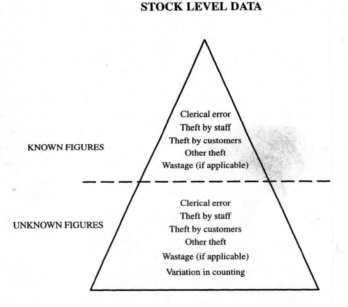

KNOWN FIGURES

Clerical error
Theft by staff
Theft by customers
Other theft
Wastage (if applicable)

UNKNOWN FIGURES

Clerical error
Theft by staff
Theft by customers
Other theft
Wastage (if applicable)
Variation in counting

As loss data is averaged between stores and over time, it moves further and further away from a useful measure of theft activity. Usually of course, there are other indications that a store has a problem with theft, other than simple loss figures. Incidents of aggression towards staff may be high. Indeed, research by Beck, Gill and Willis has demonstrated a link between shop theft activity and violence towards staff.[8] In addition, store detectives may report high numbers of shop thieves being apprehended (though this of course, does not necessarily mean that theft activity is high). However, the majority of retailers use shrinkage figures as their main source of information about theft activity within a store.

This paper aims to highlight some of the most common errors that can occur in retail stock systems, using evidence from a study of one retail company. It demonstrates the impact of data corruption and suggests how to identify common errors and how to reduce them, so that a more reliable picture of theft activity can be determined. This should help security managers refine their data collection system, to give a more accurate reflection of the losses in-store and to avoid inappropriate security responses. It will also be of use to researchers and practitioners interested in quantifying the level of theft activity.

Methodology

The research on which this paper is based was conducted in a medium-sized casual clothes retailer, over a twelve-month period.[9] It followed on from a previous project with the same company, which examined the impact of CCTV on shop theft.[10] During this project it became apparent that data integrity was an issue and the company subsequently sponsored an in-depth review of its data systems and processes. This review was designed to identify if data integrity was a problem within the company, the scale and impact of the data corruption and methods of eliminating or reducing data problems. The research was conducted with the co-operation of the loss prevention department and focused on data relating to losses. The aim was to strengthen the reliability of data so that real losses could be identified and acted upon. In order to do this, the most common data problems affecting the company were first examined and are explored below.

Common problems with inventory data

Data errors can occur throughout a stock control system. To illustrate this, the following list examines some of the most common types of error that occur. Some of these errors are common to many types of retail business, while others may be specific only to clothing retailers, or even to this particular company's processes.

Initial input of data
Orders sent to the supplier may contain typing mistakes, while errors may also occur when new style codes are entered onto the computer.

Delivery system
The supplier may pick the wrong items (by style, size or quantity) or produce an incorrect packing note. Errors in delivery to the warehouse (under or over-delivery and theft) may not be noticed. The warehouse may split stock incorrectly, complete the Goods Received Note (GRN) incorrectly, send packed boxes to the wrong stores, produce an incorrect packing note or simply delay delivery.

At the store
The store may sign for an incorrect number of boxes. When checking deliveries, discrepancies from the packing note may be missed or recorded incorrectly (assuming that the packing note is correct). Errors may occur at the till if the items cannot be scanned (eg the bar code has fallen off, is damaged or the code is not on the till file). This leads to manual input using a code from the code book, use of a 'dump' code or scanning of a similar item which does possess a bar code.

Updating stock information via the tills
At the end of every day, electronic information about sales is transferred to a central computer via the till. Records of inter-branch transfers (IBTs) and goods returned to the warehouse are also sent. At the same time, adjustments, such as new codes or price reductions, are sent to the till from the head office computer. Errors may occur during file transmission. The files may not arrive, may be delayed, incomplete or corrupted.

Stocktake
A stocktake is designed to reconcile differences between (computer) records of stock and an actual physical count of what is in-store. Full stocktakes can be prohibitively time-consuming and expensive to conduct. Often, cycle-counting is used instead. This has the advantage of nullifying natural data degradation due to the effects of stock transactions over time.[11] However, cycle-counting may be inappropriate when a store has problems with variation in counting: that is, if the act of counting creates more errors in the data than would have existed if the stock had not been counted at all. This problem was highlighted by a double stocktake conducted specifically for the project.

Staff conducted a full store stocktake in the normal manner using hand-held bar code scanners but were not told that a recount was planned. A second team of staff entered the store immediately after the stocktake had finished and recounted all the stock, again using hand-held scanners. Both of these data sets were then compared to the computer records. It was found that there were significant differences between the two counts. One team appeared to overlook counting a considerable amount of stock and to mix sizes, though neither the first nor second count exactly matched the computer records. Overall, only 88.4% of stock was counted the same between the first team and the second team. Hence, a difference of 11.6% was introduced simply due to variation in counting. This experiment also showed that some stock types appeared easier to count than others and this was primarily due to the quality of bar coding.

The impact of variation in counting on stocktake data is difficult to quantify, as it depends on the experience of staff doing the stocktake, the time allowed for the stocktake to be done and the quality of supervision. The following general examples illustrate these points.

First, even with the advantages of bar code technology, human error can impact significantly on the validity of stocktake data. Stock may be accidentally over-counted, which will cause an apparent over-stock in the computer records. This means that stock will not be replenished correctly until the records are corrected at the next stocktake, which may result in lost sales. Conversely, stock may be under-counted or accidentally missed. This gives the appearance of greater losses than there actually are in the store, which may be (incorrectly) attributed to theft. Under-counting leads to excessive replenishment until the following stocktake and can have associated costs in stockpiling goods that may not be sold. The subsequent stocktake will often show a reflexive positive stock. That is, the computer records have been adjusted to show less stock than is actually in store. When it reappears in the next stocktake (assuming that it is counted correctly this time), the computer believes it has gained stock. This type of reflection is a very good indicator that (apparent) losses are not due to theft but rather are a product of data error.

Second, unless strict procedures are in place and they are policed properly, staff will find the easiest route to achieving a set task or not do it at all. Stocktakes are monotonous and time-consuming and it is therefore not surprising that 'short cuts' are often found. Staff may not realise the impact that these deviations from set procedure can have on stock data. For example, if there is a large pile of similar-looking items, it is much quicker to scan the first one and then repeat this for the total number in the pile rather than scan them individually. But if the pile does not contain the same size or style of goods, then size or style mix-ups will result. It is hard to spot if staff are doing these sorts of short cuts, though it can be quite apparent in the stocktake report.

Third, not all stock can be scanned using a bar code scanner. Bar codes fall off or get damaged and codes may not be recognised by the system. This leads to stock being manually identified and written down and then manually entered into the stock report later on. This can lead to writing errors and data entry errors.

Finally, reconciling the store data with information from the rest of the company can be a problem. Company 'cut-offs' (stock that is not yet in-store but has been credited on the computer) have to be reconciled, stock put through as an IBT excluded from the report, returns identified, etc. In short, the stock report has to be 'tidied up'. Though the impact of each of the errors described above may be small, the cumulative impact can be considerable. This has important implications not just for sales and merchandising but also for loss data, as the total impact of this data error can mask losses due to theft.

It is common for stocktake data to be averaged both across lines or styles and over time. This means that negative stock will be balanced out by positive stock to give one overall figure. This is often done under the assumption that errors are likely to be reflexive. That is, one size may be up because another is down within the stock report and one stock report may be positive because the previous one was negative due to miscounting.[12] But, for example, if a store has been receiving extra stock through IBTs without the correct paperwork being processed, then theft activity may be missed. An examination of the computer records alone would not highlight the theft problem in this store because it is being masked by the effect of data error. Conversely, miscounting or other process errors during stocktakes can give the incorrect appearance of a theft problem in a store when in fact there is little theft activity.

One example from the research is when a store processed the paperwork for a batch of stock which was being returned to the warehouse, without also putting it through the till. Since the paperwork was complete, the boxes (quite correctly) were not counted in the stocktake. But because this information was not put through the till, the computer records were not updated. When the stocktake report was examined, the store appeared to have a £1257 loss and at first glance this looked like a result of shop theft (because the stock were all returns, there was no consistency in size or style which would have immediately indicated a clerical problem). It was only by accident that this error was noticed. This is a prime example of how data error can appear to be theft, unless the figures are rigorously checked.

As these examples have shown, using stocktake data alone to estimate theft is problematic when data used to produce the comparative figures may be unreliable. Lower loss levels may be a product of reducing data error, rather than any significant change in the rate of theft. So how can the level of real theft be distinguished among all this data corruption?

Identifying data corruption and isolating theft

Unfortunately, isolating the true level of theft is not easy. Various techniques have been employed by researchers to quantify shop theft levels. Store shrinkage figures, recorded numbers of shop thieves, official police statistics, aggregated retail loss figures,[13] self-reported offending,[14] direct observation,[15] and repeated systematic counting[16] have all been used with varying degrees of success. As has been shown, store shrinkage figures can become unreliable due to the cumulative effects of data error. Using records of the number of shop thieves apprehended is also unreliable, as, arguably, they only serve to show how good store staff are at spotting offenders. The same problem of under-recording is found with official police statistics. Only a small number of shop thieves are caught and of those, even less are reported or subsequently prosecuted. As self-reported offending research demonstrates, shop theft activity is probably much greater than the police figures would suggest and this is supported by the findings of direct observation studies. So the problem is that most sources of data on shop theft are hampered by under-reporting or unreliability. However, some methods are available to reduce the impact of data error and non-reporting.

One of the best ways to minimise data error when looking at theft, is to bypass the normal stock control system entirely. This method was used by Buckle and Farrington with their 'Repeated Systematic Counting' and has also been examined by Beck and Willis (see paper in this volume). Buckle and Farrington used a method which relied on counting specified items daily, identifying losses due to non-theft causes and thereby deriving the theft level. Their study showed that in this particular company, only 3% of total shoplifting losses of major items were being recorded and in the worst store, almost a third of minor items were stolen. Shoplifting was much higher than had been anticipated. This method provides a useful snapshot figure to compare to computer stock records, in order to quantify how far out from reality the stock records are (both due to theft and data error).

This type of daily counting has also been used to investigate other theft problems. Losses of certain targeted items were graphed twice weekly for employees in one grocery store in Sweden. This resulted in reduced losses, although it was not known if this was due to reduced employee theft or to increased staff observation of high risk items.[17] A similar counting principle was used by Masuda to intensively target high-loss merchandise in an electronic and appliance retailer.[18] This was part of an audit strategy to expose internal theft trails and direct limited resources towards theft-prone areas. He found that an apparent 'diffusion of benefits' occurred, where merchandise other than that targeted also showed reduced losses.

Clearly, regular counting of high-risk items can provide useful data if managed appropriately. However, this method is time-consuming and requires a high level of supervision in order to work. Problems with variation in counting stock, which were highlighted previously, can have a disastrous effect on any manual count system such as this. Identifying corruption due to incorrect deliveries, IBTs or other movement of stock also requires great care. This type of intensive method is useful to provide extra evidence that a particular store has a problem with theft, especially when shrinkage figures are unreliable, but it is probably impractical to use on anything other than a periodic basis.

Identifying and minimising data corruption

We have seen that reducing the impact of data error on stock figures is an important objective both for crime management and for sales. To achieve this, data error needs first to be identified and then, if possible, minimised. Five key stages in this management process are outlined below:

(1) *Identify if there is a problem with data integrity and the scale of the problem:*
  * look for reflexive variation in stocktake reports;
  * conduct repeat stock counts and compare to computer records.

(2) *Identify causes:*
  * review stock control processes at all stages (supplier to customer);
  * identify frequent process errors and those with most impact on the business.

(3) *Review the existing error-reporting processes:*
  * are reporting processes being followed, and are there any gaps in reporting?
  * Are errors simply corrected or are causes investigated and rectified?

(4) *Reduce or eliminate process errors:*
  * define areas of responsibility, record errors, correct errors and provide feedback;
  * make data integrity a high-profile issue.

(5) *Review data integrity:*
  * monitor data integrity and react quickly to new data problems.

As the summary list notes, the process begins with a measurement of how good the existing data is. This can be in the form of a simple graph, showing variation from computer records at a stocktake. Or, an experimental daily stock count can be conducted to determine theft levels and the discrepancy from stock records. This is a very useful measure but it needs to be strictly controlled in order to gain reliable figures. This stage highlights whether the company has a problem with data collection and the scale of the problem.

If there is a problem, the next stage is to identify where the problem lies. Minimising data corruption is predominantly a management issue. Processes need to be reviewed at all stages of the stock system, to ensure that there are no loopholes which allow theft or data corruption. Where errors can occur, checks should be in place to report and correct problems. Of course, procedures may appear to be in place already but often staff are not following them correctly, either due to ignorance, unwillingness or, perhaps, dishonesty. In addition, where data error is a problem, it is often difficult to identify specific factors which cause the error. In this situation, general data management needs to be reinforced and possible areas of corruption systematically tested and eliminated. This is a slow process, but the potential benefits are great.

Conclusion

This paper has attempted to demonstrate some of the most common ways that stock data becomes corrupted and to show the implications of this error in quantifying theft levels. The importance of this problem for security should not be underestimated. To reduce shop theft, security must be accurately targetted to problem stores, areas or merchandise. It seems obvious that putting expensive security into a store without a theft problem is a waste of money and effort, yet relying on poor loss data may unintentionally cause this sort of mistake. Indeed, increasing the risk for offenders using a target-hardening approach is bound to fail if the wrong target is hardened! As the research has shown, store shrinkage figures are often an unreliable indicator of theft activity. Shrinkage figures may hide theft problems or may give the impression of greater losses than are actually occurring. This suggests that loss prevention managers must become much more critical of simple shrinkage figures before reacting to them.

Moreover, it should not be forgotten that the implications of poor data go beyond the security department. Indeed, improving stock data gives more reliable estimates of loss, allows more accurate buying and ensures that the correct stock is in-store to be sold. This means that data integrity is more than a simple loss prevention issue; it is one that affects the profitability of the business as a whole, and it should be recognised as such.

Notes

1   Vicky Turbin is a research officer at the Scarman Centre for the Study of Public Order, 154 Upper New Walk, Leicester, LE1 7QA. Tel: (0116) 2525706; fax: (0116) 2525766 (email: vjt4@leicester.ac.uk).

2   Brookes, C. and Cross, C. (1996) *Retail Crime Costs 1994/95 Survey*. London: British Retail Consortium.

3   Ibid.

4   Gill, M. (1994) Introducing Crime at Work. In Gill, M. (ed.) *Crime at Work*. Vol. I. Leicester: Perpetuity Press.

5   There is variation in recording practice for the term 'shrinkage'. Some retailers will include known losses due to crime whilst others will exclude such figures. The figures may also include wastage, clerical error and mark-downs. (BRC, 1996:20).

6   Masuda, B. (1992) Displacement vs Diffusion of Benefits and the Reduction of Inventory Losses in a Retail Environment. *Security Journal.* Vol. 3, No. 3, pp 131-136.

7   Brookes and Cross, op cit.

8   Beck, A., Gill, M. and Willis, A. (1994) Violence in Retailing: Physical and Verbal Victimisation of Staff. In Gill, M. (ed.) op cit, pp 83-101.

9   The author would like to acknowledge the invaluable assistance of Simon Reade and Chris Chappill (Loss Prevention Department), during this research project.

10   See Gill, M. and Turbin, V. (1998) CCTV and Shop Theft: Towards a Realistic Evaluation. In Norris, C., Armstrong, G. and Moran, J. (eds) *Surveillance, CCTV and Social Control.* Aldershot: Gower. Also, Gill, M. and Turbin, V. (1998) Evaluating 'Realistic Evaluation': Evidence from a Study of CCTV. In Tilley, N. and Painter, K. (eds) *Crime Prevention Studies.* Vol. 10. Monsey, New York: Criminal Justice Press.

11   Neeley, P. (1987) Simple Mathematics Applied to Inventory Accuracy. *Production and Inventory Management.* Vol. 28, pp 64-68.

12   There are also business implications to ignoring reflexive stock. If the previous report was incorrect but computer stock was adjusted to match that report, then for the intervening period until the next stocktake (or cycle-count) the store has incorrect stock. This means that for a maximum period of 13 weeks in this company (though it may be much longer in other companies) stock is being incorrectly replenished. There is also no guarantee that the following stocktake will correct these errors, particularly if they are due to process errors which have not been identified.

13   Brookes and Cross, op cit.

14   Butler, G. (1994) Shoplifters' Views on Security: Lessons for Crime Prevention. In Gill, M. (ed.) op cit, pp 56-72.

15   Buckle, A. and Farrington, D. (1984) An Observational Study of Shoplifting. *British Journal of Criminology.* Vol. 24, pp 63-73.

16   Buckle, A., Farrington, D., Burrows, J., Speed, M. and Burns-Howell, T. (1992) Measuring Shoplifting by Repeated Systematic Counting. *Security Journal.* Vol. 3, No. 3, pp 137-146.

17   Carter, N., Holmstrom, A., Simpanen, M. and Melin, L. (1988) Theft Reduction in a Grocery Store through Product Identification and Graphing of Losses for Employees. *Journal of Applied Behaviour Analysis.* Vol. 21, pp 385-389.

18   Masuda, op cit.

Chapter 3

High Risk, Low Risk: The Use of Data in the Identification of Potential Targets of Commercial Crime Offenders

Kate Bowers and Alex Hirschfield[1]

An important part of the process of increasing the effort and the risk to offenders who commit crimes against commercial premises is the identification of the potential targets of those offenders. Without such knowledge it is unlikely that even the most effective crime detection and prevention measures will have a substantial deterrent effect. This chapter examines the way in which information relating to victimisation can be used to identify the potential targets of commercial crime. The strengths and weaknesses of using Recorded Crime and survey information in this process are discussed. The chapter then goes on to describe some practical issues connected with the implementation of a crime prevention initiative (the Safer Merseyside Partnership's Small Business Strategy) on the basis of such information. The chapter concludes with a discussion of the importance of well-structured evaluation of such initiatives in order to further our knowledge of 'what works' in the prevention of crime.

Introduction

For many years, residential properties have been the focus not only of academic research into crime and crime patterns, but also of practical efforts to alleviate the problems of crime against individuals and properties. Research has recently turned to the problems of crimes against businesses and other commercial properties, and possibly as a result of this, crime prevention techniques have also begun to address the issue of business crime.

This raises the question of how the practitioner can identify properties that may be particularly vulnerable; in other words, single out Felson and Cohen's[2] 'suitable targets' of business crime. And then, once identified, to understand how the risk and/or the effort associated with the perpetration of a crime by an offender can be increased sufficiently to make it a less desirable target.

Not least of the obstacles associated with the implementation of such a scheme is the lack of availability of documentation laying out good practice in the area of business crime prevention. Much of the documentation that does exist forms part of the Home Office Crime Prevention Unit Series. These papers have, for example, described crime prevention initiatives within specific shops, such as a music store,[3] particular types of shop such as chemists,[4] Asian-run small shops,[5] sub-post offices,[6] and particular types of area, for example, industrial estates[7] and shopping centres.[8] Some of this work has focused on small businesses in general.[9] More recently, details of the implementation of the Small Business and Crime Initiative (SBCI), which aimed to decrease incidents of crime within the business community of two areas of Leicester, have become available.[10] However, as the editor outlined in introducing this book, much still needs to be done to establish what works most effectively in deterring crime against businesses in particular circumstances.

Other problems lie in the attitudes of members of the business community to crime prevention, in particular, its relatively low priority compared with the drive towards profitability. Furthermore, the work described in this chapter, which has been conducted on Merseyside, UK, has found that business managers often tolerate a certain level of crime as unavoidable, a phenomenon that is less likely to be found within the residential community.

There is also the serious problem of the lack of reliable information in a useful form relating to characteristics of businesses in a particular area and the level of crime from which they suffer. Recent Home Office literature has highlighted the need for police forces to have means of identifying repeatedly victimised individuals and properties.[11] This has proved to be a challenge from the point of view of domestic burglary, where address matching is relatively straightforward. The identification of repeat commercial burglary has more problems still, due to the various ways in which a commercial address can be represented. This issue will be examined later. There is the added problem of the determination of the number of businesses in operation in a particular area at a particular point in time. Such information is required in order to establish the prevalence rate of a type of business crime. Due to the nature of the establishments there is a substantial amount of turnover of businesses, which makes it difficult to maintain accurate figures for use in such analysis.

The use of information relating to the vulnerability of businesses to victimisation is an integral part of the crime management process. Research has shown that concentrating upon buildings (and indeed individuals) that have already been the subject of victimisation is an effective way of deterring further crime, since such buildings (and individuals) have a higher probability of being victimised again, especially in the short term.[12] Without such information it is difficult to make predictions about the possible targets of crime and hence to identify the premises on which we have to focus in order to increase the risk and effort to offenders through crime detection and prevention measures.

In order to develop a comprehensive strategy which can be targetted, monitored and evaluated effectively, access to the information described above in some form is essential, whether it is collected as primary information or supplied to practitioners as secondary information. Until the issue of data sharing between organisations is formalised, as it may well have to be with the implementation of the Crime and Disorder Act, the means by which this information is collected and the accuracy of this information are likely to vary greatly between different business crime initiatives.

The idiosyncrasies of projects aimed at deterring crime against business mean that each experience will require the formulation of a method which meets its own needs. The SBCI has shown how a successful initiative can be implemented in two small areas of Leicester. In this case every business in the defined area of interest has been considered. However, how can a strategy with limited resources be implemented most effectively in a larger area of interest, for example, at district or even county level? Research has shown that properties that have a history of victimisation are more likely to be victimised subsequently,[13] but what other criteria can be used to channel available resources into the business community?

The remainder of this paper addresses the issue of targetting, monitoring and evaluating a small business initiative which operates at county level, namely the Small Business Strategy of the Safer Merseyside Partnership.

Background

The Safer Merseyside Partnership (SMP) is a nine-year Single Regeneration Budget (SRB)-funded initiative covering the period 1995-2004 which is aimed at reducing levels of crime on Merseyside. The Small Business Strategy (SBS) is one of several programmes supported by the SMP. The SBS aims to tackle crime and improve community safety and the competitiveness of the local economy by increasing the security of businesses through the use of crime prevention techniques, and by introducing detection measures where businesses have experienced disproportionately high levels of crime.

In its early stages, the SBS operated a system whereby businesses across Merseyside were invited to apply for a grant. The application was then considered by a surveyor, who assessed the security of properties that appeared to be particularly vulnerable and recommended improvements. The major problem with this phase of the SBS was the disproportionate level of demand that was created by the use of an open-ended application strategy. Making everybody eligible for a grant in such a large geographical area as Merseyside, inevitably meant that as the scheme gained more public exposure the demand would eventually outweigh the available resources. Moreover, many of the businesses that needed urgent attention were not made aware that they would be eligible for a SBS grant.

For these reasons, a review of the SBS was conducted and recommended a second phase to the SBS in which businesses that were particularly vulnerable would be identified by the SMP and approached with an offer of assistance. It was considered important that the revised method have the following characteristics:

- a targetting system that identified the *need* that businesses had for crime prevention or detection measures (ie that identified the rate of victimisation and repeat victimisations to businesses);

- a system that could prioritise areas of the greatest need;
- a system that could be of benefit to as many residents as possible;
- a strategy that could be carried out at a steady pace to increase the efficiency of the target-hardening processes.

The revised strategy had to prioritise areas of need within the county. There are over 30,000 businesses across the whole of Merseyside. It would be an unmanageable task to try to visit and assist all of these businesses. Due to the frequency of victimisation of businesses it would be a major task just to visit all the businesses that had experienced crime. Therefore, it was important to identify a manageable subset of Merseyside's businesses that were in particular need of crime prevention assistance. It was also important, due to the objectives of SRB-funded initiatives, to produce a strategy that would benefit as many residents as possible within the most disadvantaged areas.

The identification of vulnerable businesses

In order to identify a manageable subset of businesses to consider assisting, the first objective of the scheme was to acquire a comprehensive list of businesses covering the whole of Merseyside. This was eventually obtained by approaching each of the five Local Authority Districts of Merseyside and asking for computerised copies of their firms' databases. Each district database contained information relating to the address of each business, the size of each business and a description of the activity of each business. This information was fed into a Geographical Information System (GIS), which enabled the location of each business to be cross-referenced with other geographical information. Through this process those businesses that fell into a particular urban policy priority area could be identified.

A preliminary sift of this database in order to obtain a manageable subset of properties, identified all the businesses on Merseyside with the following attributes:

- those that were small and had fewer than 25 employees;
- those that were within an European Union Objective One area;
- those that were within a residential area;
- those that were of a certain type (eg retail outlets, newsagents, etc).

The reasons for this choice of criteria were as follows: firstly, small businesses are more vulnerable since they have less resources to channel into crime prevention; larger businesses often have a central resource for security and many head offices produce guidelines which instruct staff in methods of dealing with incidents of crime. Secondly, businesses in Objective One areas were prioritised because these are the most deprived areas of Merseyside, which need to maintain their social fabric and employment opportunities and require assistance with both the economic and social regeneration of their communities. Thirdly, businesses in residential areas were seen to be a priority since they are vital to the well-being of the local community; if businesses in a residential neighbourhood are not thriving, the area is often seen as a less desirable place to live. Lastly, businesses of a certain type were seen to take priority in this phase of the SBS. These included: shops and retail establishments, manufacturing establishments, wholesalers, premises used for storage of goods, offices, private day nurseries, some service-based businesses, some leisure and entertainment establishments and some health care establishments.

Table 1 shows the number of businesses in each district which met the criteria of the preliminary sift.

Table 1. Businesses meeting research needs

District	No. of businesses within district	No. of businesses that are small and within residential Objective 1 area	Representative pilot study	Main phase of Survey
Sefton	6,084	127	2	51
Knowsley	1,015	82	1	33
St Helens	4,354	185	2	74
Wirral	8,539	857	10	340
Liverpool	10,306	1,266	15	502

Risk assessment of businesses

The preliminary sift of businesses resulted in a more manageable subset of establishments to assess for possible assistance. The next stage of the process was to identify establishments that were in particular need of crime prevention or detection measures. Primarily, risk assessment was to be based upon levels of burglary and repeat burglary reported to Merseyside Police by the business establishments. Therefore a method of identification of repeat burglaries against commercial premises was devised. A detailed account of this work can be found elsewhere.[14] However, there are several issues associated with the use of police data determining the level of repeat burglaries against commercial premises, and in the use of this information in connection with crime prevention.

*   There is a problem with the classification of the victimised property as a business or otherwise. This is because the police only separate crime records relating to burglary into 'residential' or 'non-residential' burglary. As a result all schools, public buildings, health services and businesses, for example, will be present in the crime records that need to be analysed. So far, the identification of different types of business has only been performed manually. It would be difficult to write a computer program that would separate out different types of property.

- There is also a problem with the way in which repeat victimisations are identified for businesses. This is because a business can be addressed in more than one way: for example, *The Green Room Cafe, Banks Road* might also be addressed as *121 Banks Road*. This could result in a proportion of the repeat burglaries being missed unless great care is taken.

- There is a further risk of under-reporting of incidents of commercial burglary. Victimised businesses may not feature in the crime records due to the fact that they have not reported the incidents to the police.

- Other information about crime risk is needed to augment the repeat burglary information, such as other types of victimisation experienced by the establishment, levels of loss associated with incidents and the number and quality of security devices the business has already installed.

- Lastly, there is a problem with the supply of police information. A strategy which aims to assist particularly vulnerable buildings needs current information on the crime affecting those buildings. The police data available to the SMP at the time of the revisions to the strategy was for the period 1994 to 1995. More recently, updates have been provided, but until consistent information can be provided and analysed on a regular basis, the SBS will need to search for and use other sources of information.

For these reasons the revised SBS assessed the vulnerability of businesses using results from a victimisation survey. The survey was designed to ask business managers about the following:

- The history of victimisation of the business (eg levels of burglary in the previous year).
- The cost of crime.
- Current security measures installed and maintained by the business.
- The age of the business.
- The organisational structure of the business (is it a free-standing business or part of a larger organisation?).
- The location of the business premises.
- Fear of crime experienced by the management and the staff.

The questions in the survey were taken from various sources. Many of the questions mirrored those asked by the Commercial Victimisation Survey conducted by the Home Office.[15] Some questions were also based on those included in the SBCI mentioned earlier. This has the advantage that it allows comparisons of the experience of crime within different areas and across different levels of resolution.

It was decided that a survey which covered all of the 2,517 businesses that were identified from the initial sift was impractical, given the resources provided for the SBS. For this reason, a sample of 1,000 randomly chosen businesses were surveyed. The random sample proportionally represented the overall number of eligible businesses in each district (see Table 1). In order to identify which of the 1,000 properties visited were most at risk, a scoring mechanism was devised in a pilot phase of the survey. This mechanism awarded points to businesses that:

- had an extensive history of victimisation, especially repeat burglary;
- had few or inadequately installed security measures;
- were free-standing businesses with no central support or central crime prevention strategy.

The mechanism was designed so that it could be easily processed by a surveyor on the business premises. The pilot survey enabled thresholds to be set which separated businesses into three different risk categories: low-risk, medium-risk and high-risk properties. The thresholds were set to enable the SMP to regulate the number of properties falling into medium and high risk and hence the number of properties that were given assistance.

Target hardening and crime detection

Those businesses that were identified as high or medium risk were asked if they would like to be visited by a Crime Prevention Officer (CPO) from their district. In the medium-risk case general advice is given about securing the premises. In addition to this, those properties falling into the high-risk category can be offered some financial assistance in target hardening their premises or, for particularly high-risk properties, the installation of a detection measure. No action is taken in the low-risk properties.

Therefore, the target hardening/crime detection process has two elements. First, some high-risk properties receive help with physical crime prevention measures or detection measures. The following types of assistance can be given:

Target hardening:
- help with the installation of CCTV cameras;
- provision of roller shutters for shop fronts;
- provision of rear entrance target hardening;
- provision of security mirrors;
- provision of other target-hardening devices up to the value of £1,500.

Crime detection devices:
- covert CCTV;
- forensic traps (eg smart water);
- enhanced directed patrolling;
- NEMCO alarms.

Physical measures can be valuable in securing properties or detecting crime. However, both medium and high-risk businesses were also involved in the second phase of target hardening, which dealt with the human element of crime prevention. Unfortunately, much crime prevention to date has concentrated on the use of physical devices without considering the role of managers and other individuals responsible for the security of the property. The SMP has recognised that the physical target hardening of a business alone will not necessarily be a particularly effective method of crime prevention. Therefore, each visit involves an individual crime risk assessment of the business and concentrates on problem-solving techniques that would be relevant to the particular business in question. The approach taken is generally very much a problem-oriented one. It is the belief of the SMP that such advice is just as effective as more expensive physical target hardening at reducing the levels of crime experienced by businesses; a belief that is reinforced by the experiences of the SBCI.

Preliminary findings from the small business survey

Several issues have been identified from the surveying process:

- There is a high rate of turnover of businesses. Approximately one third of the sample could not be contacted due to the fact that the organisation had moved from the address specified on the database or had closed down. This is an important issue when constructing crime rates based on the number of businesses in an area.

- A proportion of the organisations said that the manager was unavailable or too busy to participate in the survey after several visits by the surveyor.

- In many instances, there was a positive response to the survey and business managers were only too happy to set up a meeting with the Crime Prevention Officer. Many felt they had had little help with or advice on crime prevention from other sources.

To date, 121 meetings with Crime Prevention Officers have been organised; 87 of these businesses fall into the high-risk category and the remaining 34 fall into the medium-risk category. At the time of writing, the CPOs were currently making the final visits to the identified high and medium-risk properties. The SMP is currently receiving confirmations of acceptance of grant aid by the high-risk businesses. Figure 1 is a flow diagram of the process by which properties receive help.

Monitoring and evaluation

It is important with any initiative to have a rigorous method of evaluation. The University of Liverpool has taken on the role of evaluator of the SBS. A database has been set up at the University which holds information collected by the surveyors in the selection process. This database includes the businesses that have not had target-hardening assistance as well as those that have. A follow-up survey, carried out one year after the initial survey will collect information from all the businesses originally surveyed. This will enable a comparison of the levels of crime experienced by those who did and those who did not receive assistance from the SMP.

Figure 1: Small business strategy flow chart

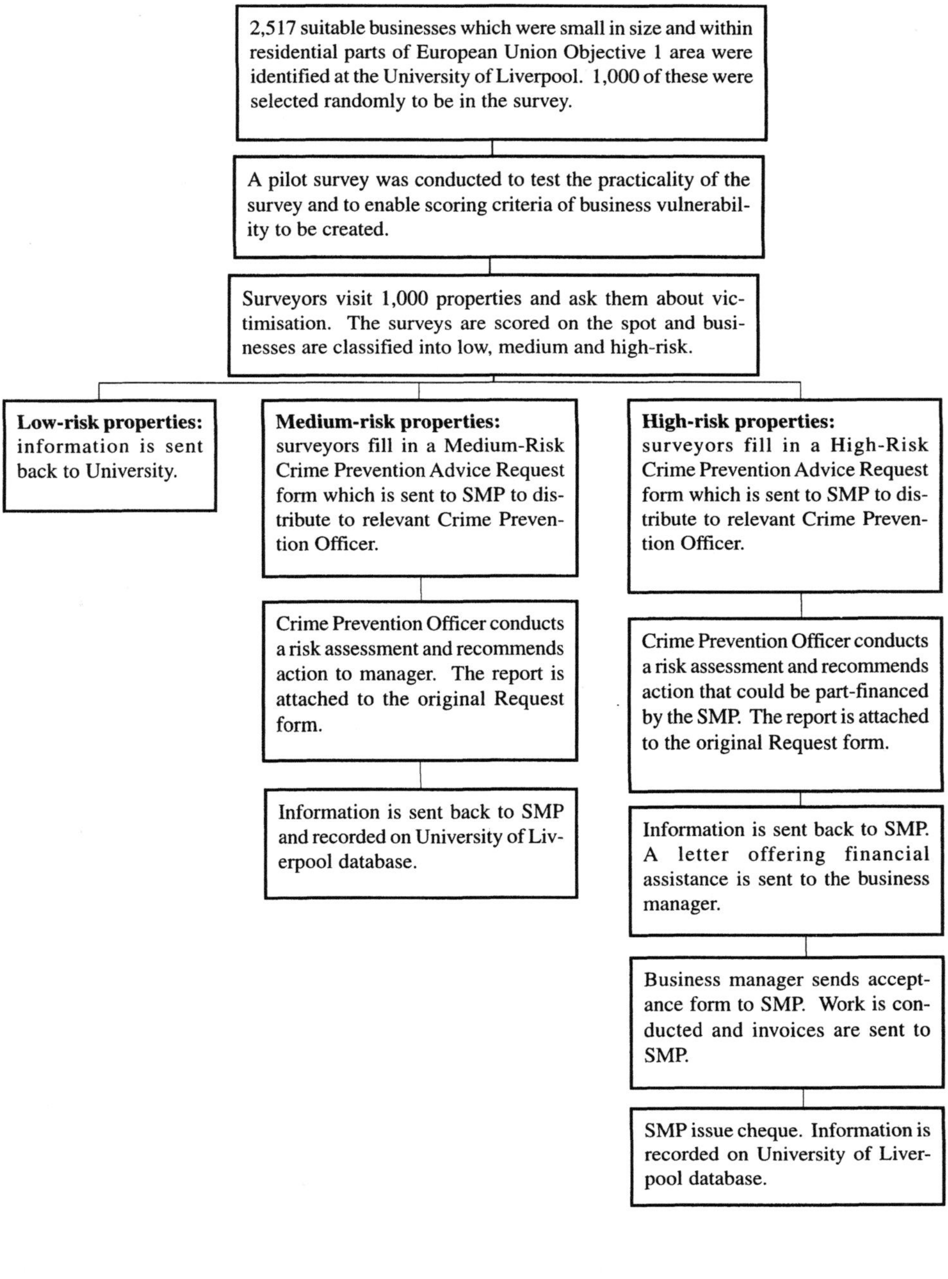

2,517 suitable businesses which were small in size and within residential parts of European Union Objective 1 area were identified at the University of Liverpool. 1,000 of these were selected randomly to be in the survey.

A pilot survey was conducted to test the practicality of the survey and to enable scoring criteria of business vulnerability to be created.

Surveyors visit 1,000 properties and ask them about victimisation. The surveys are scored on the spot and businesses are classified into low, medium and high-risk.

Low-risk properties: information is sent back to University.

Medium-risk properties: surveyors fill in a Medium-Risk Crime Prevention Advice Request form which is sent to SMP to distribute to relevant Crime Prevention Officer.

High-risk properties: surveyors fill in a High-Risk Crime Prevention Advice Request form which is sent to SMP to distribute to relevant Crime Prevention Officer.

Crime Prevention Officer conducts a risk assessment and recommends action to manager. The report is attached to the original Request form.

Crime Prevention Officer conducts a risk assessment and recommends action that could be part-financed by the SMP. The report is attached to the original Request form.

Information is sent back to SMP and recorded on University of Liverpool database.

Information is sent back to SMP. A letter offering financial assistance is sent to the business manager.

Business manager sends acceptance form to SMP. Work is conducted and invoices are sent to SMP.

SMP issue cheque. Information is recorded on University of Liverpool database.

A longitudinal analysis of individual properties will establish whether the high, medium and low-risk properties have experienced any incidents in the year following the initial survey. Hopefully, the high and medium-risk properties will show a decrease in the number of crimes they have experienced and therefore indicate that overall, crime risks have decreased since the intervention period of the SBS. It will also be possible to investigate the effectiveness of different crime prevention strategies using this information. For instance, the level of crime experienced by properties that have been provided with new roller shutters could be compared to those that have received window locks or reinforced doors. Analysis can also help to establish whether crime prevention advice is more cost-effective, in terms of deterring crime, than assistance towards physical target-hardening measures. Such individual level analysis can therefore look at some of the more direct effects of SBS intervention upon levels of crime experienced by businesses.

Information from Merseyside Police's crime reports will also play a central role in the evaluation process. As mentioned above, data relating to non-residential burglary and other types of crime against businesses such as shoplifting and robbery has been acquired for the period before the SBS commenced. Analysis of these data alongside the survey data will allow a baseline to be established, to which comparisons will be made on completion of the initiative.

The Recorded Crime information covers a time period of just under three years before the commencement of the second phase of the SBS. This information can be processed to allow change over time to be monitored. Figure 2 shows the number of commercial burglaries committed in each quarter (three-month period) of the time period available for the whole of Merseyside. It is apparent from this Figure that overall the number of commercial burglaries committed on Merseyside has decreased over the last few years. If this trend continues, it will be encouraging for the SBS, but also very difficult to attribute the decline to the introduction of the revised SBS in an environment where crime levels are already declining.

Figure 2: Number of commercial burglaries

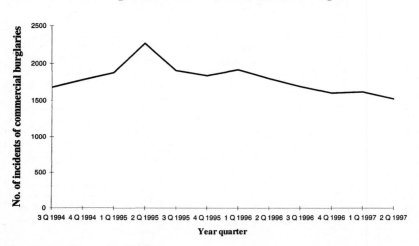

Figure 3: Commercial burglary rates

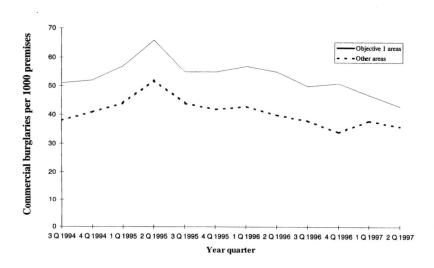

In order to examine the effect of the SBS in more detail, it is necessary to compare the way in which the level of crime changes over time within the SBS operational areas to other areas of Merseyside. In order to do this effectively, we need to compare crime *rates* within the operational areas to other areas. Figure 3 therefore shows commercial burglaries per 1,000 commercial premises per quarter for Merseyside's Objective One areas in comparison to all other areas of the county. Figure 3 shows a similar story to Figure 2: there was a peak in the commercial burglary rate both inside and outside Objective One areas in the second quarter of 1995, and over the past three years there has been a substantial decline in the number of commercial burglaries committed. However, the commercial burglary rate in the Objective One areas is unanimously higher than in other areas. The level of commercial burglary within the Objective One areas also increased in the fourth quarter of 1996, when commercial burglary in other areas was at its lowest for the entire time period. It is also clear that the rates for the two types of area have been converging since 1997. Sustained, closer convergence after the SBS initiative was implemented would be another indication that the initiative was successful.

However, the evaluation can be more specific still and calculate the commercial burglary rate for residential parts of Objective One areas. This is possible using a GIS to establish the number of crimes and the number of premises that fall within these areas alone. This can be compared with the crime rate in non-residential Objective One areas and other areas. Figures 4a and 4b show the results from this analysis. These Figures demonstrate that there are two very different pictures emerging from the Objective One areas. Figure 4a shows that the commercial burglary rate in the non-residential areas is very similar for the Objective One areas and the other areas of Merseyside. Although the rates within the priority areas are generally slightly higher, there are year quarters where the burglary rate for the rest of Merseyside is actually greater than the rate within the priority areas (the first and fourth quarter of 1995). The non-residential area burglary rates also follow the trend seen in Figures 2 and 3, with a general decline in the rates over the three-year period.

Figure 4a: Commercial burglary rates in non-residential areas

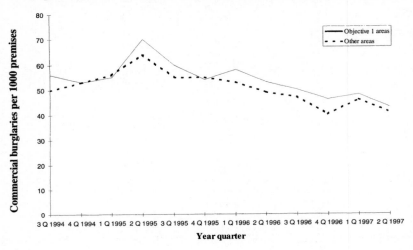

Figure 4b: Commercial burglary rates in residential areas

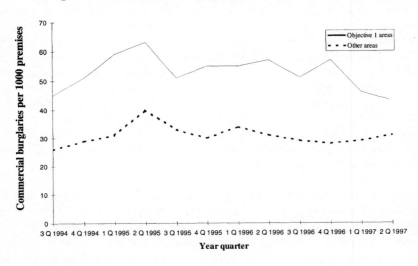

It is obvious, however, from Figure 4b that it is within the residential areas that the differences in the burglary rates lie. The commercial burglary rates within the residential areas of Objective One areas are very much higher than for such areas across the rest of Merseyside. In fact, in many cases the rate within the residential priority areas is over twice that elsewhere. Furthermore, the rate within the residential priority areas is very similar to that within the non-residential priority areas, and this is certainly not the case in the rest of Merseyside. It is also interesting to observe from Figure 4b that the general decline in commercial burglary is far less pronounced in the residential areas of Merseyside. This evidence suggests that the SMP is concentrating resources in the areas of Merseyside that do have particular problems with commercial burglary.

The Figures discussed above help give a context to the way in which commercial burglary rates may or may not decrease with the implementation of the SBS in its particular operational areas. It is a process of taking all the evidence into account which will allow conclusions to be drawn as to whether the initiative has been successful. The evidence put forward here is only part of the evaluation process: there is the need to gather evidence concerning other crime types, such a shoplifting or robbery, since the initiative also aims to reduce the incidence of these crimes where possible.

The Figures do address another problem which may arise as a result of the SBS to a certain degree: that of displacement of crime to other areas. If there is a general decrease in commercial burglary in the residential parts of Objective One areas and an increase in the non-residential parts, and this trend is not observed in other areas of Merseyside, it may be the case that some crime has displaced from the residential parts of Objective One areas to the non-residential parts. However, this sort of analysis may fail to pick up any local changes in crime patterning. Displacement may be more of a problem in specific areas where the scheme operates. In order to address this issue a more detailed spatial analysis of crime patterns over time which uses GIS technology is required.

A GIS system that is undergoing development at the University of Liverpool (details forthcoming) investigates the issue of displacement on a disaggregate level. The system intends to give a picture of crime patterning in regions just outside the priority area of an initiative as well as examining the crime patterning within it, in order to establish whether crime is displacing into adjacent areas. The maps can be created for time periods before, during and after the intervention of an initiative, which allows the investigator to identify the location of the problem areas within and adjacent to an initiative priority area over time.

This approach has obvious applications in the longitudinal evaluation of the side effects of an initiative such as the SBS. It has the added advantage that the situation *within* a priority boundary can be analysed. As mentioned above, the SBS operates in the residential parts of Objective One areas. It should be possible to monitor any shift in the distribution of non-residential burglaries between the residential and non-residential parts of specific priority areas using such an approach.

Finally, some consideration of the effects of other initiatives which may be running in the operational areas of the SBS is required. This is very often difficult to quantify, not least due to the fact that it is seldom possible to be aware of all the schemes running in an area as large as Merseyside.

Summary

This chapter has described how one of the key issues in increasing the risk and effort involved in committing crime against businesses is the identification of premises that have a disproportionate risk of being victimised. The ability to identify such businesses relies on the collection of accurate information relating to the victimisation history of commercial premises. A crucial part of the crime management process is to get to the potential targets of an offender, before the offender does. Without identifying such vulnerable targets the best crime detection and prevention measures in the world will prove ineffective. We have seen how information from various sources can be used to identify such targets. Once the risk is identified, deterring as much crime as possible is a balance of crime prevention and crime detection, and an approach which uses both of these methods is often advisable. The Safer Merseyside Partnership Small Business Strategy is an example of such an approach.

Crime prevention can usefully be seen as a combination of physical security devices such as roller shutters or burglar alarms and individual assistance regarding the particular needs of an establishment. Business managers need to be made aware of ways in which the management of crime prevention can influence the effectiveness of measures. For instance, CCTV cameras are not likely to be effective unless they are monitored properly.

A further concern is that the value of such approaches is often undetermined due to the fact that there are few examples of well-evaluated schemes. It is important to record the progress of individual premises assisted by the scheme, and to compare any change in crime risk with other premises that did not receive assistance. Such monitoring can be particularly useful in distinguishing between the effectiveness of different crime prevention or crime detection measures. It is also important to monitor levels of crime in the operational area of a scheme in relation to other control areas with similar characteristics. The possibility of displacement of crime to other areas should also be addressed.

Such detailed monitoring and evaluation depends upon the availability of sufficient information and of the necessary analysis tools, such as Geographical Information Systems or crime pattern analysis programmes. To date, access to such facilities has been very limited. With the introduction of the Crime and Disorder Act, the issue of data sharing and processing will start to be addressed more formally and hopefully this will lead to the emergence of well-evaluated crime prevention initiatives aimed at the business community.

Notes

1   Kate Bowers is a PhD. student and Alex Hirschfield a senior researcher in the Department of Civic Design, University of Liverpool, Abercromby Square, L69 3BX.

2   Cohen, L. and Felson, M. (1979) Social Change and Crime Rate Trends: A Routine Activity Approach. *American Sociological Review.* Vol. 44, pp 588-608.

3   Ekblom, P. (1986) *The Prevention of Shop Theft: An Approach Through Crime Analysis.* Crime Prevention Unit Paper 5. London: Home Office.

4   Laycock, G. (1984) *Reducing Burglary: a Study of Chemists' Shops.* Crime Prevention Unit Paper 1. London: Home Office.

5   Ekblom, P. and Simon, F. (1988) *Crime and Racial Harassment in Asian-Run Small Shops: The Scope for Prevention.* Crime Prevention Unit Paper 15. London: Home Office.

6   Ekblom, P. (1987) *Preventing Robberies at Sub-post Offices: An Evaluation of a Security Initiative.* Crime Prevention Unit Paper 9. London: Home Office.

7   Johnston, V., Leitner, M., Shapland, J. and Wiles, P. (1994) *Crime on Industrial Estates.* Crime Prevention Unit paper 54. London: Home Office; see also Johnston, V., Leitner, M., Shapland, J. and Wiles, P. (1994) Crime, Business and Policing on Industrial Estates. In Gill, M. (ed.) *Crime at Work.* Vol. I. Leicester: Perpetuity Press.

8   Phillips, S and Cochrane, R. (1988) *Crime and Nuisance in the Shopping Centre: a Case Study in Crime Prevention.* Crime Prevention Unit Paper 16. London: Home Office.

9   Tilley, N. (1993) *The Prevention of Crime Against Small Businesses: The Safer Cities Experience.* Crime Prevention Unit Paper 45. London: Home Office.

10   Wood, J., Wheelwright, G. and Burrows, J. (1997) *Crime Against Small Business: Facing the Challenge.* Swindon: Crime Concern.

11   Bridgeman, C. and Hobbs, L. (1997) *Preventing Repeat Victimisation: the Police Officers' Guide.* London: Home Office.

12   Chenery, S., Holt, J. and Pease, K. (1997) *Biting Back II: Reducing Repeat Victimisation in Huddersfield.* Crime Detection and Prevention Series Paper 82. London: Home Office.

13   Farrell, G. and Pease, K. (1993) *Once Bitten, Twice Bitten: Repeat Victimisation and its Implications for Crime Prevention.* Crime Prevention Unit Paper 46. London: Home Office; see also Chenery, S. Ellingworth, D., Tseloni, A. and Pease, K. (1996) Crimes Which Repeat: Undigested Evidence from the British Crime Survey 1992. *International Journal of Risk, Security and Crime Prevention.* Vol. 1, No. 3, pp 207-216; and Gill, M. (forthcoming) The Victimisation of Business: Crimes Which Repeat and the Indicators of Risk. Accepted for publication in the *International Review of Victimology.*

14   Bowers, K., Hirschfield, A. and Johnson, S. (1998) Victimisation Revisited: A Case Study of Non-Residential Repeat Burglary on Merseyside. *British Journal of Criminology.* Vol. 38, No. 3, pp 429-52.

15   Mirrlees-Black, C. and Ross, A. (1995) *Crime Against Retail and Manufacturing Premises: Findings from the 1994 Commercial Victimisation Survey.* Home Office Research Study 146. London: Home Office.

Chapter 4

Commercial Crime, Crime Prevention and Community Safety: A Study of Three Streets in Camden, North London

Matt Hopkins and Nick Tilley[1]

Research has indicated that businesses suffer from higher rates of victimisation than households. This produces high consequent financial losses from crime. In the light of these findings, interest in business victimisation, the costs of crime to businesses and how businesses can reduce their risks of victimisation has grown amongst both academics and practitioners. This chapter reports the findings of a research project which investigated commercial crime on three streets in the London Borough of Camden. First,the rates of business victimisation and the impact of crime on businesses are discussed. Second, the efforts of businesses to increase the risks of crime for offenders through installation of crime prevention measures are considered. Finally, business involvement in community safety and the problems encountered when trying to increase it are discussed.

Introduction

This chapter summarises the findings of a commercial victimisation survey commissioned by Camden Council (and supported by Safer Cities) to investigate small businesses' experience of, and involvement with, community safety issues such as harassment and criminal acts.[2] The enquiry focused on three streets where particular concerns about crime against businesses had been raised.

There were four key objectives to the research. The first was to investigate business experience of crime, intimidation and harassment in the previous 12 months. The second was to investigate the impact of crime and harassment upon the business and individual members of staff. The third was to examine the extent of business involvement in current crime prevention and community safety issues, and the fourth was to assess how businesses might become involved in these issues.

A comprehensive face-to-face interview with all businesses in the target streets willing to take part in the survey was asked for, because of the potential significance of crime for planned local area regeneration efforts. With regard to the size of the crime problem, it was recognised that police data might be inadequate for identifying issues and planning preventive responses: for example, not all offences are reported and of those reported not all have been recorded; records of crimes have not routinely distinguished commercial victims from non-commercial ones; and there have been difficulties in accurately assigning incidents to particular locations.

This chapter will consider variations in crime experiences and the impact of crime in the three streets. It confirms earlier research findings which have revealed generally much higher rates of victimisation of business premises compared to domestic households, though it also shows that problem patterns are highly localised. The chapter will go on to discuss how businesses are involved in crime reduction and increasing risks for potential offenders through the installation of preventive measures and participation in community safety. It will then assess the problems encountered when trying to involve businesses in community safety.

The three streets

The three streets under review were geographically removed from each other: Petunia Street, in the Somers Town area; Bluerose Street, in the Regent's Park area and Redaster Crescent, in the Gospel Oak area. Petunia Street and Bluerose Street are located close to St Pancras and Euston railway stations. Redaster Crescent is situated in a quieter residential area ten minutes walk' from Chalk Farm tube station.

All three streets are around half a mile in length. Only Bluerose Street had regular road traffic passing through. The business composition in each street consisted largely of small independent retailers and service providers: 68% of businesses employed between 1-4 staff, while only 7% employed over 20 or more. However, the appearance of the three streets varied. Petunia Street and Redaster Crescent had a mixture of newsagent, off-licence and cafe-type businesses that seemed to be economically marginal. Several of the shops on both Petunia Street and Redaster Crescent were disused and both streets had areas of graffiti. Both Petunia Street and Redaster Crescent had a street market (Petunia one day per week and Redaster two days per week), which increased the opportunity for street crime and petty theft from market stalls. By contrast, Bluerose Street appeared to be more affluent. It is well known, especially for its long-established Indian restaurants which draw custom from all over London.

All three streets were close to areas of low-income housing and known to have crime problems. Petunia Street and Bluerose Street had witnessed severe racial tension in the early 1990s, which culminated in the racially motivated murder of Richard Everitt in Somers Town in 1995. Redaster Crescent had acquired a reputation for petty crime such as street robbery on market days, and people were often found drinking on the street.

Patterns of crime, intimidation and harassment

The requirement of the research was not only to gauge the level of crime on the three streets, but also to compare these findings with relevant ones from the Commercial Victimisation Survey (CVS) and the Small Business and Crime Initiative survey (SBCI), which have become standard reference points in this type of research.[3] The 1994 CVS was a national victimisation survey of manufacturers and retailers, conducted by the Home Office. The SBCI was a demonstration project examining crime against small businesses carried out in Leicester, and dealt with all business types. Comparisons are made with the most relevant subsets of the CVS and SBCI data, generally retailers with ten or fewer workers in regard to the CVS, and services and retailers in the case of the SBCI survey.

As with previous research in this area, it proved necessary to survey businesses in the three streets to assess their crime problems.[4] The Three Streets survey drew on questions used in the CVS and SBCI research.[5] An effort was made to conduct interviews with representatives from all businesses trading in the three streets and an overall response rate of 84% (n=87) was achieved. In each street over 85% of the respondents were either owners or managers. The fieldwork for the project was carried out between 21 September and 11 October 1997.[6]

The findings below present the prevalence, incidence and concentration of crime in the three streets. Prevalence (P) measures the number of businesses within the given population which were victimised once or more than once, incidence (I) measures the number of offences suffered; and concentration (C) measures the average numbers of offences committed against each victim.[7]

The relationship between prevalence, incidence and concentration can be described with the simple equation: I = PC. Data for prevalence and incidence are presented as rates per 100 businesses.

Table 1. Prevalence rates for offence types across the three streets (absolute numbers given in brackets)

Offence type	Petunia Street	Bluerose Street	Redaster Crescent	All three
Abuse	37 (10)	47 (13)	66 (21)	51 (44)
Customer theft	37 (10)	36 (10)	66 (21)	47 (41)
Fraud by outsiders	19 (5)	54 (15)	66 (21)	47 (41)
Criminal damage	37 (10)	29 (8)	28 (9)	31 (27)
Burglary (with entry)	7 (2)	32 (9)	16 (5)	18 (16)
Violence	22 (6)	11 (3)	25 (8)	20 (17)
Robbery	11 (3)	4 (1)	0	5 (4)
All crime*	70 (17)	86 (20)	78 (25)	71 (62)

*Excludes customer theft and abuse.

Table 1 shows that across the three streets 71% of businesses experienced at least one incident excluding customer theft and abuse. The highest rate was in Bluerose Street and the lowest in Petunia Street. The highest prevalence rate for all offences was for abuse, customer theft and fraud. These three offence types were particularly prevalent on Redaster Crescent with 66% of businesses experiencing at least one of each. The most prevalent crime on Bluerose Street was fraud (54%), with abuse, customer theft and criminal damage being the most prevalent on Petunia Street.

Table 2. Incidence rates for offences types across the three streets

Offence type	Petunia Street	Bluerose Street	Redaster Crescent	All three
Fraud by outsiders	59 (16)	157 (44)	119 (38)	113 (98)
Criminal damage	100 (37)	104 (29)	94 (30)	110 (96)
Violence	56 (15)	29 (8)	60 (19)	48 (42)
Burglary (with entry)	7 (2)	57 (16)	16 (5)	26 (23)
Robbery	11 (4)	4 (1)	0	5 (5)
All crime	304 (75)	432 (102)	419 (109)	387 (286)

Table 2 shows that the overall incidence rate for all crime was 387 per 100 businesses. Therefore if all incidents were spread evenly across 100 businesses, each business would be expected to be victim of 3.87 incidents a year. The incidence rate was highest in Bluerose Street (432 per 100), closely followed by Redaster Crescent (419 per 100). Excluding customer theft and abuse, where estimates cannot be made because in some businesses incidents occurred so often they were unable to estimate their frequency, the highest incidence rates were for fraud and criminal damage, at 113 and 110 per 100 businesses respectively.

Table 3 shows that on average a victim of crime on any of the three streets would suffer 4.6 incidents in one year. The highest rate was found on Redaster Crescent, where a victim would expect to experience 5.4 incidents in one year. Despite the high incidence rates for fraud, the highest number of incidents per victim was for criminal damage with an average of 3.5 incidents a year. This figure was constant across all streets, with an average of 3.7 on Petunia Street, 3.6 on Bluerose Street and 3.3 on Redaster Crescent. There were also high concentration rates for fraud and violence at 2.4 and 2.5 respectively for all streets combined. Again, these rates were similar for each street, except for fraud on Redaster Crescent, which had a lower rate than the other two. Excluding the more common incidents of abuse and customer theft, it is notable that 11 of the businesses suffered 46% of all the crimes identified in the survey.

When compared with other surveys, it emerged that there was a great deal of minor crime and nuisance across all three streets. The Commercial Victimisation Survey and the Small Business and Crime Initiative survey both found higher prevalence rates for burglary (CVS= 22, SBCI=40, Three Streets=18), as well as higher incidence and concentration rates than the three streets. However, the three streets had higher prevalence rates for criminal damage, customer theft, fraud, violence and abuse.

Within the three streets the prevalence rates for external fraud in Bluerose Street and Redaster Crescent were unusually high by SBCI and CVS standards. Taking all crimes together, the three streets shared a similar overall crime rate to that found in other studies, though - as indicated - their distribution has some distinctive characteristics.

Table 3. Concentration rate for offence types across the three streets

Offence type	Petunia Street	Bluerose Street	Redaster Crescent	All three
Burglary (with entry)	1	1.8	1	1.4
Criminal damage	3.7	3.6	3.3	3.5
Robbery	1	1	0	1.3
Fraud by outsiders	2.5	2.9	1.8	2.4
Violence	2.5	2.7	2.8	2.5
All crime	4.4	5.1	5.4	4.6

The impact of crime on businesses and their staff

Financial losses from crime
The financial impact of crime against businesses was examined in terms of both the average loss per incident and the average loss per victim.

Table 4. Average loss per incident in pounds

Offence type	Petunia Street	Bluerose Street	Redaster Crescent	All three
Burglary (with entry)	800	3,284	625	3,073
Criminal damage	35	324	83	138
Fraud by outsiders	32	31	12	24
All*	72	788	102	260

* This excludes customer theft.

Table 4 shows the average financial loss per incident from various crime types. Overall, the average loss per incident was £260, though the figure for Bluerose Street was much higher than the other two streets. Incidents of burglary led to the highest average losses. Again Bluerose Street lost most per incident.[8] When compared to the CVS and the SBCI the average losses for an incident of burglary tended to be higher in the three streets at £3,073 per incident compared to £790 in the CVS and £1,158 in the SBCI survey. However, the average loss per incident for criminal damage and fraud was substantially lower than for these comparison surveys.

Table 5. Average losses per victim in pounds

Offence type	Petunia Street	Bluerose Street	Redaster Crescent	All three
Burglary	800	6,240	1,000	4,419
Criminal damage	130	1,175	278	489
Fraud	102	92	22	57
All	228	3,086	367	1,412

Table 5 shows that the average total of crime losses per victim over the 12-month period was £1,412. On average, burglary cost victims £4,419 per year, with the highest losses on Bluerose Street. Criminal Damage cost victims on Bluerose Street £1,175, which is substantially higher than on Petunia Street or Redaster Crescent. In contrast to Bluerose Street, overall financial losses from crime to businesses in Petunia Street were relatively low, with an average of £72 per incident (excluding customer theft) and £228 per victimised premises.

Bluerose Street not only had an atypically high rate of burglary, as Table 1 shows, but it also revealed unusually high losses per incident. At an average of £3,284 per burglary incident, the losses were over three times the average for small retailers in the CVS, and more than twice those found in the SBCI survey. The loss per victimised premises was £6,240. This was over three times the average found in the CVS and SBCI surveys. Bluerose Street also experienced high costs in relation to criminal damage. At £324 the average cost per incident was higher than that found in the other two streets in the survey. The average cost per victimised premises was very high at £1,175.

Though there was a great deal of low-level crime and nuisance in Redaster Crescent, as well as more major crime, this did not lead to very high financial losses. The average cost of crime per victim in the area was £367, which was higher than Petunia Street but rather lower than that in Bluerose Street, or that found in other comparative research.

Other crime impacts
In addition to the financial cost of crime to businesses, the human costs of crime against businesses can also be substantial. The Three Streets Project considered these in several ways. Businesses were asked about various responses to crime: whether crime had ever caused them to consider relocation; how they perceived the local consequences of crime; how they perceived local crime problems; and times when workers were particularly worried about crime.

In total, 30% of businesses claimed they had considered relocating due to the effect of crime, and 29% had considered ceasing trading. Businesses in Redaster Crescent were most likely to have considered relocation or ceasing trading. Over three-quarters of businesses (80%) thought that crime had damaged the image of the local area and 54% saw crime as an obstacle to business growth. Over 80% of businesses in Petunia Street and Redaster Crescent saw crime as damaging the local area and 65% on Bluerose Street and 60% on Redaster Crescent saw crime as an obstacle to business growth.

Businesses were also asked about their perceptions of general crime and nuisance problems such as youths hanging around, vandalism or racial tension. Youths hanging around were seen as the most serious problem on all of the three streets, with 74% of businesses viewing the problem as serious or fairly serious. Crime was viewed as the second most serious problem overall, with 70% of respondents describing it as serious or fairly serious. There were some distinct variations in perceptions of problems between streets. Crime was viewed as the second most serious problem on Redaster Crescent and Bluerose Street, whereas graffiti was viewed as the second most serious problem on Petunia Street. It is also worth noting that drinking in public was seen as a significant problem on Redaster Crescent by 56% of businesses. Racial tension was viewed as a significant problem on Bluerose Street, with 55.2% of businesses seeing this as a fairly serious problem. And empty and boarded-up premises were seen as significant problems on both Petunia Street and Redaster Crescent, but not on Bluerose Street.

As had also been found in the SBCI survey, businesses were most worried about crime when staff were alone on the premises or in the evenings. However, there were variations between streets here. In Petunia Street 39% of businesses said they were most worried about crime when leaving staff alone on the premises, as did 24% in Redaster Crescent and only 6% in Bluerose Street. Only 11% of businesses in Petunia Street and 4% in Redaster Crescent were most worried during evening times, compared to 61% in Bluerose Street. These differences may reflect varying trading patterns of the business populations in the three streets. Bluerose Street businesses were more likely to trade during the evening and were therefore less likely to leave workers on their own on the premises.

Increasing the risks for offenders. Business involvement in crime prevention and community safety

The survey identified clear crime problems in the three streets, and over two-thirds of businesses viewed crime as a serious or fairly serious problem. As a result, one may expect business involvement in crime prevention/ community safety to be high. This was assessed in two ways, first by consideration of physical security measures installed in the business (such as alarm systems and CCTV); and second by participation in relevant partnerships such as traders' associations or business watch.

Physical security
Overall, 51% of businesses responding to the survey had an intruder alarm and security shutters at the front of the premises, whilst external CCTV, internal shutters or dummy CCTV were least prevalent, with under 10% overall having any of these. This shows that the Camden businesses were less likely to have alarms than those in the SBCI survey, though they were more likely to have security shutters.[9] There were some variations be-

tween streets. Businesses on Redaster Crescent seemed to be the most security conscious, with 59% having an alarm, 56% shutters, 53% bars or grilles and 50% a panic alarm. Only 30% of businesses on Bluerose Street had alarms (compared to 52% on Petunia Street and 59% on Redaster Crescent); 50% of businesses on Redaster Crescent had a panic button (compared to only 33% on Petunia Street and 21% on Bluerose Street); and only 11% on Petunia Street had CCTV (as compared to 25% on Bluerose Street and 28% on Redaster Crescent).

Whether security is installed due to victimisation, the perceived risk from crime, or the ability to afford it is unclear. Given the apparent problems on Redaster Crescent with abuse and violence, the relatively high number of businesses with panic alarms is unsurprising. Businesses on Petunia Street may not have installed CCTV because they were the most economically marginal of the three streets. The fact that Bluerose Street had the lowest proportion of businesses with alarms might go some way to explaining why it had the highest rate of burglary, though it is unlikely to be the only factor.

Present participation in partnerships
In addition to installing physical security, businesses in all three areas were involved in traders' associations, though there was no evidence of a business watch scheme on any street. The traders' associations were groups of businesses from the same locality which met to discuss shared problems, including those to do with crime. However, it was unclear how often the associations met, who led the associations and what they did to reduce crime. They tended to be reactive rather than proactive (with the possible exception of Bluerose Street) and their survival seemed to depend on Council servicing or leadership from especially committed individuals.

Future prospects for business involvement in community safety partnerships

The local authority were interested in businesses' views as to how they thought community safety could be improved and who should be responsible for community safety.

Businesses were given a list of eight initiatives designed to improve community safety such as CCTV, business watch and private security guards. They were than asked to rank their top three options for improving community safety or if they wished, they could add any options that did not appear on the list.

Table 6 shows which measures respondents thought would be most effective in improving community safety. The most popular choice was CCTV, with 68% viewing it as the most effective potential measure. The second most popular option was for 'cleaner streets', which 13% of businesses favoured. Only 1% of businesses saw schemes such as business watch as effective. There was little variation between streets. On all streets CCTV was the most favoured option, followed by 'cleaner streets' on Petunia Street and Bluerose Street and private security on Redaster Crescent. The CCTV option is clearly problematic for streets with smallish independent businesses. CCTV is expensive to install and very costly to run effectively. Where cost-sharing arrangements between public and private sector bodies are required (as in CCTV Challenge),[10] it will be very difficult for streets of the sort examined in the Three Streets Project to raise the private sector contribution and to compete effectively.

Table 6. Percentage of respondents stating which of the following measures would be most effective in improving community safety

Community safety measures	Petunia Street	Bluerose Street	Redaster Crescent	All three
CCTV in public places	64.7	77.8	60.7	68
Cleaner streets	17.6	11.1	10.7	13
Well-lit streets	0	7.4	10.7	6.9
Private security patrols	0	0	11	4.2
Fewer boarded-up shops	5.9	0	3.6	2.8
More contact with neighbours	5.9	0	3.6	2.8
Fewer empty houses	5.9	0	0	1.4
Business watch	0	3.7	0	1

The respondents were also given a choice of groups who may be able to improve community safety, including the local authority, adjoining businesses, adjoining householders and businesses of the same type in the area. They were then asked if they thought the respective groups could provide a 'great deal', 'a little help', 'not much help' or 'no help at all' in improving community safety.

As Table 7 shows, overall the local authority was most commonly believed to be able to do most to improve community safety, with 44% of businesses saying it could provide a 'great deal' or a 'little help'. On Petunia Street and Bluerose Street the local authority was most frequently deemed to be able to provide most help. Only on Redaster Crescent was the most favoured option for local businesses to work with other adjoining businesses. Here, 50% of businesses thought this would provide the most help in improving community safety. Bluerose Street appears to offer rather little support for work with other businesses, though this may reflect the fact that it was considered that matters were already being addressed through the relatively active traders' association.

Table 7. Percentage of respondents stating that the following could provide 'a great deal' or 'a little help' in improving community safety

Various groups	Petunia Street	Bluerose Street	Redaster Crescent	All three
Local authority	56	39	38	44
Adjoining businesses	33	14	50	33
Adjoining householders	33	18	25	22
Businesses of same type	7	14	38	21

The difficulties in stimulating businesses' own involvement in community safety issues should not be underestimated. In the SBCI survey, notwithstanding dedicated efforts to persuade businesses to work in partnership with each other, there was felt to be only limited success. Similarly, a report of Phase One of the Safer Cities programme noted substantial problems in involving the business community actively.[11] Where there is one or more large store, especially when part of a group which has significant crime prevention interests, there may be leadership and also a willingness to bear many of the staff and incidental costs of a partnership. In none of the three streets examined in this study, with the possible exception of Bluerose Street, is it likely that both leadership and this form of material support would be available.

There are various reasons why it will be difficult to involve small businesses in community safety, and findings in the Three Streets Project are likely to hold in other areas also:

• Small independent businesses have few staff, work long hours and will find it difficult to put time and effort into general community safety issues.

• Small independent businesses are preoccupied with short-term economic survival.

• When engaged in similar activities local businesses are in competition with one another.

• There is significant suspicion of local residents in some cases.

• There is a high turnover of some businesses.

• Some businesses feel intimidated by sections of the community.

• A large proportion of small business owners live some distance from where they trade — less than a third in the three streets lived in their trading areas.

• Many issues relating to community safety are not under the control of businesses (appearance of the streets, empty premises, graffiti, quality of community relations).

• There is a tendency for businesses to develop private responses to crime risk and to expect the Council to take care of collective ones.

Despite the obstacles, there may be opportunities for involving businesses on the three streets in community safety. Many recognised that there are crime and nuisance problems on the streets, and as Table 7 shows, a significant proportion believe that some form of collective action to prevent crime would be beneficial to the business community. Many acknowledged that other businesses (and in some cases householders) might be of assistance in crime reduction. Many businesses expressed a willingness to become involved in community safety issues — 75% said they would be willing to meet to discuss local problems. The study also found that businesses had previously met to discuss community safety in traders' associations. These associations could be utilised further to develop community safety action.

There were, nevertheless, many businesses (44%) where it was believed that the responsibility for managing crime should be assumed solely by the police and other public authorities. Trying to encourage these to become involved in community safety issues will be difficult.

It appears that if widespread long-term small business involvement in community safety issues is wanted, significant 'carrots', continuing support, and practical help will be needed. The introduction of measures producing quick tangible gains for businesses could be expected to encourage participation. Businesses will also need sensitive leadership and guidance in developing partnerships. As part of this, the commercial aims of businesses and the problems faced by small enterprises will need to be fully acknowledged. Though there might be indirect commercial benefits from businesses' becoming involved in issues which do not directly and immediately impinge on their profitability, it will be difficult to draw in more than the occasional public-spirited business owner or manager. There is, however, more scope for stimulating partnerships directly addressing community safety issues affecting the businesses themselves.

Conclusion

There is growing evidence that businesses suffer high levels of crime and substantial losses from it: victimisation rates are certainly substantially higher than those for households.[12] Whilst all business sectors experience these high crime rates, it is also becoming clear that patterns vary widely by sector. Most notably (and unsurprisingly) in businesses dealing with the general public, such as retailers and service providers, there are substantially higher rates of violence and abuse than in other sectors, and it is retailers that suffer the highest rates of customer theft.[13] It is significant that the three streets surveyed in Camden were dominated by retailers and service providers.

Whilst the numbers of businesses surveyed in each street are low, what the Three Streets research brings out is that there is significant variation in crime problems across fairly similar streets of independent traders. For example, Bluerose Street businesses experienced much higher prevalence, incidence and concentration rates for burglary than those on the other two streets, and suffered much higher losses from crime. Redaster Crescent businesses suffered substantially more customer theft, abuse and violence than the other two streets. Petunia Street businesses suffered less fraud, abuse, and customer theft, but more criminal damage than the other streets. Moreover, though 'youths' were a common concern to businesses across all three streets, litter and graffiti were a particular issue in Petunia Street, drinking in public an issue in Redaster Crescent, and racial tension an issue for Bluerose Street. Finally, whilst there were significant concerns about empty/boarded-up premises in Petunia Street and Redaster Crescent, this was a much less significant problem in Bluerose Street.

The contexts furnished by the three streets also suggested variations in potential for implementing measures and yielding benefits from differing responses to problems. Therefore a uniform approach to crime reduction or increasing the risks for potential offenders could not be taken across the three streets.

Bluerose Street is well known and cosmopolitan, and housed a few large, relatively successful businesses alongside the small ones. It was suggested to the Council that there is probably scope for further self-financed improvements in security to reduce losses, in addition to collective action through the relatively robust traders' association. There was a very high commitment to the installation of CCTV, which had been supported by both the local authority and the Government Office for London. This had floundered, however, through businesses' reluctance or inability to provide the necessary financial support. The wider local partnership, of which Bluerose Street forms a part, had already been addressing issues to create a safer, more prosperous place in which to work and live, and was believed to have been successful already in reducing problems.

Petunia Street appeared to be struggling economically, with many empty premises, few customers, and an air of unkemptness. Yet, the construction of a large hotel at the southern end, the opening of the British Library just round the corner and the prospect of inward investment of substantial public monies (some £600,000) meant that its longer-term economic future looked bright. New crime problems could be expected, of course, with the anticipated increased trade, but so too could provision of improved security. At the time of the survey, however, the predominance of very small, relatively recent and seemingly sometimes struggling businesses probably explains the difficulties in forming a self-sustaining traders' association, which could act as an effective focus for collective efforts to reduce crime.

Redaster Crescent served and is immediately surrounded by blocks of local authority housing, within an otherwise affluent part of north London. Crime problems were perceived to be substantially more serious than on the other two streets, with 84% of respondents believing them to be serious or fairly serious (compared to 52% and 68% respectively on Petunia Street and Bluerose Street), and a similar proportion believing that crime damaged the image of the area. The street had the most serious difficulty with empty premises. A higher proportion of the businesses had considered relocation, ceasing trading or changing opening hours because of crime than businesses on either of the other two streets. Yet, unlike Petunia Street, there did not appear to be any major developments about to change the fortunes of the street. Perhaps because of this, businesses on Redaster Crescent had already had more security devices fitted than the other two streets. They also expressed greatest willingness to attend meetings and work with other businesses in the area to try to address local crime problems, many of which were to do with abuse which was not particular to individual concerns. There was certainly scope for crime-related environmental improvements to the area (for example improved lighting to dark corners, and regular cleaning of graffiti), as well as drawing the businesses into crime prevention partnership.

For any real prospect of success, attempts to address business crime problems will need to be sensitive to very local problems and the economic, social and physical circumstances presented in them. It is to Camden's credit that having identified a number of streets which appeared to have crime problems, they commissioned carefully targetted research to try to inform decisions about what could be done for and with businesses to reduce their crime problems.

Notes

1   Matt Hopkins is a researcher and Nick Tilley Professor of Sociology, in the Crime and Social Research Unit, Nottingham Trent University, Burton Street, Nottingham. NG1 4BU.

2   This paper summarises findings presented at greater length in Tilley, N., Burrows, J., Hopkins, M., Taylor, G. and Webb. S. (1997) *Camden's 'Three Streets' Project*. A Report for Camden Council. Nottingham: Nottingham Trent University and Morgan Harris Burrows.

3   Mirrlees-Black, C. and Ross, A. (1995) *Crime Against Retail and Manufacturing Premises: Findings from the 1994 Commercial Victimisation Survey*. Home Office Research Study 146. London: Home Office; Wood, J., Wheelwright, G. and Burrows, J. (1997) *Crime Against Small Business: Facing the Challenge — Findings of a Crime Survey Conducted in the Belgrave and West End Areas of Leicester*. Swindon: Crime Concern.

4   See Mirrlees-Black, C. and Ross, A. (1995) and Wood et al (1997), op cit.

5   Ibid.

6   The fieldwork was conducted by Hopkins, M., (Nottingham Trent University), Webb, S., (Morgan, Harris and Burrows) and Taylor, G. (Small Business and Crime Initiative).

7   This definition is that drawn by Farrell, G. and Pease, K. (1993), *Once Bitten, Twice Bitten: Repeat Victimisation and its Implications for Crime Prevention*. Crime Prevention Unit Paper 36. London: Home Office.

8   However, the figures for costs of burglary in Petunia Street are not very meaningful, given that there were only two incidents.

9   76% of businesses in the SBCI survey had an alarm and 28.5% had shutters.

10   This was a competition for Home Office support for installing CCTV in public areas, to complement funds being raised locally.

11   Tilley, N. (1992) *Safer Cities and Community Safety Strategies*. Crime Prevention Unit Paper 38, London: Home Office.

12   See, for example, the papers collected in Felson, M. and Clarke, R. (eds) (1997) *Business and Crime Prevention*. Monsey, New York: Criminal Justice Press; also the Introduction to this Volume.

13   See Wood et al (1997), op cit.

Chapter 5

The Extent and Nature of Homicide and Non-fatal Workplace Violence in the United States: Implications for Prevention and Security

Bonnie S. Fisher, E. Lynn Jenkins and Nicolas Williams[1]

Workplace violence has been recognised in the United States as a significant problem facing workers and employers. Interest in the area has come from a number of sectors, including the media, academia, as well as government research agencies. Our goal is to provide a better understanding of workplace violence in the United States through: a review of the workplace violence research to date in the US; a secondary data analysis of the National Crime Victimisation Survey that examines the extent of violent victimisations while the respondent was working or on duty, characteristics of such victimisations, and the reporting behaviour of the victims; and a discussion of the implications of the results of these studies and our NCVS results for homicide and non-fatal violence prevention and security in the workplace.

Introduction

Violence in the workplace has been labelled a 'significant public health problem' and has emerged as a vital safety issue for the 130 million plus members of the US labour force.[2] Problems that relate to workplace violence including workers' compensation claims,[3] insurance costs, lost productivity, counselling for employees, grievances, lawsuits, and extra security may also intensify as employment continues to grow in the US.

Over the last two decades, the media has routinely fuelled the public's fears by spotlighting incidents of workplace violence.[4] The popular press continues to highlight celebrated violent incidents such as employees and supervisors being shot and killed by fellow or former employees, a disgruntled lover seriously assaulting an ex-lover, or a depressed person gunning down employees at random. Headlines like those in *The New York Times* that read 'Dismissed Worker Kills 4 and Then Is Slain' and 'Postal Worker Shoots Three and Kills Self' continue to capture the attention of the public and to create the perception that employees, customers, and clients are in imminent personal danger in the workplace.[5] These events are often covered to the exclusion of the routine killings of taxicab drivers, police officers, and convenience store and other retail workers, which, in reality, constitute the real workplace violence issue in the US. In addition, professional associations through their trade journals have frequently reported on the magnitude and sources of workplace violence, as well as on efforts to develop guidelines to manage and prevent violence in the workplace.[6]

Beyond its newsworthy appeal, workplace violence has also captured the attention of the US Congress, federal agencies such as the National Institute for Occupational Safety and Health (NIOSH), the Bureau of Labour Statistics (BLS), and the Bureau of Justice Statistics (BJS), and other interested parties such as private insurance companies (eg the Northwestern National Life Insurance Company) and researchers.[7] Their interests have generated several conferences, a wide range of private sector anti-violence training programmes, as well as published studies regarding the magnitude of and risk factors associated with different types of homicide and non-fatal workplace violence.

Our goal is to provide a better understanding of workplace violence in the US. To this end, this chapter has three main sections: first, a review of the workplace violence research to date in the US; second, a secondary data analysis of the National Crime Victimisation Survey that examines the extent of violent victimisations while the respondent was working or on duty, characteristics of such victimisations, and the reporting behaviour of the victims; and third, a discussion of the implications of the results of these studies and our NCVS results for homicide and non-fatal violence prevention and security in the workplace. Our secondary analysis adds to the sparse yet growing body of workplace violence research by providing national-level estimates of five types of violence in seven professional categories and compares and contrasts these estimates and characteristics of the victimisations across these professional categories.

The magnitude of violence in the workplace

Estimates of workplace violence vary dramatically across different studies for six main reasons. First, the definition of the term 'workplace' differs across studies. Some studies define workplace as the worksite while others define it as while the victim is working or on duty. Still others define workplace as related to work. Second, what types of crimes are included in defining violence also varies. Some studies only examine the most extreme form of violence, homicide, while others examine one or more different types of non-fatal violence such as aggravated assaults, simple assaults, sexual victimisation (eg rape, sexual assault, harassment, threats), and robbery. Third, there is variation in terms of the time period covered by the studies. Some studies employ a longitudinal design (eg 1980-1992) while others employ a pooled cross-sectional design covering a few years (eg 1987-1992) or a cross-sectional design covering a single year. Fourth, some studies are a case study of one city or state or one industry or occupation. Others are at the national level and examine multiple industries or occupations. Fifth, the source of the data varies by study. The various sources include: death certificates, injury reports, incident reports from the victim, and press releases from wire services. Last (and related to reason five), some studies use data that represent a census of acts of violence while others use a sample of individuals to generate their estimates.

Below, we summarise the major findings from studies that use national-level data to examine the magnitude and characteristics (both job-related and incident-related) associated with workplace violence in the US. Although the noted methodological differences between the studies preclude direct comparisons, taken as a whole, however, they do highlight patterns of workplace violence that are present in spite of the methodological differences.

Homicide in the workplace
Two federal agencies collect and analyse data to determine the number and characteristics of workplace homicides. First, data from the National Traumatic Occupational Fatalities (NTOF) Surveillance System[8] sponsored by NIOSH indicated that 9,937 workplace homicides occurred from 1980-1992; a number that decreased during the 1980s but began to increase in the 1990s.[9] Using NTOF data, Jenkins[10] reported that homicide has become the second leading cause of occupational injury death, exceeded only by motor vehicle-related deaths. The data also indicated that workplace homicides are not evenly distributed across industries. High-risk industries include taxicab services, liquor stores, gas service stations, and detective/protective services.[11]

The Census of Fatal Occupational Injuries (CFOI) collected by the BLS is the second major source for data on workplace homicide. These data indicate that of the 6,112 job-related fatal injuries in 1996, 15 per cent were homicides (N=912). This places homicide second only to motor vehicle accidents as a source of workplace fatalities, supporting the evidence from the NTOF data.[12]

While the media has led the public to believe that many workplace homicides are committed out of passion and anger by someone known to the victim(s), the CFOI data revealed a very different reality. Eighty per cent of the homicides at work were committed during a robbery or another crime, presumably by a person(s) unknown to the victim(s), while only twenty per cent were committed by disgruntled co-workers, clients, or personal acquaintances (eg husband/ex, boyfriend/ex, or relative). These victims included cab drivers, convenience-store clerks, owners of inner-city bodegas, and pizza delivery drivers.[13]

Similar to the NIOSH results, the BLS also presented results using the CFOI data that showed that no occupation is immune from workplace homicide. Occupations with the highest risk of workplace homicide included taxicab drivers and chauffeurs, gas station attendants, sale counter clerks, and public services (police and detectives).[14] Workers at greatest risk generally are those who handle money, work alone or in small numbers, work either late at night or early in the morning, work in high-crime areas, guard valuable property, and/or work in community settings (eg taxicab drivers and police officers). Ironically, however, the cash stolen is often a nominal amount.[15]

Southerland et al[16] used content analysis of news releases about incidents of potentially lethal and lethal workplace violence to estimate the magnitude of work-related violence.

While their results are subject to the criticism of being based on a highly selective sample (only violence significant enough to make the national news services), their results do provide information about the characteristics of the violent offender, which is not available from either the NIOSH or BLS data sources. They found that the typical offender is a male US citizen, between the ages of 26-45 years old (median = 33 years old), and equally likely to be white or non-white.[17]

Similar to the media's general coverage of workplace violence, they reported that of the 246 incidents, 42% involved a current employee and 15% involved an ex-employee.[18] Like the trend reported in the NIOSH study, Southerland et al reported that incidents of potentially lethal and lethal workplace violence decreased in the late 1980s and then began to increase in the early 1990s.[19]

These national-level studies add to our understanding of the extent and trends in fatal violence in the workplace, who is most at risk, and the characteristics of the offender. Despite their methodological differences, common themes emerge: homicide in the workplace is a reality and those employed in certain types of work are more at risk than others.

Non-fatal violence in the workplace
Three federal agencies collect data on the extent and nature of non-fatal workplace violence. First, the BJS has provided annual criminal victimisation estimates since 1972.[20] Several researchers have used this data to examine the magnitude and characteristics of workplace victimisation. Using data from the 1987-1992 National Crime Survey (NCS), Bachman reported that approximately one million people annually were victims of non-fatal violent incidents while at work or on duty. These violent incidents included rape, robbery, aggravated assault, and simple assault, and accounted for 15% of the more than six and a half million acts of violence experienced by US residents aged 12 years and older. She also reported that more than a third (36%) of the incidents happened in commercial establishments.[21]

Using the same data and time frame as Bachman, Fisher reported that most of these workplace victimisations were simple assaults (62% of the victimisations annually), followed by aggravated assaults (28.3%), robberies (9%), and rape (1.3%).[22] She also reported that males were on average close to three times as likely to experience a crime of violence as females. Her research also showed that workplace theft outnumbered workplace violence almost three to one across all years (2.5 million compared with 0.8 million on an annual average basis).[23]

Using data from the 1973-1981 NCS, Block, Felson and Block estimated occupation-specific crime victimisation rates per 1,000 employees for 246 occupations for robbery and assault. They found that certain occupations were consistently among the most victimised: first, sheriffs, police, amusement and recreational workers, table clearers, and dishwashers had the highest risk of assault; second, table clearers, amusement and recreational workers, taxicab drivers, dishwashers, and newspaper deliverers were among the most often robbed.[24]

The second source of data on non-fatal workplace violence comes from the Annual Survey of Occupational Injuries and Illness (ASOII) published by the BLS.[25] The BLS reported that in 1992, about 22,400 workers were injured seriously enough in non-fatal assaults in the workplace to require days away from work to recuperate. Women were the victims in 56% of these assaults. The BLS further reported that non-fatal violent acts which took the form of 'hitting and kicking' accounted for almost half (47%) the non-fatal assaults.[26]

As with the Block et al result, the BLS reported variation in the risk across industries. Almost two-thirds of non-fatal assaults occurred in service industries, such as nursing homes, hospitals, and establishments providing residential care and other social services. Retail trade industries such as grocery stores and eating and drinking places accounted for about one-fifth of these assaults.[27]

The third source of national-level violence data is sponsored by the Federal Bureau of Investigation (FBI) in its Uniform Crime Report (UCR). The FBI collects and aggregates data only on crimes known to the police. In 1995, the FBI reported that 'nonresidential' incidents constituted just over one-fifth of all robberies.[28] Unfortunately, their data cannot be used to disaggregate work-related assaults or homicides. Another commonly cited estimate of the number of non-fatal workplace assaults (defined as physical attacks) comes from a survey conducted by the Northwestern National Life Insurance Company.[29] Their data revealed that approximately 2.2 million workers had been physically attacked on the job between July 1992 and July 1993. Their study also found that 25 per cent of the workers were harassed, threatened, or physically attacked during this time.

Despite their methodological differences, these studies tell a consistent story: non-fatal violence is not uncommon in the US workplace. Like the workplace homicide studies, these studies reveal a common theme: those employed in certain types of work are more at risk of victimisation than others. We now turn to a brief discussion of the job characteristics that researchers have found are related to a high risk of violence.

Risk factors associated with non-fatal workplace violence
A limited amount of research, mostly in criminology, has been done that examines risk factors associated with non-fatal workplace violence, defined mostly in terms of workplace assaults.[30] Most of the studies are descriptive, with very few having a theoretical framework.[31] Taken together, these studies reported that several features of the workplace and characteristics of the tasks performed were more related to the risk of workplace assault than a worker's demographic characteristics. Using a routine activity framework and the 1982 Victim Risk Supplement to the National Crime Survey (NCS), Lynch[32] reported that four features of the tasks and workplace that increased a worker's risk of victimisation included:

- face-to-face exposure to a large number of people (exposure);

- mobility-routine travel (local and extra-local) or no single worksite (guardianship);

- handling money (target attractiveness);

- the employee's perceived dangerousness[33] of the workplace and the neighbourhood where employed (proximity to potential offenders).

Using a lifestyle and routine activity framework and methodology modelled after the NCS, Collins et al[34] conducted a victimisation survey of a sample of Washington DC residents and found results similar to those of Lynch related to the risk of violent victimisation. Specifically, two job activities associated with violent workplace victimisation were:

- dealing with the public (exposure);

- delivery of passengers or goods (exposure).

The previously discussed research provides an overview of the magnitude and risk factors associated with homicide and non-fatal assaults in US workplaces. Still lacking within the non-fatal research are national-level estimates for different types of workplace violence and a description of the characteristics of the incidents across professional categories. We present such estimates and descriptions as previous research has consistently shown variation in the risk of workplace violence across type of job. In doing so, we add to the limited, yet growing, body of workplace violence research.

Methods

Our results are from a secondary data analysis using the NCVS.[35] We use this dataset because the NCVS collects individual-level and incident-level information about crimes reported and those not reported to the police from an ongoing, nationally representative sample of households in the US.[36] To date, with the exception of the Lynch and Collins et al papers in the 1980s, little is known about characteristics of criminal victimisations that happen when the victim is working or on duty. We use this incident-level data to estimate the extent and nature of workplace violence across seven types of work (medical, mental health, law enforcement, at a teaching institution, retail trade, transportation, and other)[37] and to examine their characteristics. This work extends our understanding of workplace violence by examining magnitude differences and similarities for five types of violence across three years, sex, type of work and selected incident-level characteristics (ie characteristics of the offender and of the victimisation experience). For this chapter, only incidents where the respondent replied that the incident had happened while 'working or on duty' to the question 'What were you doing when this incident (happened/started)?' were included in our analysis. Note that this definition of 'workplace' does not necessarily mean that the incident happened at the worksite. This definition, however, does provide the broadest range of possible employment situations and will give an appreciation of the breadth of the workplace violence problem.[38] Survey responses from the 1992-1994 NCVS were used to generate the estimates presented in the Tables. The estimates in the Tables are annual averages across these three years.

Types of crimes defined

We analysed five types of violent crimes using the standard BJS definitions: rape, sexual assault, robbery, aggravated assault, and simple assault. The estimates include both completed and attempted victimisations. For some types of crimes, threats were also included in our estimates. For example, threats of rape and sexual assault were included in the estimates of rape and sexual assaults, and aggravated assaults included threats with a weapon. Technically a person could experience an incident while on duty or at work outside the US if his or her job required such travel. We excluded these incidents as well as series crimes from our analysis.[39]

Findings

The magnitude of violence while someone is working or on duty

As seen in Table 1, on average across the three years, over 1.85 million violent crimes were committed annually while someone was working or on duty.[40]

Table 1. Type of crime occurring while working or on duty by annual average and sex

Type of crime	Annual average % (n)	Annual average: males % (n)	Annual average: females % (n)
Rape	0.9 (16,660)	0.3 (3,309)*	2.2 (13,351)
Sexual assault	1.8 (33,930)	0.2 (2,911)*	5.0 (31,019)
Robbery	4.5 (82,820)	4.9 (60,275)	3.7 (22,545)
Aggravated assault	21.1 (391,503)	23.2 (287,660)	16.9 (103,842)
Simple assault	71.7 (1,329,791)	71.4 (885,344)	72.2 (444,446)
Crimes of violence	100.0 (1,854,704)	100.0 (1,239,499)	100.0 (615,204)

* Estimate is based on 5 or fewer sample cases. This notation is employed in subsequent Tables.

We see that the frequency of occurrence across types of workplace crimes is not uniform.[41] Simple assault such as an attack without a weapon that resulted in no injury or in only a minor injury (eg bruises, black eyes, or cuts) was always the most frequently occurring crime. This was roughly three times as frequent as the next most frequently occurring crime, aggravated assault (71.7% compared with 21.1%). Robbery, and rape and sexual assault were the least likely crimes to occur (4.5% and 2.7%, respectively).

Crimes of violence committed against males, on average, outnumbered crimes of violence committed against women by about two to one (1.2 million compared with 0.6 million).

This ratio is higher than that between males and females for comparable types of violence regardless of location in 1994 of about 1.3 to 1 (6.0 million compared with 4.4 million).[42]

The pattern of violent crimes committed against males and females in the workplace was similar: simple assault was the most frequently occurring victimisation, followed by aggravated assault. For females, sexual victimisations (rape and sexual assault), on average, ranked as the third most frequently occurring victimisation (7.2%), followed by robbery (3.7%). For males, the opposite victimisation pattern prevailed: robbery ranked as the third most frequently occurring victimisation (4.9%), followed by sexual victimisations (0.5%).

Magnitude of violence by type of work

We next turn to detailing how workplace violence varies within and across type of work. First, the patterns of victimisations within the different types of work are similar, as simple assaults constitute the majority of workplace violence within each profession (specifically, 86.4% at a teaching institution, 84.6% in the medical profession, 77.9% in the mental health profession, 75.7% in the law enforcement profession, 70.7% in other professions, 59.1% in the retail trade profession, and 58.6% in the transportation profession).[43] Second, Table 2 presents violent victimisation estimates across type of work, and reveals that the highest frequency of workplace violence occurred in the retail sales (17.5%), and law enforcement (17.4%) professions, although in many instances the victimisations occurred in professions not explicitly asked about on the NCVS survey (the other professions category comprised 40.0% of the victimisations). The transportation profession had the lowest frequency of all types of violence (4.4%).

Third, Table 2 reveals that workers in particular professions are more likely to be victims of particular crimes than others. For example, the retail trade profession had the second highest frequency of rapes, robberies, and aggravated assaults (the other professions had the highest of all three); the transportation profession had the third highest frequency of robberies; the law enforcement profession had the third highest frequency of aggravated assaults; and the medical and mental health professions had the second and third highest joint frequency of rapes and sexual assaults. This suggests that risk of different types of violence varied markedly between different types of work.

Characteristics of the offender

We next examine who is committing the workplace violence, using self-reported information from the victim. The majority of the victimisations (85%) across the professions involved a single offender.[44] The medical profession had the highest — 96.1% of the violent victimisations — and the transportation profession had the lowest — 70.5% of the violent victimisations.[45] Except for robbery committed against those employed at a teaching institution, or those in the retail sales and transportation professions, the majority of all the other victimisations committed involved a single offender. Furthermore, the perpetrator was a male in a majority of the single-offender violent incidents, white (63%), and over 30 years old (49%).[46]

Table 2. Type of crime while working or on duty by type of work

Type of crime	Type of work						
	Medical	**Mental health**	**Teaching**	**Law enforcement**	**Retail**	**Transport**	**Other**
	% (n)	**% (n)**	**% (n)**	**% (n)**	**% (n)**	**% (n)**	**% (n)**
Crimes of violence	8.2 (152,314)	5.3 (97,657)	7.2 (132,381)	17.4 (322,312)	17.5 (323,884)	4.4 (80,978)	40.0 (740,375)
Rape	5.0 (790)*	20.8 (3,298)*	0.0 (0)*	6.5 (1,034)*	28.7 (4,555)*	4.8 (758)*	34.2 (5,425)
Sexual assault	29.2 (9,897)*	6.9 (2,330)*	5.4 (1,827)*	2.2 (743)*	6.8 (2,296)*	0.0 (0)*	49.6 (16,838)
Robbery	0.8 (680)*	0.0 (0)*	6.2 (5,097)*	1.0 (837)*	26.6 (22,000)	13.0 (10,767)	52.5 (43,439)
Aggravated assault	3.1 (12,113)	4.1 (15,964)	2.8 (11,080)	19.4 (75,761)	26.5 (103,619)	5.6 (21,976)	38.6 (150,990)
Simple assault	9.7 (128,834)	5.7 (76,065)	8.6 (114,377)	18.4 (243,937)	14.4 (191,414)	3.6 (47,477)	39.5 (523,683)

As can be seen in Table 3, the percentage of single-offender violent crimes committed by strangers and non-strangers were essentially the same. Among the non-strangers, someone at work was involved in 64.0 per cent of the victimisations (calculated from information in Table 3), while intimates and relatives were very rarely involved in workplace violent victimisations.

There are substantial differences in the relationship of the victim to the offender across the different types of crime. For example, someone at work was involved in 54.9% of the rapes, and nearly three-quarters of the sexual assaults. Someone at work was the second most frequent offender in aggravated assaults and simple assaults (23.4% and 33.7%, respectively). On the other hand, 87.5% of the robberies, and 62.0% of the aggravated assaults involved a stranger.

Finally, when we concentrate on simple assaults, we find considerable variation in the relationship of the victim to the single offender across type of work. While 47.3% of all such simple assaults were committed by a stranger, across the professions the percentage committed by a stranger ranges from 84.4% in law enforcement to 14.6% in the mental health profession. The percentage of workplace simple assaults committed by someone at work was relatively constant across the professions (33.7%), with the mental health profession being on the high end (48.8%), and the law enforcement profession being on the low end (8.4%) of the distribution. Finally, very few simple assaults in the workplace were committed by intimates or relatives (0.9 and 0.8%, respectively).[47]

Table 3. Type of crime while working or on duty by relationship to victim in single-offender victimisations

Type of crime	Relationship to victim				
	Stranger % (n)	Intimate[a] % (n)	Someone at work %[b] (n)	Relative % (n)	Non-relative[c] % (n)
Crimes of violence	50.3 (653,845)	1.0 (12,999)	31.8 (413,237)	0.8 (10,739)	16.1 (209,101)
Rape	6.9 (723)*	0.0 (0)*	54.9 (5,742)	0.0 (0)*	38.2 (4,004)*
Sexual assault	20.6 (5,094)*	0.0 (0)*	74.0 (18,275)	0.0 (0)*	5.3 (1,315)*
Robbery	87.5 (31,193)	2.7 (956)*	0.0 (0)*	0.0 (0)*	9.8 (3,493)*
Aggravated assault	62.0 (151,272)	1.3 (3,118)*	23.4 (57,058)	1.1 (2,613)*	12.3 (29,916)
Simple assault	47.3 (465,563)	0.9 (8,925)	33.7 (332,162)	0.8 (8,126)	17.3 (170,374)

[a] This category includes spouse at the time of the incident, ex-spouse at the time of the incident, boyfriend or girlfriend, or ex-boyfriend or girlfriend.
[b] This category includes someone at work such as a fellow employee or a customer, patient, client, etc.
[c] This category includes a friend or ex-friend, room-mate, boarder, schoolmate, neighbour, or other non-relative.

Offenders drinking and/or using drugs

A substantial number of offenders who were strangers to the victim were believed to be drinking and/or using drugs during the commission of the crime. Specifically, the results in Table 4 show that in 36.7% of the crimes of violence committed by a stranger(s), the offender was drinking and/or on drugs.[48] In the majority of violent crimes against members of the medical and law enforcement professions committed by a stranger(s), the offender was drinking and/or on drugs (50.2% and 53.2%, respectively). Members of the transportation profession had the smallest percentage of violent crimes committed against them by such a stranger(s) (14.6%).

Table 4. Type of crime while working or on duty by type of work: percentage of victimisations where a stranger(s) was drinking and/or on drugs[a]

Type of Crime	Type of work							
	All	Medical	Mental health	Teaching	Law enforcement	Retail	Transport	Other
	% (n)	% (n)	% (n)	% (n)	% (n)	% (n)	% (n)	% (n)
Crimes of violence	36.7 (319,149)	50.2 (35,712)	34.4 (3,969)*	23.3 (6,366)*	53.2 (116,803)	32.9 (67,005)	14.6 (7,421)	28.6 (81,873)
Rape	100.0 (723)*	-[a]	-	-	-	-	-	100.0 (723)*
Sexual assault	42.6 (2,168)*	-	-	100.0 (751)*	-	0.0 (0)*	-	38.8 (1,417)*
Robbery	26.0 (18,325)	-	-	100.0 (3,641)*	0.0 (0)*	18.9 (3,405)*	20.4 (2,192)*	24.4 (9,087)
Aggravated assault	32.6 (73,470)	73.50 (5,130)*	0.0 (0)*	0.0 (0)*	43.3 (24,309)	29.0 (20,398)	24.4 (3,544)*	27.5 (20,089)
Simple assault	39.5 (224,463)	47.7 (30,582)	43.2 (3,969)*	9.3 (1,974)*	56.9 (92,494)	37.6 (43,202)	6.6 (1,685)*	29.52 (5,557)

[a] Indicates that there were no crimes committed of that particular type of crime and involving that type of work.

Repeat offender(s) by type of work

Most victimisations did not involve a repeat offender(s),[49] although as the estimates in Table 5 reveal, this varied across the professions.[50] For example, 24.4% of the simple assaults and 24.1% of the sexual assaults against the medical profession were committed by a repeat offender(s). At teaching institutions, 46.6% of the aggravated assaults were committed by a repeat offender(s), followed by 28.8% of the simple assaults. The transportation profession followed a similar pattern — 16.5% of the aggravated assaults were committed by a repeat offender(s), followed by 15.5% of the simple assaults. For law enforcement, only 7.7% of the simple assaults (the highest percentage) for this profession were committed by a repeater(s). In the retail sales profession, sexual assault and simple assault were the two types of crimes where a repeat offender(s) was most frequent (28.6% and 14.9% of the victimisations, respectively). In other professions, simple assault had the second largest percentage of a repeat offender(s), followed by aggravated assault (21.8% and 19.3%, respectively).

Table 5. Type of crime while working or on duty by type of work: percentage of victimisations involving repeat offender(s)[a]

Type of Crime	Type of work						
	Medical	Mental health	Teaching	Law enforcement	Retail	Transport	Other
	% (n)	% (n)	% (n)	% (n)	% (n)	% (n)	% (n)
Crimes of violence	23.2 (35,175)	32.0 (30,690)	29.9 (39,605)	6.5 (19,794)	12.1 (38,016)	13.4 (10,441)	20.0 (141,368)
Rape	0.0 (0)*	67.0 (2,208)*	_[b]	0.0 (0)*	0.0 (0)*	0.0 (0)*	59.5 (3,229)*
Sexual assault	24.1 (2,387)*	100.0 (2,330)*	0.0 (0)*	0.0 (0)*	28.7 (658)*	-	0.0 (0)*
Robbery	0.0 (0)*	-	28.6 (1,456)*	0.0 (0)*	10.8 (2,368)*	0.0 (0)*	3.5 (1,495)*
Aggravated assault	13.0 (1,579)*	25.4 (4,053)*	46.6 (5,168)	2.8 (2,044)*	7.2 (7,055)	16.5 (3,234)*	19.29 (26,523)
Simple assault	24.4 (31,209)	29.8 (22,099)	28.8 (32,981)	7.7 (17,750)	14.9 (27,934)	15.5 (7,207)	21.8 (110,122)

[a] Offenders who have committed a crime or made threats against the victim more than once.
[b] Indicates that there were no crimes committed of that particular type of crime and type of work.

Characteristics of the victimisations

The NCVS data includes numerous other characteristics of the workplace victimisations. Below we highlight incident-level characteristics that have implications for crime prevention and security.

Use of a weapon
In 23.3% of all the violent workplace victimisations a weapon was present. The transportation profession had the highest frequency of a weapon being present (38.4% of the victimisations), followed by the retail sales profession (34.5%), other professions (23.1%), and the law enforcement profession (22.9%).[51]

The presence of others
Nearly 74% (73.6%) of all the victimisations happened when someone else was present. Within all the professions, a majority of the acts of violence, with the exception of rape, involved the presence of someone else. Victims in the mental health profession and in the law enforcement profession were the most likely to be victimised when someone else was present (83.9% and 81.2%, respectively). Those in the transportation profession were the least likely to have someone present (57.1%).[52]

Reporting crimes to the police

Over half (52%) of the victimisations went unreported to the police. In all the professions, the three most likely crimes not to be reported were: sexual assault (82.6%), simple assault (58.9%) and rape (45.1%).[53] Victims in the mental health profession were the least likely to report violent victimisation to the police (71.2% of the victimisations), followed by the those employed at a teaching institution (64.3%), and the medical profession (63.4%). It is not too surprising that victims in the law enforcement profession were the most likely to report their victimisations to the police: only 23.2% of their victimisations went unreported.[54]

Overall, the three most common reasons for not reporting a violent victimisation to the police were: the respondent dealt with it in another way (48%), some other reason (27%), and the incident was not important enough (20%).[55]

Implications for security and crime prevention

Our results support previous homicide and non-fatal workplace violence research findings: no one is immune from experiencing a violent act while working or on duty, and those employed in or at certain types of work are more likely than others to experience different types of violence. Our data show that the risk of such violence victimisations and their characteristics vary considerably by type of work. While much work is being done to examine the magnitude of workplace violence, the next steps need to be taken. As our overall findings suggest, more research is needed to examine the characteristics of the job tasks performed and how offender characteristics affect the risk of experiencing an act of violence. We believe the challenge to employers, researchers, and policy makers is to understand the types and causes of workplace violence, and the offending and incident characteristics besetting employees before initiating costly preventive measures and increasing physical security. In this way, workplace crime prevention or security strategies can move from broadly-based appeals to be careful about crime, to programmes whose resources are invested effectively and strategically to specifically make employees safer. This approach may require data collection and analysis, but it has the decided advantage of being the 'best bet' towards reducing workplace violence because there is little, if any, empirical data to support the notion that any single crime prevention or security measure can prevent workplace violence.

We are reluctant to draw broad, sweeping implications for crime prevention and security efforts for two reasons. First, residential crime prevention evaluations have found that generic strategies may not be effective in preventing or reducing incidents. Indeed, the residential crime prevention literature, crime prevention and security efforts are more than just 'implanting' the latest generic crime prevention or security measure or programme into any situation. Researchers have convincingly shown that such an approach does not necessarily result in reducing crime, and, in fact, the opposite may happen and indeed has happened. Given the variation in the frequency of the different types of crime while someone is working or on duty, their characteristics pose challenges for those developing and implementing workplace violence prevention and security policies and programmes.

Tailoring strategies to fit the type of crime and type of work may be a more judicious first step, since the one thing that is clear is that no single strategy will be effective and appropriate in all workplaces. Second, the nature of our data does not allow us to examine the effects of either individual-level or institution-level (eg workplace) crime prevention and security efforts — an area in much need of good evaluations. The temporal ordering in this relationship is critical to understanding 'what works' under which job conditions and against what types of crimes. Only by assessing this relationship can our knowledge and understanding be put to good practice for preventing violence and securing a safer workplace.

In line with tailoring strategies to certain types of crime and types of work, situational crime prevention techniques should be considered. In principle, situational crime prevention reduces the opportunities for crime and increases the risk for the offender. This approach is based on the presumption that offenders 'rationally' select their targets and that the chance of victimisation can be reduced by: increasing the physical effort for offending (target hardening, controlling the access, deflecting offenders, and controlling facilitators); increasing the risks of an offender being caught (entry/exit screening, formal surveillance, surveillance by employees and others, and natural surveillance); reducing the anticipated rewards of offending (removing the target, identifying property, removing inducements/ temptation, and denying benefits); and inducing guilt or shame (rule setting, strengthening moral condemnation, controlling disinhibitors, and facilitating compliance).[56]

In a report issued by NIOSH, several aspects of the situational approach were incorporated into their three main suggestions for prevention strategies.[57] First, physical environmental design strategies such as the use of machines that make cashless transactions possible by using debit cards or automatic teller account cards could be introduced in settings where cash is currently exchanged between employees and customers (eg in transportation and retail settings). Second, administrative controls that include staffing plans and work practices (such as escorting patients and prohibiting unsupervised movement within and between clinic areas) were recommended. Increasing the number of staff on duty may also be appropriate for certain types of jobs (eg retail or in teaching institutions) during certain times of the day and night. The use of security guards or receptionists to screen persons entering the workplace or photo identification to identify who belongs and who does not may also be appropriate for certain types of jobs. Third, behavioural strategies for employees could include offering awareness and educational programmes on the risks of violent victimisations and training procedures should a victimisation occur, as well as developing written workplace violence policies that include procedures for reporting and responding to violence, and encouraging employees to report crimes to the police.

This last point, reporting crimes to the police, should not be overlooked as a means to increase the risk for the offender. Our results show that just over half of the victimisations went unreported to the police, and for certain types of violence (eg sexual assaults), an even higher proportion went unreported. As the NIOSH report explains, the first priority is to establish a system for documenting violent incidents in the workplace so that assessing the nature and magnitude of workplace violence in a given workplace and quantifying the risks can be accomplished and the information analysed. Such data could then be used to assess situational actions to reduce or mitigate the risks of workplace violence and implement a reasonable intervention strategy. Without employees reporting these incidents, such data is lost and cannot be used to make the workplace safer for all.

Notes

1   The authors' names appear in alphabetical order. Bonnie S. Fisher is an associate professor at the University of Cincinnati in the Department of Political Science in Cincinnati, Ohio, USA. E. Lynn Jenkins is a senior scientist at the National Institute for Occupational Safety and Health in Washington DC. Nicolas Williams is an associate professor at the University of Cincinnati in the Department of Economics. Any questions about the context of the chapter should be addressed to Bonnie Fisher (email: Bonnie.Fisher@uc.edu).

2   United States Department of Health and Human Services (1996a) HHS Press Release. Online. http://www.cdc.gov/niosh/violpr.html, 18 July.

3   'Workers' Compensation' is a government programme in the US that seeks to replace lost income in the event of lost work time due to a workplace injury.

4   Larson, E. (1994) Trigger Happy: A False Crisis: How Workplace Violence Became a Hot Topic. *The Wall Street Journal*, October 13, 1994.

5   *The New York Times*, 20 December 1997.

6   See, among others: American Society for Industrial Security. (1997) ASIS Online: Workplace Violence. http://www.asisonline.org/stat1/html, 8 December; Minter, R. (1995) Violence Finds a Voice. *Occupational Hazards*, December, p 7; Roberts, S. (1994) Violence a Big Threat to Workers, Study Says. *Business Insurance*. Vol. 28, issue 31, p 35.

7   Collins J., Cox B., and Langan, P. (1987) Job Activities and Personal Crime Victimization: Implications for Theory. *Social Science Research*. Vol. 16, pp 345-360; Fisher, B. (1997) *Analysis and Report of the National Crime Victimization Survey 1992-1994: A Summary Report to DHHS, PHS, CDC, NIOSH, and ALOSH*. Cincinnati, OH: University of Cincinnati; Fisher, B. (1996) *Analysis and Report of the National Crime Victimization Survey 1987-1992: A Summary Report to DHHS, PHS, CDC, NIOSH, and ALOSH*. Cincinnati, OH: University of Cincinnati; Lynch, J. (1987) Routine Activity and Victimization at Work. *Journal of Quantitative Criminology*. Vol. 3, No. 4, pp 282-300; Southerland, M., Collins, P., and Scarborough, K. (1997) *Workplace Violence: A Continuum from Threat to Death*. Cincinnati, OH: Anderson Publishing Company.

8   NTOF is a death certificate-based census of traumatic occupational fatalities in the US, with data from all 50 states and the District of Columbia. NTOF includes information concerning all workers aged 16 or older who died from an injury or poisoning and for whom the certifier noted a positive response to the *injury at work?* item in the death certificate.

9   United States Department of Health and Human Services (1996b) *Violence in the Workplace: Risk Factors and Prevention Strategies*. Cincinnati, Ohio: Department of Health and Human Services, Centers for Disease Control and Prevention and National Institute for Occupational Safety and Health, DHHS (NIOSH) Publication No. 96-100, Table 1.

10   Jenkins, E. (1996) Workplace Homicide: Industries and Occupations at High Risk. *Occupational Medicine*. Vol. 11, No. 2, pp 219-225.

11   United States Department of Health and Human Services (1996b), op cit, Table 8.

12   United States Department of Labor. (1997) *BLS NEWS: National Census of Fatal Occupational Injuries, 1996.* Washington, DC: United States Department of Labor-97-266, August 7, 1997. The fatality census uses multiple data sources such as death certificates, workers' compensation reports and claims, Occupational Safety and Health Administration files, and new articles to compile the most complete count of fatal work injuries that is possible.

13   Larson, op cit, p A11; United States Department of Labor, op cit.

14   United States Department of Labor, op cit, pp 45-46 and Table 7; Toscano, G. and Weber, W. (1995) Violence in the Workplace: Patterns of Fatal Workplace Assaults Differ from Those of Non-fatal Ones. http://stats.bls.gov/osh/cfar0005.pdf, p 44, Table 3.

15   Toscano and Weber, op cit, pp 43-45.

16   Southerland et al, op cit, pp 15-19. They used press releases from the Associated Press (AP) and United Press International (UPI) wire services during the years 1976 to 1994. They restrict their analysis to 'definite cases of potentially lethal work-related violence.' This is defined as an incident that meets each of the following conditions: 1) lethal violence was possible but did not necessarily involve an injury; 2) there must be some connection between the assailant and the workplace; and 3) at least some potentially violent action took place in the 'workplace.'

17   Ibid, pp 36-37.

18   Ibid, p 39, Figure 2.8.

19   Ibid, p 33, Figure 2.3.

20   See the Methods section below for a discussion of this data. The NCS was used by the BJS from 1973-1992, after which the redesigned NCVS was introduced. The changes in the instruments preclude any direct comparisons between the NCS estimates and the NCVS estimates.

21   Bachman, R. (1994) *Violence and Theft in the Workplace.* Washington, DC: US Department of Justice, Office of Justice Programs, Bureau of Justice Statistics, July, NCJ-148199.

22   Fisher (1996), op cit, pp 6-7.

23   Fisher (1996), op cit, pp 8-10.

24   Block, R., Felson, M. and Block, C. (1985) Crime Victimization Rates for Incumbents of 246 Occupations. *Sociology and Social Research.* Vol. 69, No. 3, pp 442-451, especially Table 1.

25   United States Department of Labor, op cit, pp 45-47. The ASOII is an annual survey of approximately 250,000 business establishments in the private sector. Excluded from the sample are the self-employed, small farmers, and government workers (eg police and other law enforcement officers).

26   Ibid, p 43.

27   Ibid, p 46.

28   Federal Bureau of Investigation. (1995) *Crime in the United States.* Washington, DC: US Department of Justice.

29   The Northwestern National Life Insurance Company (1993) *Fear and Violence in the Workplace: An In-House Survey.* Chicago, IL: The Northwestern National Life Insurance Company. Caution must be exercised as their estimates were based on interviews with only three per cent of the sample of 600 who reported being attacked.

30   Castillo, D. and Jenkins, E. (1994) Industries and Occupations at High Risk for Work-related Homicides. *Journal of Occupational Medicine.* Vol. 36, pp 125-132; Collins et al, op cit; United States Department of Labor, op cit.

31   For exceptions, see Wooldredge, J., Cullen, F. and Latessa, E. (1992) Victimization in the Workplace: A Test of Routine Activities Theory. *Justice Quarterly.* Vol. 9, No. 2, pp 325-335; Lynch, op cit, pp 282-300.

32   Ibid, pp 285-295.

33   Ibid, p 288 and Appendix. Lynch defines the term 'dangerousness' as the employee's perception of his/her safety from crime while on the job and in the neighbourhood in which he/she works.

34   Collins et al, op cit.

35   To obtain population estimates, we weighted the data using the 1990 Census weights provided in the NCVS data set.

36   Bureau of Justice Statistics (1997) *Criminal Victimization in the United States, 1994.* Washington, DC: United States Department of Justice, Office of Justice Programs, Bureau of Justice Statistics; and Bureau of Justice Statistics (1996) *Criminal Victimization in the United States, 1993.* Washington, DC: US Department of Justice, Office of Justice Programs. The Bureau of the Census administers the NCVS to all individuals aged 12 or older living in a sample of approximately 50,000 housing units throughout the US. The final sample contains more than 90,000 individuals. Each housing unit remains in the sample for three and a half years, with each of the seven interviews taking place at six-month intervals. Each eligible member of the housing unit is questioned about their victimisation experiences within the six-month bounding period. The NCVS has consistently obtained a response rate of about 95 per cent.

37   In the survey, individuals are asked whether their job falls into one of 27 different categories. We aggregated these into seven professional categories for two reasons. First, although the NCVS is a large sample, some cell sizes became very small when all 27 categories were used, and reliable victimisation estimates could not be made. Second (and related to the first reason), we wanted to ensure that our estimates were meaningful with respect to different types of work.

38   Ninety-three per cent of all incidents where the respondent was working or on duty occurred at the worksite.

39   We did this for three reasons. First, we were primarily interested in the at-work or on-duty experiences in the US. Second, there were too few cases to analyse with any degree of reliability: there were only six unweighted violent crimes from 1992-1994 that occurred outside the US while the respondent was working or on duty. Third, series crimes (ie six or more similar but separate events which the respondent is unable to describe separately in detail to an interviewer) occurred infrequently; there were a total of 278 unweighted violent series crimes from 1992-1994.

40   This is substantially higher than the frequently cited Bachman results (op cit), and can be explained primarily by the redesign of the instrument. The percentage increase in the

estimated number of workplace violent crimes after the redesign is higher than the percentage increase in comparable types of all violent crimes regardless of location (123% increase compared with 49%).

41   The ranking of crimes within each of the three years mirrored the annual average ranking.

42   Bureau of Justice Statistics, op cit, p 7.

43   These and other similar results are documented in Fisher (1997), op cit, and are available upon request from the first named author.

44   Here we concentrate on victimisations involving a single offender both because they comprise the vast majority of all crimes, as well as because of the difficulty of classifying and interpreting victimisations where some offenders had one particular characteristic, and the remainder had different characteristics.

45   Fisher (1997), op cit, p 24, Table 9.

46   Ibid, p 20.

47   Ibid, p 27, Table 12.

48   Both single-offender and multiple-offender incidents are included in these estimates.

49   Offenders who have committed a crime or made threats against the victim more than once.

50   Both single-offender and multiple-offender incidents are included in these estimates.

51   Fisher (1997), op cit, p 23, Table 8.

52   Ibid, p 50, Table 33.

53   Ibid, p 66, Table 45.

54   Ibid, p 66, Table 46.

55   Ibid, p 65.

56   Clarke, R.V. and Homel, R. (1997) A Revised Classification of Situational Crime Prevention Techniques. In Lab, S. (ed.) *Crime Prevention at a Crossroads*. Cincinnati, Ohio: Anderson Publishing Co, pp 17-30. And the editor's introduction to this book.

57   United States Department of Health and Human Services (1996b), op cit, pp 14-15.

58   Ibid, pp 15-16.

Chapter 6

In Defence of Farms: an Agrarian Crime Prevention Audit in Rutland

Gavin Sugden[1]

Farm crime is an area of research widely ignored by criminologists. Yet the agricultural industry is a major enterprise valued in excess of £31,000 million, and reports from a wide range of sources indicate that British farms (and the British countryside) are suffering some of the highest levels of crime in their existence. This chapter examines crime and crime prevention on farms in the county of Rutland in central England; it seeks to identify the types of solutions that farmers introduce to combat common problems, while recognising that farms, by their very nature, are difficult to protect.

Introduction

This chapter examines how farmers in the county of Rutland in central England are increasing the risks for potential offenders. Essentially, the chapter reports on a crime prevention audit identifying issues pertinent to the defence of farms, and farmers' attitudes and practices. Farmers are business people and their farms are their livelihood, yet the very nature of farms, large isolated estates, makes them notoriously difficult to protect against a background where there is concern about the movement of crime away from inner-city areas, to the city outskirts and towards rural communities.[2] The data produced were obtained during an in-depth crime survey conducted by the author in 1996. The survey examined the levels of crime on farms in Rutland, and then recorded a range of details on crime prevention techniques and strategies. This chapter covers those aspects of farm security which impinge directly on the offender.[3]

In 1995, the Lincolnshire Police in the UK confirmed that 'one of the most rapid growth areas of crime' had been within the rural community.[4] At the same time, the NFU Mutual — the insurance arm of the National Farmers' Union — reported that the cost of farm theft in 1994 had risen to £13.8 million and that rural burglaries had now reached record levels.[5] The president of the NFU was himself quoted in the *British Farmer Services Supplement* as saying that 'theft, trespass and other similar crimes [which] used to be chiefly urban problems ... have spread to our own doorstep',[6] and recent enquiries at the NFU Mutual head office[7] have indicated that vehicle thefts and criminal damage are now prevalent offences on farms right across the UK. Even in the absence of empirical data, it can clearly be seen that farms are becoming increasingly susceptible to crime.

One of the key reasons behind these figures lies in the fact that the British countryside has never been easier to access. The growth in ownership of the private motor car, coupled with the extensive road network, has made day trips to the countryside an everyday occurrence; yet the rural way of life continues, at least to an extent, to be open and unguarded. This may be something of a transitional period as the rural community comes to terms with this greater accessibility; nevertheless, the net effect has been to make rural areas increasingly vulnerable to crime, and has forced the average farmer in the UK to afford security issues a higher priority than may have been the case a decade or so ago.

This chapter therefore provides a snapshot of life on farms in the distinctive region of Rutland. The survey covered the period 1994-1996 and involved detailed interviews with over 40 farmers. Rutland is an agricultural county, with almost 90 per cent of the land area being devoted exclusively to the business of farming; however, it was also selected for study because its geographical shape and size (some 400 sq km) made it an achievable area to cover in detail within the time constraints of the project. It is not claimed that Rutland is representative of the UK as a whole; nor is it suggested that research data from Rutland can be extrapolated to determine agrarian-security policies and practices nationwide. Nevertheless, the findings detailed in this chapter may be indicative of agricultural crime and security management techniques in other parts of the country, and they should serve to highlight areas of specific concern within the general farming community of central England and show how the risk for offenders is potentially on the increase.

The chapter takes the form of a security audit; it looks at a number of factors relevant to security and discusses the survey findings (both the researchers' observations and the farmers' comments). Such an audit, ascertaining the present position, is a prerequisite for deciding what courses of action would be appropriate to improve the security and safety of farms and the people who work on them. While normally each farm would carry out its own audit or risk assessment, in this paper the experiences are generalised to provide what is effectively the first overview of the state of security and crime prevention on farms (in one part of the UK). The audit covered a range of issues, and the analysis begins by considering physical security measures.

Boundaries
The physical security protection of rural farms is, on the face of it, not easy. The most common form of boundary, for 37 out of the 40 farms involved in the survey, were hedges. These were typically of hawthorn, 'backed up by electric fence and barbed wire as required'. However, not one farmer had had the boundary marked in any definitive way. The problem was highlighted by the manager of one of the larger farms (344 hectares) who reported that he had 'seven miles of roadside hedge'. From a security point of view, these hedgerows rarely proved to be a satisfactory barrier. As one farmer realistically observed, 'There is more or less open access to any part of this farm'.

Signs

Farmers were questioned as to what signs they had used to deter trespassers and would-be offenders. Seventeen had no security signs at all. The reasons given included 'we've never bothered'; 'people wouldn't take any notice'; and 'signs can be perceived as antagonistic - we don't want to get people's backs up'. While signs have been criticised for being ineffective, at least in the retail sector, the concern that they may antagonise honest people is a new limitation to this security method. Other farms, however, took a firmer line. One farmer described his warning signs as 'well produced, in good condition and unequivocal'. Seven farmers displayed *Farm Watch* signs; four farms, which were all centred on villages, had *Neighbourhood Watch* stickers, and 13 farms had signs declaring that the general area and/or the access roads were private. Other more individual signs included: *'Beware - Our Dogs Bite'*; *'Never mind the dog, beware of the owner'*; *'Beware of the Bull'*, irrespective of whether there were bulls in the field or not; and *'Beware of Snakes'*, which reportedly concentrated the minds of most ramblers and ensured that they stuck rigidly to the rights of way.

Dogs

The use of dog warning signs evoked ambivalent views from the farmers who were interviewed. The sign *'Beware of the Dog'* was seen to be a tacit admission that the owner was aware that he had a dangerous animal on his land; thus, if that dog was to bite any person, the owner would be hard put to deny his culpability. Indeed, one farmer in the survey had had a considerable claim made successfully against him when his Rottweiler bit a delivery man. Nevertheless, the survey showed that 39 of all farmers surveyed considered that dogs in general were an 'effective' or 'very effective' deterrent to potential offenders. However, only nine owners considered that *their own* dogs were 'very effective', and one in ten assessed their animals as plain 'ineffective'.

It is worth noting that, of the 40 farms inspected, only three had (comparatively) large dogs (Belgian Shepherds, German Shepherds and Lurchers). By contrast, 27 had Border Collies — the most popular choice, followed by Labradors and then Terriers. Only one farm did not have a dog, while another farmer observed that guard dogs were probably more trouble than they were worth.

Domestic security

The survey examined, so far as was possible, the security of dwelling houses on farms. A qualitative impression obtained by the researcher was that, from a physical security point of view, farmhouses in general were not particularly secure. However, most farms had compensatory measures, which included a regular presence in the farmyard area and the wide use of dogs. Nevertheless, 10 farmhouses had burglar alarms (one of which was remotely monitored), 25 had security locks on their main point of access, and 20 had window locks. In addition, 35 farms used movement (heat) activated sensor lights. Although one farmer did have a dummy camera, there was no working CCTV on any farm. However, one farm operated a six-station remote sensing system (in lieu of cameras), where the PIR detector heads relayed a signal back to a control unit which generated an audible alarm. A brief examination of this equipment suggested that it had considerable merit.

Security of farm buildings
Farm buildings, by their very nature (large, open and widespread), are plainly difficult to secure. Most farmers endeavoured to lock their most vulnerable areas — the chemical store and the workshop — but were generally less able to protect the large, open farm sheds. Four farms had no designated workshop as such, but, of the remainder, 27 had workshops that were secured (at least to some extent), and three farms, all with remote farmyards, had workshops which were alarmed. Two farms had solid barriers that swung across their farmyards' access roads and were locked into place (to prevent vehicle or trailer thefts at night), and at least 16 had movement activated lights in the yards around their farm buildings. One farmer described his security thus:

> All the buildings with anything of value in them are locked. The workshop and other vulnerable areas are also locked. Within the workshop there is a locked metal grid cage, and outside there are movement activated lights.

However, another, at the other end of the spectrum, observed, 'It's not a particularly tidy farm, all a bit of a mess really ... The only thing with a lock on it is the spray shed'. Quite clearly, therefore, individual security standards were something of a variable factor.

Vehicle security
Eighteen farmers interviewed admitted that they occasionally left keys in the ignition of vehicles that were not in use, and one farmer admitted leaving his vehicle keys with his vehicles at all times. Tractors and similar machinery generally had common keys, and one farmer disclosed how to start a tractor with a nail. Thus there appeared to be a widespread metaphoric shrug when it came to securing farm machinery. Indeed, only one farmer had made a specific effort to fit immobilisers to all his tractors. Four-wheel drive vehicles, however, were infinitely better secured, with most modern vehicles having alarms and/or immobilisers.

The biggest impetus to improved vehicular security had clearly come from the NFU Mutual. They had advised all farmers in the region that, if the keys were left in a vehicle and that vehicle was subsequently stolen, then the NFU Mutual would simply not pay the insurance. Such firm rules were seen as possibly the only way to change the inbuilt cultural ethos of the farming community; as one interviewee remarked when asked about removing keys from vehicles: 'Once upon a time, you wouldn't even have thought about it'. Two farmers used a vehicle tracking device (*Tracker*) on their four-wheel drive vehicles.

Property marking
Thirty-one farmers questioned did not mark their professional or domestic property in any way. Only four farmers marked their workshop equipment, and only three farmers used ultra-violet markers on their personal property. One farmer, however, had conspicuously marked most of the valuable and attractive items in his house with his postcode using a thick indelible pen. Seven of the sample had a photographic record (of sorts) of their private property, and two had taken a selection of representative photographs of their animals. Two further farmers had filmed their machinery and workshop tools.

Inventories were widely used, but on a sliding scale of thoroughness. Two large estates both had comprehensive inventories and conducted annual stock checks. Most other farms kept at least two general registers: one was the Valuation Schedule, which was predominantly for accountancy purposes; the second was a general list of major items, which was compiled for reasons of insurance.

Animal marking, particularly for sheep, centred on tagging, ear-notching and/or some type of distinctive paint. However, none of these methods was deemed to be permanent. Ear tags could be removed, notching could be altered or added to, and distinctive paint was seldom other than temporary (indelibly marking the wool meant that it depreciated in value). Tattooing was only used on pig breeding stock, pedigree sheep (where a Charollais ram might fetch £1,800) and certain herds of suckler cows. Dairy cows and horses were freeze-branded, although, in the case of the cows, the branding was predominantly for management rather than security purposes. Overall, however, the survey appeared to cover a period of transition in animal marking and identification. The scare caused by BSE and CJD will almost certainly require every cow — and perhaps sheep — to be positively identifiable and its life history to be fully recorded. Permanent marking would therefore seem to be the way ahead, and this should in turn directly increase the risk to offenders by leading to greater accountability for animal stocks.

Farmers were asked how often they carried out a headcount of their livestock. Cattle were checked daily by all except three farms, two of which preferred a twice-weekly count and one a monthly count in the company of an audit team. Sheep counting varied from farm to farm: eight farmers claimed to count their sheep on a daily basis; the majority, however, reported that they counted their sheep no more than monthly or even two-monthly.

Insurance
Farmers were asked to what extent they relied on insurance as a means of loss prevention. Three farmers said 'Not at all'; one of these explained: 'I've got very little insured ... [since] I don't believe in insurance'. Fourteen farmers claimed to rely on insurance 'to a limited extent', and 15 reported that they relied on insurance 'to a certain extent'. As one farmer noted: 'Everything that counts is insured, but if we had a problem area we'd sort it out'. Only eight of the sample stated that they relied on insurance to a great extent. Twenty-two of the sample had made one or more insurance claims as a result of criminal actions during the last two-year survey period, with one farmer submitting a total of six separate claims (all settled). Finally, the level of expense that farmers said that they were prepared to suffer before considering the submission of an insurance claim averaged out at about £200 (range: nil to £500).

Surveillance and image
Of the sample of farmers interviewed, 36 said that on average they 'patrolled' their farm at least once per day. On the arable farms during the winter months, farmers might only visit their fields weekly; conversely, at certain times of the year, such as during the harvest, they tended 'to almost live in the fields'.

Few farmhouses provided a satisfactory overview of the surrounding farmland. Indeed, some two-thirds of the sample could see no more than 20 per cent of their farmland from their primary residence and/or main farmyard. Many farms were an agglomeration of scattered fields, some up to five or ten miles apart, and less than half the farms claimed to be *ring-fenced* (all in one block). A considerable effort had therefore been made by the NFU regional office to introduce *Farm Watch* schemes in the district. Fifteen farmers stated that they were part of the *Farm Watch*; however, only two farmers rated the scheme to be of any value, the remainder considering it ineffective and superficial. Farmers were tempted to lay the blame for this at the feet of the police, although it could be argued that it is primarily a system run *by* farmers *for* farmers.

The survey examined whether any farms had a particularly distinctive image. Those adjacent to the Tri-National Tornado Airbase at Cottesmore, the Seaton viaduct and the Roman archaeological site(s) invariably attracted a high profile by association. Less dramatic but nevertheless eye-catching features, reported by a cross-section of the sample, included the following:[8]

- attractive house or farm buildings;
- river frontage, lake or reservoir;
- wild deer;
- scenic and attractive farm setting;
- public rights of way;
- disused railway line;
- lay-bys and picnic areas;
- farm(s) on the skyline;
- messy or derelict buildings;
- rarer farm animals (ie pedigree sheep, pedigree cattle, llamas, etc).

Firearms
Thirty-seven of all farmers possessed at least one firearm as defined by Section 57 of the *Firearms Act 1968*. All 37 owned shotguns, at an average rate of nearly four per farm. In addition, 22 of those farmers who had firearms also had in their possession at least one .22 rifle. Some 20 air rifles and two air pistols were declared, together with two starting pistols and one antique pistol. Seven farmers covered by the survey owned high-powered shooting rifles, and at least one of the shotguns was a pump-action design. Farmers confirmed that all firearms were properly secured in approved cabinets when not in use.

When asked if they would deliberately take a firearm with them when investigating what they suspected could be a serious crime, 20 of those who possessed firearms said that there was at least a possibility that they would. Indeed, six of those with firearms declared that they would definitely take a firearm with them. When asked if they might be prepared to take their firearm to a confrontation with a criminal, six of those with firearms said that they would be prepared to use their firearm, and a further six admitted that it was possible that they might. Two qualitative comments were particularly noteworthy during this set of questioning. The first was by one of the farmers who owned a high-powered rifle: 'If the police don't provide a decent service, you're going to end up with vigilantes if you're not careful'. The second observation, however, is from the other end of the spectrum, and referred to one special occasion: 'I took my shotgun out to an incident once — but never again. I could have shot someone, and the thought of what might have happened scared me'. Clearly, the culture of gun use which is so much a part of some rural communities has very serious implications for would-be offenders, and for farmers too, where the legal implications of using a firearm could be serious.

Communications

The survey examined (in brief) the concept of *risk communication*. Farmers were asked from what sources they learnt about farm crime. Two factors stood out from these results. First, the majority of farmers appeared to learn most about farm crime by talking to fellow farmers — 'on the grapevine' as one farmer put it — or from local periodicals specialising in farming matters (although other types of media could also prove informative). Second, the *Farm Watch* and the local police crime prevention officer proved to be amongst the least effective. These findings are displayed in Table 1.

Interviewees were asked to what extent they encouraged their staff to be security conscious. Seven farmers said 'to a limited extent'; 13 claimed 'to a certain extent'; and 20 stated that they encouraged their staff 'to a great extent' to be security conscious.

Table 1. Methods of risk communication (against number of farmers)

Source of information	Always	Often	Occasionally	Rarely	Never
Talking to fellow farmers	1	22	14	1	2
Local periodicals (ie *East Midlands Farmer & Grower)*	-	12	20	5	3
By learning about crime in general and then relating it to life on your farm	-	9	19	9	3
National periodicals (ie *Farmers Weekly)*	-	9	18	9	4
Being a victim of crime yourself	-	7	15	15	3
Newspapers	-	5	16	16	3
National Farmers Union data	-	4	17	11	8
The local police (other than the local crime prevention officer)	-	4	12	13	11
Groups such as Farm Watch	-	1	6	9	24
Radio	-	-	8	16	16
Your local crime prevention officer	-	-	7	12	21

Table 2. Attitudes and perceptions (against number of farmers)

Statement	Strongly agree	Agree	Don't know/ no particular view	Disagree	Strongly disagree
Farmers have to face up to and deal with farm crime themselves rather than rely on the police	4	29	4	3	-
Security only becomes an issue after an incident when we then consider how to prevent a recurrence	4	25	2	8	1
The local police have little influence over farm crime	4	29	2	5	-
Crime is on the increase in Rutland	2	29	6	3	-
Burglary in Rutland is a problem	2	27	8	3	-
Criminals will eventually find their way past most security systems	1	38	-	1	-
The police are ineffective when it comes to dealing with farm crime	1	27	7	5	-
Farmers tend not to think about security on a day-to-day basis	1	20	1	15	3
Criminal activity on my farm *has been* a problem	1	10	4	21	4
Ramblers are a considerable nuisance	1	7	4	28	-
Farmers are irresponsible when dealing with security	-	31	6	2	1
I think that some of the contractors who work on my farm are not completely honest	-	3	6	31	-
Crime on my farm *is* a problem	-	3	2	35	-

Attitudes and perceptions

The research examined a number of basic attitudes and perceptions. The sample was asked to comment on a number of qualitative statements, and a Likert scaling was used to categorise the answers which are shown in Table 2. The majority of farmers agreed that they lived in a district where crime was on the increase. At the same time, the general assessment appeared to be that the police were ineffective when it came to dealing with farm crime, and that they had little influence on this specialised field of offending. Thus 33 farmers acknowledged that farmers had 'to face up [to] and deal with farm crime themselves rather than rely on the police'. However, despite this realistic appraisal, the majority of the sample admitted that (a) farmers tended 'not to think about security on a day-to-day basis', (b) farmers were 'irresponsible when dealing with security' and (c) that security only really became 'an issue after an incident when ... [they then considered] how to prevent a recurrence'.

The Table suggests at least one explanation for this apparent apathy: 35 of the sample considered that crime on their farm 'was not a problem'. The overall impression was that while crime was getting worse it tended to be on other farms.

Finally, farmers were asked what they perceived to be the greatest criminal threat to their farm. The majority suggested that theft-related offences were their greatest threat; however, these offences encompassed at least seven sub-categories, ranging from the theft of livestock to the burglary of farmhouses. By far the most distinctive individual concern was arson: 'Crops are very vulnerable to a box of matches', acknowledged one farmer; 'it's such an easy crime to commit'. Indeed, other research has confirmed that the agriculture sector is comparatively more at risk of arson than other sectors.[9]

Security equipment

The level of expenditure on security equipment by the sample of Rutland farmers during the last two financial years was investigated and recorded. Some 20 farmers questioned had spent less than £500 on security equipment during the period 6 April 1994 to 5 April 1996, confirming that farmers reflect the general attitude of other commercial enterprises in placing a low priority on security issues. At the same time, however, 11 had spent in excess of £1,000, and two farms from the sample had spent over £5,000 on security related-equipment.

An analysis of the crime prevention equipment which farmers had bought revealed a wide cross-section of security items. These are listed below in Table 3 in order of prevalence, with the number of farmers who purchased each listed item detailed alongside.

When asked about the cost-effectiveness of the security equipment that they had purchased in general, a number of farmers criticised the design and use of immobilisers. 'Immobilisers are nothing but a nuisance', remarked one interviewee, whilst another considered that 'The first immobilisers were a gimmick ... [and] weren't good enough for the job'. The only other criticism of security equipment concerned movement-activated lights: 'Our sensor lights were cheap and soon stopped working ... Cheap equipment is just not *worth it.*'

Table 3. Crime prevention equipment purchased by farmers

Equipment	Number of farmers
Chains and padlocks	27
Movement-activated lighting	21
Fencing	7
Gates	6
Non-movement-activated lighting (including floodlighting)	5
Tracker	3
Immobilisers	3
Burglar alarm(s)	3
New windows/window locks	3
Strengthened workshop	2
New doors; combination locks; remote sensing equipment; new signs; new door locks	less than 2

Farmers were also questioned as to whether they had ever taken professional security advice prior to purchasing crime prevention equipment. Three farmers said that they had discussed the issue with the local police; one had followed the advice of the NFU, and another — the largest estate — had employed a security consultant for one day. Three farmers followed the advice of the company specialists selling alarm equipment to them; all other farmers bought security equipment independently, relying on their general perceptions of the risk. Farmers were asked if they had ever carried out a cost-benefit analysis of the security measures that were in use on their farms. Only three farmers admitted that they had formally done so, but more than half the interviewees explained that they would normally conduct such an analysis 'at the back of their mind'. 'Farmers are businessmen', one respondent explained, a view corroborated by a second farmer: 'We are in business... [We have to] weigh up the pros and cons'.

Relationship with the police
All farmers were questioned about their relationship with Leicestershire Constabulary in general and the Rutland Local Policing Unit (ie the local police) in particular. Twenty-five of the sample believed that the police could do more to combat rural crime, but there was a widespread acknowledgement that, without an increase in resources, there was little scope for an improvement in the existing service. Thirty-one of the sample had requested the services of the police during the reporting period, and at least 97 crime-related calls had been made to the Leicestershire Constabulary, the majority of which were responded to positively.

Conclusion

The risk to offenders on farms, at least in the Rutland area, is clearly significant. Crime awareness would appear to be increasing, and crime prevention is certainly becoming a consideration within the region. On the evidence put forward, most farmers in Rutland *are* taking steps to lessen the vulnerability of their buildings, their equipment and their stock. Yet, farmers could hardly be considered overly security conscious, although in this respect they typify businesses generally.[10] While farmers recognised that crime was an emerging concern, they felt as though it was something that was more likely to prove problematic for others.

Although risk management techniques were clearly discernible, they were basic and most farmers did not appear to have fully come to terms with their vulnerability. Set against this, however, was the unpredictability of the farm environment, which presents the real risk for offenders. In fact, much security resulted from management practices. For example, risks were indicated by the finding that most farms were continually staffed; there were high levels of natural surveillance; some farmers mounted random patrols of their farms on a regular and often daily basis; almost all farms had dogs, and while not all were considered by farmers to be good guard dogs they would nevertheless raise the alarm should security be threatened; security devices (alarms, locks, sensors, etc) were clearly becoming the norm; and almost every farmer had ready access to firearms — with a sizeable proportion prepared to use their weapon in dealing with crime if they deemed the circumstances of the incident warranted it. This clearly represents a real risk for offenders, but for farmers too.[11]

There is considerable potential for farmers to increase the risk for offenders, and to adopt and adapt situational techniques to meet their own (very different) circumstances. Some farmers had found warning signs to be a useful technique, and others had been prompted to change behaviour because of the threats of insurance companies. Farms are a distinctive type of business, with a distinctive culture; they thus present an interesting challenge to security experts, and offer an important area of research for those who want to learn more about the theory and practice of crime prevention.

Notes

1   Gavin Sugden is contactable via the Scarman Centre for the Study of Public Order, University of Leicester, The Friars, 154 Upper New Walk, Leicester, LE1 7QA, UK.

2   See, for example, Matthews, R. and Francis, P. (1995) *The Relative Decline of Urban Crime.* Paper Presented to the British Sociological Association Annual Conference, University of Leicester, 10-13 April; Shapland, J. and Vagg, J. (1988) *Policing by the Public.* London: Routledge.

3   For details of the level of crime experienced by farmers in Rutland, see Sugden, G. (forthcoming) Farm Crime: Out of Sight, Out of Mind. *Crime Prevention and Community Safety: An International Journal.*

4   See *Tackling Countryside Crime,* a promotional video released by the Lincolnshire Constabulary in 1995.

5   Hornsby, M. (1995) Theft cost farmers £14 million. *The Times,* 4 July.

6   Sir David Naish, June 1995.

7   By the author, 6 February 1996.

8   The researcher, it should be noted, identified expensive farm machinery, especially trailers, left unattended and insecure in at least four easily accessed farmyards.

9   Gill, M. (1999) The Victimisation of Business: Indicators of Risk and the Direction of Future Research. *International Review of Victimology*. Forthcoming.

10   Ibid.

11   As, of course, is the case of the farmer who uses any unlawful force.

Chapter 7

Sales and Security: Striking the Balance

Adrian Beck and Andrew Willis[1]

This study reports an investigation of product theft in the electrical retail sector using an innovative methodology which involved tagging all small goods available for sale in ten stores (part of a national chain) over a two-week period. The study explores the number and value of goods sold and stolen by product type and location in the store. It adds an empirical dimension to the theoretical work of Clarke[2] and others which identified the importance of opportunity in understanding offending behaviour and the potential for situational crime prevention in the retail sector.[3] The study offers some evidence that location of product is associated with levels of loss and it also suggests that retailers can make an informed choice about an acceptable trade-off between sales and security.

Introduction

Crime and crime prevention in the retail sector are relatively under-explored areas, but there are emerging data about the scale and nature of the problems.[4] The retail sector is one of the largest and most dynamic parts of the United Kingdom's economy.[5] By the mid-1990s the industry had a turnover of £187 billion or 14% of the nation's gross domestic product (GDP) and it employed 2.4 million persons or 10% of the British workforce in some 328,000 retail outlets.[6]

The British Retail Consortium (BRC) report on retail crime and its costs covering the financial year 1995–96, was based on a survey of 48,000 UK retail outlets with a combined turnover of over one-half of all retail sales.[7] The total annual costs of retail crime were estimated to be £1.9 billion – £1.4 billion sustained as a result of known or suspected criminal incidents and a further £450 million of expenditure on security hardware and security services. Against annual sales of £187 billion this was equivalent to 1.13 per cent of total retail turnover. Crime costs amounted to an average loss of £85 from each household in the country.

More specifically, retailers witnessed or could establish 5 million instances of customer theft, with 1.6 million offenders apprehended and just over one million referred to the police, but with only 276,000 offences recorded as such by the police. The BRC survey estimated customer theft in 1995/96 as costing £653 million – £211 million lost due to witnessed incidents and £442 million lost to unwitnessed cases of customer theft; and within these figures the value of stolen electrical goods could be as high as £146 million. Earlier retail crime surveys have pointed to near-identical findings.[8] The data are un-equivocal – the criminal threat to the retailer in general, and the electrical retailer in particular, is substantial, whether this is measured by the number of incidents or the direct costs of stock loss.

Methodology

These figures are a useful (albeit alarming) indicator of the extent and value of shoplifting losses but because they rely on witnessed offences and detected offenders they cannot be seen as an accurate measure. The picture of retail crime is imperfect and incomplete unless and until undetected (or successful) crime is entered into the equation. This poses a fundamental problem because undetected crime is that about which little or nothing is known. This directs attention towards a methodology which offers a more complete and robust measure of criminal activity. This has rarely been attempted. The primary objective here was to explore the extent to which the 'design factor' or the position of small electrical items (called 'essentials' in the trade) in stores contributed to shoplifting losses. Essentials are small items such as audio tapes, video tapes, films, headphones, batteries and plugs. It examined the hypothesis that 'ease of access' to goods would be associated with higher levels of sales and shoplifting, and that less accessible product would be sold and stolen at lower levels.

The approach adopted is known as 'repeated systematic counting'.[9] It involves three steps. First, all product at risk of being stolen is counted and then marked prior to the start of the trading day. Secondly, during the trading day, whenever product is sold the tag is removed and the sale verified. Thirdly, at the end of the trading day, the stock on display is checked against the initial tally. Any discrepancy between the sum of the verified sales and the stock remaining at the end of the day, and the initial count of product on display, can be attributed to stock loss due to theft.

The study was conducted in ten stores selected as a representative sample of a national electrical retailer. Shoplifting was measured by counting all items available for sale on Thursdays, Fridays and Saturdays over a two-week period. The research team attached a small sticky label to all essentials at risk of being stolen. Whenever an item was sold, given away or used in-store, the staff were asked to peel off the label and stick it on a tally sheet held by the till. Shoplifting was measured each day by comparing the number of missing items with the number sold, given away or used in-store. All goods were tagged with colour-coded sticky labels in order to identify product sold or stolen by type and a parallel colour code was used to identify product sold or stolen by location.

This fastidious approach permitted a fourfold analysis of sales and losses – by number, by value, by product type and by location. The project was in part a replication of a 1990 study[10] which explored the theft of similar goods from stores in the same company, differing only in that the earlier study concentrated on the ten'worst' stores (those known to be suffering high losses). It is important not to underestimate the technical difficulties of operationalising the 'repeated systematic counting' methodology, or its labour-intensive nature. Every item available for purchase had to be tagged with the appropriate colour-coded sticker before sales. At the point of sale, all goods had to have the tag removed and then re-stuck to a tally sheet. Furthermore, at the end of trading, there had to be a total for goods sold (stickers removed and coded), goods unsold (stickers in place) and goods missing – presumed stolen.

Goods sold and stolen by number and value

Initial data on shop theft of small items are presented as a percentage of goods lost expressed as a function of the total number of goods sold and goods stolen (Table 1), with all figures rounded to the nearest whole number. For all stores and all small items, 1,403 items were sold and 165 items were stolen, giving an overall rate of stock lost due to theft of 10% by number. There was considerable variation by store, with a rate ranging from 2% to 16%. The earlier study found an overall rate of stock loss due to theft of 16% by number for similar items, but this study concentrated on known high-risk stores rather than a representative sample of all stores.

Table I. Number of goods sold and stolen by store

Store	Number sold	Number stolen	Per cent stolen
A	55	5	8
B	148	2	2
C	211	21	9
D	115	13	10
E	126	10	7
F	135	10	7
G	128	20	14
H	287	56	16
I	138	21	13
J	60	7	10
All stores	1,403	165	10

Additional data sets the value of losses due to theft within the context of overall sales (Table 2). These findings relate only to the value of sales and losses of packs of video and audio cassettes. These were chosen because they represented the bulk of small items sold. The proportion of goods stolen is given as a percentage of the total value of goods sold and goods lost.

Table 2. Value of audio and video goods sold and stolen by store

Store	Video			Audio		
	Sold £	Stolen £	Stolen Per cent	Sold £	Stolen £	Stolen Per cent
A	89	34	28	126	11	8
B	289	35	11	126	11	8
C	661	67	9	347	27	7
D	207	21	9	182	45	20
E	251	14	5	82	8	9
F	345	9	2	89	0	0
G	717	50	6	169	29	15
H	347	38	10	259	36	12
I	284	95	25	261	29	10
J	235	35	13	116	13	10
All stores	3,425	398	10	1,757	209	11

For all stores, the total value of video sales was £3,425, with losses of £398 giving an overall rate of stock loss due to theft of 10%. The total value of audio sales was £1,757 with losses of £209 giving an overall rate of stock loss due to theft of 11%. Although the total value of video sales was double that of audio sales, the proportion of items stolen by value was nearly identical. Some stores were more vulnerable than others. With respect to video cassettes, the percentage losses were greatest in Store A (28%) and Store I (25%). With respect to audio cassettes, the percentage losses were greatest in Store D (20%) and Store G (15%). If the figures for video and audio are combined, the total value of sales was £5,180, with losses of £607 giving an overall rate of stock loss due to theft of 10% by value. Again, these data are in contrast to the earlier study, which identified an overall rate of stock loss due to theft of 27% by value for similar items in high-risk stores (although the findings are not so different if the two sets of high-risk stores are compared).

Goods sold and stolen by type of product

It was also possible to identify sales and losses by type of product, including data on the type of product with the highest sales and the type of product which was stolen most frequently, together with the rate of stock loss due to theft by product. Not all essentials are stolen at the same rate and it is important to identify the items most at risk. The findings on sales and losses by number, together with the distribution by product type, are presented in Table 3. The most straightforward way to understand loss due to theft is to calculate the number of units stolen as a percentage of the total number of units (sold and stolen).

Table 3. Number of goods sold and stolen by type of product

Product	Number sold	Number stolen	Per cent stolen
Audio tapes (5 or less)	357	45	11
Audio tapes (6 or more)	99	12	11
Video tapes (4 or less)	270	25	8
Video tapes (5 or more)	120	11	8
Films	193	11	5
Headphones	129	23	15
Other	235	38	14
Total	1,403	165	10

Within the overall picture (1,403 items sold and 165 items stolen, giving an overall rate of shop loss due to theft of 10% by number), the rate of loss for audio tapes was slightly above average – 11% for both small and large packs. In contrast, the rate of loss for video tapes was noticeably below average – 8% for both small and large packs. Films were stolen at a rather less than average rate (5%). The rate of loss for headphones was the highest for any product type at 15%, one-half as much again as the average rate for all products.

There was a positive correlation between units of product sold and their liability to loss due to theft (Table 4). With respect to sales by volume, if the sales of small and large packs of audio tapes and video tapes are combined, then these products accounted for nearly two-thirds (60%) of all essentials sold. Nearly one-half of all the items sold (44%) were either small packs of audio tapes (25%) or small packs of video tapes (19%). In contrast, films comprised about one-seventh of all sales (14%); and headphones accounted for 1 in 11 sales (9%).

Table 4. Relationship between goods sold and stolen by type of product

Product	Sold		Stolen	
	Number	Per cent	Number	Per cent
Audio tapes (5 or less)	357	25	45	27
Audio tapes (6 or more)	99	7	12	7
Video tapes (4 or less)	270	19	25	15
Video tapes (5 or more)	120	9	11	7
Films	193	14	11	7
Headphones	129	9	23	14
Other	235	17	38	23
Total	1,403	100	165	100

The distribution by theft is roughly similar. The total theft of audio tapes (34%) and video tapes (22%) combined accounts for over one-half of all thefts (56%). In both of these categories very many more small packs than large packs were stolen. For audio tapes, small packs accounted for over one-quarter of all thefts (27%), whilst large packs made up less than 10% of all thefts (7%) — a ratio of nearly four to one. For video tapes, small packs accounted for 15% of all thefts and large packs only 7% of all thefts — a ratio of over two to one. For both audio tapes and video tapes there was a positive correlation between the distribution of items sold and items stolen. This was not true for other items. Films comprised 14% of sales, but only 7% of thefts. Conversely, headphones accounted for only 9% of sales by number but as much as 14% of thefts.

Goods sold and stolen by location and type of product

Finally, the study generated broad information about all goods sold and stolen in relation to their in-store location and more detailed information about stock theft by product type and location. With respect to sales by location (Table 5), nearly two-thirds of product (65%) was sold from the sales counter or shelves immediately below it — sales counter (37%), middle shelf (16%) and bottom shelf (12%). Of all the goods sold from this location, over one-half was sold from the sales counter itself. Roughly 1 in 4 items were sold from displays (27%), a term which refers to goods located between major products such as video recorders and hi-fi equipment, or stacked in free-standing displays or special racks on pillars. Very few goods, less than 1 in 12 or 8%, were sold from dump bins — containers filled with stock on offer at reduced prices. The figures for goods stolen were strikingly similar. Over three-quarters of all product which was stolen (76%) was taken from the sales counter (41%), the middle shelf (19%) and the bottom shelf (16%). Of all the goods stolen from this location, over one-half was taken from the sales counter. Approximately 1 in 5 items were stolen from displays (22%). Very few goods were stolen from dump bins (2%).

Table 5. Relationship between goods sold and stolen by location[a]

Location	Sold		Stolen	
	Number	Per cent	Number	Per cent
Sales counter	480	37	63	41
Middle shelf	213	16	29	19
Bottom shelf	157	12	24	16
Display	348	27	34	22
Dump bin	109	8	4	2
Total	1,307	100	154	100

[a] Totals vary from previous Tables due to missing data

Another way of looking at the same problem is to calculate the shoplifting rate by type of product and location (Table 6). Against an average loss of 11% of audio tapes from all locations, the sales counter was most at risk (14%), followed by the middle shelf (13%) and bottom shelf (12%). For video tapes, against an average loss of 8% from all locations, the sales counter (11%) and middle shelf (10%) were most at risk. Against an average loss of 15% of headphones from all locations, the bottom shelf (18%), the middle shelf (17%) and the sales counter (17%) were most at risk. Films were most at risk on the sales counter (8%).

Table 6. Rate of goods stolen by type of product and location

Location	Audio tapes Per cent stolen	Video tapes Per cent stolen	Films Per cent stolen	Headphones Per cent stolen
Sales counter	14	11	8	17
Middle shelf	13	10	N/A	17
Bottom shelf	12	8	N/A	18
Display	10	7	4	14
Dump bin	5	3	N/A	9
Total	11	8	5	15

Discussion

The relationship between small electrical items sold and product stolen is strikingly similar, whether this is expressed for all goods lost by number (10%) or for audio and video cassettes lost by value (10%). These figures are rather less than the rates of loss identified by the Buckle et al[11] survey of high-risk stores – 16% by number and 27% by value. In the current study the rate of loss due to theft was greatest for headphones (15%) and audio tapes (11%), with a below-average rate for video tapes (8%) and films (5%). Small packs of audio and video tapes accounted for 44% of sales and 42% of thefts; customers and thieves alike showed a preference for small goods. Headphones had the highest rate of loss by number (15%) of all goods. The face-value interpretation is that easy-to-carry goods are a significant target for shop thieves and that around 1 in 10 items of stock of this type can be expected to be stolen. This presents a not inconsiderable crime threat with real costs, but it also directs attention to the ways in which product is distributed within the store and its vulnerability by location.

The sales counter was the most productive site for legitimate sales (37%) but it was also the most vulnerable location for theft (41%). Although it shifted product it did so for both honest customers and thieves. This was particularly true for audio and video tapes. Against average losses by number due to theft of 10% for all goods, the sales counter had above average losses for audio tapes (14%) and video tapes (11%). The vulnerability of the sales counter may be explained because this focal point in the store is something of a 'zone of confusion' – an area where product is displayed to attract customers but also where buyers complete their purchases (handing over cash, writing cheques or completing credit card transactions); and it is possible that the bustle of activities associated with honest buying also operated so as to allow theft to take place undetected. The diminishing losses from the shelves below the counter probably reflected the fact that larger and less portable items were located nearer to the floor, although some shop staff offered the view that the lower shelves would be high-risk areas because they were less overseen than the sales counter.

Displays were the second most vulnerable location, experiencing one in five losses by number (22%). One manager offered the view that items displayed at 'coat pocket' level were more likely to be stolen than those placed higher up on the display. Finally, dump bins were associated with low levels of sales and low rates of loss. A possible reason is that customers and thieves perceived goods in this location to be of inferior quality ('seconds' or damaged) and therefore not worth either buying or stealing. Alternatively, because the bins tended to be located in prominent positions in the stores this may have afforded high levels of natural surveillance.

The data allow a composite picture of shop theft to emerge. Even within the category of small electrical items, those most at risk were small, easily portable and relatively high value goods – small, not large packs of audio and video tapes. Product on the sales counter may be vulnerable because legitimate interactions may have facilitated illegitimate activities, and product on display may be at risk because lack of oversight may have contributed to ease of access.[12] Theft of small electrical goods represents a classic case of opportunistic offending, which is usually held to include one or more of three factors: high enticement to commit crime or the attraction of unpaid-for product; material conditions which are conducive to crime or ease of access; and benefits which can be obtained at minimal risk with low prospects of detection.[13] This has important implications for crime prevention.

Situational crime prevention would seek to reduce the benefits of offending by reducing opportunity, by minimising easy rewards and increasing the risk for offenders.[14] Physical protection through target hardening (making the at-risk product less attractive and open to would-be offenders) or target removal, would have a certain appeal to the company's security staff. As regards the theft of product from sales counters and displays, one security manager commented, albeit facetiously:

> Frankly this is aggravation I could do without. It's a big nuisance but not a threat to trading. The answer is simple – nail it down! That would stop them, wouldn't it? Sometimes I think we give it away.

It is equally clear, however, that such an approach would be far less attractive to those with responsibilities for marketing and merchandising. It is reasonable to suppose that the closer an honest customer can get to goods and examine them, the more he or she may then be prepared to make a purchase – having confirmed its suitability and quality in relation to price. Earlier work for the same national electrical retailer found that one-third of buyers (38%) and even more browsers (44%) handled product on their visit to the store;[15] and fashion retailing is even more heavily predicated on a physical interaction between potential purchaser and product.[16] But it is at this point that the interests of 'selling' and 'security' may collide, presenting a genuine dilemma. What increases the risk for offenders may at the same time prove an irritant for the honest customer. Merchandising requirements would bring the customer as close as possible to the goods for sale, whilst security considerations would maximise the distance between customers and (illegitimate) opportunities for theft; and these are seemingly irreconcilable differences.

Moreover, even where shop theft is interpreted as the product of an instrumental and considered approach to making the decision or 'rational choice' to engage in offending behaviour,[17] the low rates of apprehension and referral to the police suggest that the shopwise offender will readily calculate that the stealing odds are very much in his or her favour. For example, data from the British Retail Consortium's crime survey show that of 5 million offences witnessed or experienced by retailers, only around 1 million were referred to the police and fewer than 276,000 were recorded by the police. There is an enormous rate of attrition between known offending and formal action. There is yet more attrition between prosecution and conviction; and, even at this point, there is no certainty that any penalty will be sufficient to exercise an individual or deterrent effect. Finally, it may be unwise to categorise shop theft as being a function of rational choice, because offenders may not be calculating criminals making precise judgements about their actions and their consequences; and if retail theft is unpremeditated and unplanned, the concept of increasing the costs attendant on crime or reducing its benefits becomes instantly redundant. It is even possible that the long odds against detection could act as an incentive to criminality.

The implications for retail crime prevention are both clear and confusing. On the one hand, the systematic repeated counting methodology can be seen as a robust and useful means of moving towards hard measures against shop theft, even though it is both time-consuming and costly. It is more than 'exploratory' crime analysis[18] because it is focused on specific situational variables which relate to loss.[19] The data show high overall loss (10%) with variations between different product types and locations. Even though they are not that marked, there is limited evidence that shop theft would be reduced by moving product away from an at-risk location such as the sales counter, an area which has been identified as a crime-enhancing zone of confusion. A product relocation strategy would have some impact, probably of the order of a 1% or 2% reduction on current levels of loss against a baseline figure of around 10% loss by number. This is not insignificant and in absolute terms the benefits would increase for more expensive product. It also confirms the importance of micro-environmental aspects of shop theft and opportunity denial in controlling it.[20] Finally, following the environmental criminology developed by Patricia and Paul Brantingham, it shows that further work could be done to elaborate at-risk areas within stores, including the identification of 'nodes' or offence locations, 'paths' or routes which offenders might normally take to those locations and 'edges' or boundaries between two departments of the same store.[21] All these factors point to realistic and feasible crime prevention benefits through the design of the interior of the store. On the other hand, the opportunity to restrict loss by product placement is severely limited because of broader considerations about the relationship between selling and security.

At one extreme, if there were no goods on sale there would be no product to steal; and, at the other extreme, if all goods remained accessible and on unsupervised display, then even the normally honest customer may be tempted to steal. Somewhere in between these polar positions is a need to strike a balance between ease of access to goods for well-intentioned customers and restricted access for would-be thieves. The difficulty is that there may be an inverse relationship between the coefficient of security and the honest shopper's inclination to browse and purchase; and at some point increased security may deter both thieves and shoppers. The possibility of security threatening sales is an empirical question, however, and it suggests a new research agenda – namely the effect on shopping behaviour of customers' perceptions of security measures.[22]

To the extent that retailers wish to maximise customers' physical interaction with product as part of the process of encouraging them to make a purchase, stock losses due to theft may be considered as an acceptable trading cost. They could make an informed choice that the costs of tolerating certain levels of shop theft are compensated for by additional sales. Although there is a conventional view which expects action to be taken against crime, there is no reason why retailers should see themselves as moral guardians rather than protectors of profit. From their perspective, setting the cost of crime against profit is an example of rational choice theory in the commercial sector. The data presented above show a positive association between volume of sales and number of thefts and their distribution by location, indicating that just such an accommodation has been made, perhaps inadvertently. The 'worst case scenario' is one of low sales and high loss of high-value product. The most desirable outcome is one of high sales and low loss for both inexpensive and high-value goods. Crime analysis of items sold and stolen by location and product type is a useful first step which enables an informed decision to be made about the balance between sales, stock theft and security. At the same time, such an approach provides important clues as to how the opportunities for offenders might be decreased.

Notes

1   Adrian Beck is a Lecturer in Security Management and Andrew Willis is a Senior Lecturer in Criminology at the Scarman Centre for the Study of Public Order, University of Leicester, The Friars, 154 Upper New Walk, Leicester, LE1 7QA.

2   Clarke, R.V.G. (1980) Situational Crime Prevention: Theory and Practice. In Muncie, J., McLaughlin, E. and Langan, M. (eds) (1996) *Criminological Perspectives: A Reader*. London: Sage.

3   See Burrows, J. (1988) *Retail Crime: Prevention Through Crime Analysis*. Crime Prevention Unit Paper 11. London: Home Office; Ekblom, P. (1988) *Getting the Best Out of Crime Analysis*. Crime Prevention Unit Paper 10. London: Home Office; and Burrows, J. and Speed, M. (1996) Crime Analysis: Lessons From the Retail Sector. *Security Journal*.

Vol. 7, No. 1, pp 53-60.

4   Beck, A. and Willis, A. (1995) *Crime and Security: Managing the Risk to Safe Shopping*. Leicester: Perpetuity Press.

5   See O'Brien, L. and Harris, F. (1991) *Retailing: Shopping, Space, Society*. London: David Fulton; Cahill, M. (1994) *The New Social Policy*. Oxford: B. Blackwell; and Guy, C. (1994) *The Retail Development Process*. London: Routledge.

6   See Burrows, J. and Speed, M. (1994) *Retail Crime Costs 1992/93 Survey*. London: British Retail Consortium; House of Commons (1994) *Environment Committee, Session 1993-94, Fourth Report, Shopping Centres and Their Future, Volume I, Report, together with the Proceedings of the Committee relating to the Report*. London: HMSO; and Wells, C. and Dryer, A. (1997) *Retail Crime Costs 1995/96 Survey*. London: British Retail Consortium.

7   Wells and Dryer, op cit.

8   See Bamfield, J. (1994) *National Survey of Retail Theft and Security 1994*. Northampton: Nene College, School of Business; Burrows and Speed (1994), op cit; Forum of Private Business (1995) *Crime and Small Business*. Knutsford, Cheshire: Forum of Private Business; Mirrlees-Black, C. and Ross, A. (1995) *Crime Against Retail and Manufacturing Premises: Findings From the 1994 Commercial Vicitimisation Survey*. Home Office Research Study 146. London: Home Office; and Speed, M., Burrows, J. and Bamfield, J. (1995) *Retail Crime Costs 1993/94 Survey: The Impact of Crime and the Retail Response*. London: British Retail Consortium.

9   See Buckle, A., Farrington, D., Burrows, J., Speed, M. and Burns-Howell, T. (1992) Measuring Shoplifting by Repeated Systematic Counting. *Security Journal*. Vol. 3, No. 3, pp 137-146; and Farrington, D., Bowen, S., Buckle, A., Burns-Howell, T., Burrows, J. and Speed, M. (1993) An Experiment on the Prevention of Shoplifting. In Clarke, R.V.G. (ed.) *Crime Prevention Studies*. New York: Criminal Justice Press.

10   Buckle et al, op cit.

11   Ibid.

12   This possibility has been powerfully articulated by Felson, M. (1996) Preventing Retail Theft: An Application of Environmental Criminology. *Security Journal*. Vol. 7, No. 1, pp 71-75.

13   Some of the most important work on opportunistic offending includes Clarke (1980), op cit; Hough, M., Clarke, R.V.G. and Mayhew, P. (1980) Introduction. In Clarke, R.V.G. and Mayhew, P. (eds) *Designing Out Crime*. London: HMSO; Poyner, B. (1983) *Design Against Crime: Beyond Defensible Space*. London: Butterworths; Lab, J. (1992) *Crime Prevention Approaches, Practises and Evaluations*. Cincinnati: Anderson; and Felson, M. (1994) *Crime and Everyday Life*. Thousand Oaks, CA.: Pine Forge.

14   See Clarke, R.V.G. (ed) (1997) *Situational Crime Prevention: Successful Case Studies*. Second edition. New York: Harrow and Heston.

15   Beck, A. and Willis, A. (1991) *Selling and Security: Addressing the Balance*. Leicester: University of Leicester, Centre for the Study of Public Order.

16   Cowley, J. (1998) Hold on to Your Purse. *The Times*, 4th February.

17   See Wilson, J.Q. (1975) *Thinking About Crime*. New York: Basic Books; and Cornish, D.

and Clarke, R. (1986) *The Reasoning Criminal.* New York: Springer-Verlag.

18   Ekblom, op cit.

19   Burrows and Speed (1996), op cit.

20   Felson (1996), op cit.

21   Brantingham, P.L. and Brantingham, P.J. (1993) Nodes, Paths and Edges: Considerations on Environmental Criminology. *Journal of Environmental Criminology.* Vol. 13, pp 3-28.

22   See Michele Tonglet's paper in this volume.

Chapter 8

Consumers' Perceptions of Shoplifting and Shoplifting Behaviour

Michele Tonglet[1]

A major concern for retailers is how to increase the risk to shoplifters. This chapter reports on findings from a survey of 417 Northampton shoppers. The object of the study was to investigate consumer attitudes towards shoplifting, the factors influencing the motivations of shoplifters, and the effectiveness of shoplifting prevention measures. In all, 7 per cent of consumers admitted to shoplifting in the previous 12 months, and their behaviour was influenced by their positive amoral attitude to shoplifting and their perception that shoplifting is a low-risk, low-cost crime. Recommendations are made as to how this perception can be changed, and how the risks of shoplifting can be increased.

Introduction

A major concern for those involved with the control of retail crime is how shoplifting can be prevented by increasing the risk to offenders. The rational choice perspective,[2] on which situational crime prevention is based, hypothesises that offenders behave rationally, in that they weigh up the costs and benefits of criminal behaviour, and select the alternative with the highest utility. This suggests that people will shoplift if they perceive the benefits of shoplifting to be greater than the costs, and implies that shoplifting will be prevented by increasing the risks and costs to the offender. However, for this to be achieved a greater understanding is required of offenders' perceptions of the risks and costs of shoplifting, and of how these risks and costs, together with other factors, inhibit or encourage shoplifting behaviour.

Although recent shoplifting research has provided useful data about the effectiveness of shoplifting prevention measures,[3] and the extent and costs of shoplifting,[4] very little is known about the shoplifters themselves, or about the factors which influence their behaviour. The criminological approach, investigating the characteristics of shoplifters and causes of their criminal behaviour, has produced largely inconclusive findings. It does show that a substantial proportion of shoplifters are adolescents,[5] that shoplifters come from all social backgrounds[6] and have a variety of motivations for their shoplifting behaviour.[7] In addition, with a few notable exceptions,[8] very little attention has been paid to the factors which encourage or inhibit shoplifting, or to the values, attitudes and beliefs which influence shoplifting behaviour. This research is therefore a weak foundation on which to build measures designed to increase the risks for offenders.

Self-report surveys indicate that more than 30% of consumers have shoplifted in their lifetime, with between 10% and 20% shoplifting within the previous 12 months.[9] An alternative approach to shoplifting is to view it as consumer behaviour, albeit deviant consumer behaviour. One of the main concerns in the study of consumer behaviour is to understand how consumers make choices, and the factors influencing these choices,[10] and this requires the investigation of the beliefs, attitudes, values and norms which influence consumers' purchasing, or in the case of shoplifting, stealing decisions.

The view of shoplifting as consumer behaviour is a new approach to researching shoplifting in the UK, and provides an additional dimension to previous research in that it attempts to understand how the risks and costs of shoplifting influence the shoplifter's decision of whether or not to shoplift. To indicate how this approach can be utilised to increase the risks of shoplifting, the findings from this study will be discussed in three sections: the factors influencing shoplifting behaviour (including an evaluation of shoplifting as a rational crime), consumers' perceptions of the risks of shoplifting, and consumers' perceptions of the costs of being caught. The final section will then discuss the implications of these findings for the design of measures to increase the risks of shoplifting for offenders.

Research design

The research reported in this study was part of a larger survey of Northampton consumers during March and April 1997. Northampton was selected for the survey as it was felt to be typical of a medium-sized local shopping centre, with a good mix of both multiple and independent retailers. The questionnaires were distributed on each day of the week (including Sunday) over a two-week period, to every fourth consumer leaving selected shops in both city-centre and 'out of town' locations. The consumers were asked to complete the questionnaire at home and return it in a stamped addressed envelope, and were not required to disclose any personal details. Although every effort was made to ensure that the sample was representative of shopping activity in Northampton, the use of convenience sampling limits the extent to which the results can be generalised, either to Northampton consumers or consumers throughout the UK.

To investigate the factors influencing shoplifting behaviour, a methodology used in both social and consumer research to understand and explain behaviour, the Theory of Planned Behaviour,[11] was utilised. This theory has been successfully applied to such diverse behaviours as leisure choice,[12] driving violations,[13] investment decisions,[14] consumer purchases,[15] cheating, shoplifting and lying,[16] and is based on the assumption that people behave rationally, considering the implications of their behaviour. The theory hypothesises that behaviour is the result of intentions to perform or not to perform the behaviour, and that intentions are influenced by three factors:

- *Attitude:* the degree to which the individual has a favourable or unfavourable evaluation of the behaviour.

- *Subjective norm:* social pressures to perform or not to perform the behaviour.

- *Perceived behavioural control:* the individual's belief as to how easy or difficult performance of the behaviour is likely to be.

The relative importance of each of these factors in influencing intentions is determined by multiple regression. An additional factor, the *moral norm*, is included in this study, as it has been suggested that moral issues could be relevant to a dishonest behaviour such as shoplifting.[17]

Central to the theory of planned behaviour are the beliefs underlying the behaviour, which influence attitude, the subjective norm and perceived behavioural control. These beliefs, which relate to the outcomes of performing the behaviour and the evaluation of these outcomes, have important implications for shoplifting research as they suggest the investigation of the factors which inhibit or encourage shoplifting. The belief-based questions were constructed from the beliefs mentioned most frequently in interviews conducted with a sample of 25 Northampton shoppers one month prior to the distribution of the questionnaire. These beliefs related to the advantages/disadvantages and costs/benefits of shoplifting, groups or individuals who would approve/disapprove of shoplifting and the factors that would make shoplifting easy or difficult.

In addition to the components of the theory of planned behaviour and beliefs about shoplifting, the questionnaire also included questions on shoplifting motivation, and attitudes to shoplifting and shoplifting prevention measures. The respondents were asked to report how many times they had shoplifted and how recently they had shoplifted. Demographic information was also requested and a section inviting respondents to comment on shoplifting and shoplifting prevention and to describe their own experiences of shoplifting was included at the end of the questionnaire.

Results and discussion

Sample characteristics
1,200 questionnaires were distributed and 417 were returned fully completed, a response rate of 35%. Although the response rate is about average for a survey of this type, nothing is known about the opinions, attitudes and behaviour of the majority who did not respond, and this must be considered when interpreting the results. The demographic characteristics of the sample are shown in Table 1, and as the 'typical' shopping population of Northampton is not known, it is impossible to assess how representative the sample is. However, although Table 1 suggests the over-representation of certain demographic sub-groups (for example the under 20s, students and those with an income of less than £10,000 p.a.), it is likely that these groups will be over-represented in any sample of shoppers, as they possibly represent the consumers who have the most time available for shopping. For

example, in this survey over 55% of students, the under 20s and those with a low income said that they went shopping at least once a day.

Table 1. Demographic characteristics of the sample (n=417)

Gender	n	Per cent	Employment	n	Per cent
Male	140	34	**Full-time**	116	28
Female	277	66	**Part-time**	65	15
			Housewife/husband	45	11
			Student/at school	142	34
			Unemployed	13	3
			Retired	33	8
			Missing	3	1

Age	n	Per cent	Income	n	Per cent
Under 16	51	12	**under £10,000**	227	54
16-19	79	19	**£10,000 - £19,999**	88	21
20-29	90	22	**£20,000 - £29,999**	44	11
30-44	98	24	**£30,000 or over**	19	5
45-59	64	15	**Missing**	39	9
60-74	31	7			
75 and over	4	1			

The self-report studies discussed above suggest that over 30% of consumers have shoplifted at some time during their life, and this is supported by the findings of this study: 7% of the sample had shoplifted in the previous 12 months, 25% had shoplifted over 12 months ago and 68% had never shoplifted. To gain an understanding of shoplifting behaviour the sample was categorised into *non-shoplifters*, *past shoplifters* (shoplifted over 12 months ago) and *recent shoplifters* (shoplifted in the last 12 months). This enabled any differences in beliefs, attitudes and opinions between the three groups to be investigated, using one-way analysis of variance to determine whether these differences were statistically significant or occurring by random chance.[18] As this analysis indicated a high degree of similarity in views between non-shoplifters and past shoplifters, the discussion will focus on how recent shoplifters differ from the other two groups (although the results for all three groups are reported in the Tables). However, as only 27 respondents admitted to shoplifting in the previous 12 months, it is possible that their views are not representative of shoplifters in general, and this should be considered when interpreting the findings for this group.

Shoplifting and demographic characteristics
Previous shoplifting research[19] suggests that a substantial proportion of shoplifters are juvenile, and this is confirmed by the findings of this study. As shown in Table 2, 26% of the recent shoplifters were under 16, and 41% were between the ages of 16 and 19. Table

2 also indicates that involvement with shoplifting declines with age, as indicated by the research of Cameron.[20] Buckle and Farrington[21] suggest that males are more likely to shoplift than females, and this study reports similar findings: 39% of males admitted to shoplifting, compared to 28% of females, with 9% of the males having shoplifted in the last 12 months (as compared to 5% of females).

Table 2. Shoplifting history by age

	Non-shoplifters		Past shoplifters		Recent shoplifters	
	Number	**%**	**Number**	**%**	**Number**	**%**
Under 16	33	12%	11	10%	7	26%
16 - 19	46	16%	22	21%	11	41%
20 - 29	49	17%	34	32%	7	26%
30 - 44	69	24%	28	27%	1	4%
45 - 59	55	19%	9	9%	-	-
60 +	33	12%	1	1%	1	4%
Total	285	100%	105	100%	27	100%

Sixty-seven per cent of the recent shoplifters were students, a not altogether surprising finding in view of the fact that 87% of the under 20s (the age group most likely to shoplift) were students; however, not all the recent shoplifters under 20 were students: one was employed part-time. The remainder of the recent shoplifters were distributed almost equally among the other employment categories. Although 58% of the past shoplifters and 83% of the recent shoplifters had an income of less than £10,000 p.a., implying that people with low incomes are more likely to shoplift, or admit to doing so, than those who are better off, 67% of the respondents with an income of less than £10,000 had never shoplifted. This suggests that although economic need may contribute to shoplifting behaviour, for the majority shoplifting is not a solution to their economic problems, possibly because of their attitude to the behaviour, and this is discussed further in the next section.

Factors influencing shoplifting behaviour
To investigate which factors had the greatest influence on shoplifting intentions (and thus, by implication, behaviour), multiple regression was used.[22] Respondents were asked about the likelihood of their shoplifting in the future (shoplifting intentions) and this was used as the dependent variable. The independent variables of attitude, subjective norm, perceived behavioural control (PBC) and the moral norm explained 47% of the variation in shoplifting intentions (ie these four variables explained the reasons for almost half of the differences between shoplifting and non-shoplifting intentions in the respondents surveyed). Table 3 shows the results of the multiple regression, with the factors listed in descending order of importance for each group. The factors which have a statistically significant influence on intentions are shown in italics.

Table 3. Factors influencing intentions

Non-shoplifters	Past shoplifters	Recent shoplifters
Attitude	*Attitude*	*Moral norm*
Subjective norm	*Subjective norm*	*Attitude*
Moral norm	PBC	PBC
PBC	Moral norm	Subjective norm

Over 90% of both non-shoplifters and past shoplifters thought it unlikely that they would shoplift in the future, and the main reason for this was their negative attitude toward shoplifting, with over 85% thinking shoplifting wrong, dishonest, and a foolish way to behave. Their negative attitude is reinforced by the influence of the subjective norm (over 85% thought it *extremely* unlikely that people important to them would approve of them shoplifting) and by their strong moral views (over 80% agreed that shoplifting is morally wrong and against their principles).

However, the recent shoplifters held significantly different views. Fifty-two per cent of this group thought it likely that they would shoplift in the future, and the main influence on their intentions was the moral norm. Less than 50% of the recent shoplifters thought shoplifting to be morally wrong, and only 44% stated that shoplifting is against their principles. Their amoral view of shoplifting is supported by their attitude, with only 48% thinking shoplifting bad, and only 56% thinking shoplifting wrong. In addition, only 63% thought shoplifting to be dishonest, suggesting that a substantial proportion of recent shoplifters do not view shoplifting as a crime. Indeed, 89% of the recent shoplifters also thought shoplifting exciting, and this view of shoplifting as exciting behaviour is supported by the fact that 91% of all respondents and 100% of the recent shoplifters thought people shoplift because it's an exciting thing to do.

Although perceived behavioural control was not a significant influence on intentions for any of the three groups, 51% of all respondents and 85% of recent shoplifters thought that there are plenty of opportunities to shoplift, and 78% of recent shoplifters felt that shoplifting is easy. Therefore, despite retailers' efforts to prevent shoplifting, it is still perceived as an 'easy' and 'available' crime, and this is confirmed by the finding that 84% of all respondents and 96% of the recent shoplifters thought it likely that people shoplift because they have the opportunity to do so, and because they have easy access to the goods they want to steal. The view that shoplifting is an opportunistic crime is supported by the fact that recent shoplifters had significantly more opportunities for shoplifting than the other two groups (82% of recent shoplifters used shops at least once a day, compared to 44% of non-shoplifters and 64% of past shoplifters).

As previously discussed, central to the theory of planned behaviour are the beliefs about the behaviour which influence attitude, the subjective norm and perceived behavioural control. The beliefs identified as being relevant to shoplifting related to the financial outcomes of shoplifting, the likelihood and consequences of being caught, and the opinions of other people.

Deterrence theorists[23] have become increasingly interested in the contribution of informal sanctions to the success of deterrence measures, and this study investigated the role played by the opinions of others in influencing and deterring shoplifting behaviour. Family, friends and the police were identified as the people most likely to influence shoplifting behaviour, with over 80% of all respondents thinking it likely these three groups would not approve of shoplifting. However, the recent shoplifters were significantly less likely than the other two groups to be influenced by the opinions of their family, friends and the police, with 45% stating that doing what the police think they should do is bad. In addition, the recent shoplifters were significantly more likely to have friends that approved of shoplifting, and 44% stated that their friends often encouraged them to shoplift. This suggests that recent shoplifters may have little respect for authority, and that it is probably unlikely that they will be dissuaded from shoplifting by the sanctions of their family, friends and the legal system.

The financial consequences of shoplifting relate to the economic benefits of the behaviour, in that shoplifting enables people to get things without paying for them and to save money. Eighty-three per cent of the recent shoplifters had an income of less than £10,000, and in addition, 74% of this group stated that they were often short of money, and 85% agreed that being short of money would encourage them to shoplift. These findings suggest that shoplifting is economically motivated, and as shown in Table 4, the majority of recent shoplifters were likely to view shoplifting as a 'good' solution to their economic problems. Although 41% of the non-shoplifters were also frequently short of money, for them shoplifting was not an acceptable alternative, undoubtedly because of their anti-shoplifting views, and the influence of people important to them. However, the past shoplifters had a more favourable view of the economic benefits of shoplifting and this could have influenced their previous shoplifting behaviour.

Table 4. Benefits of shoplifting - percentage of respondents agreeing with statements

Statements	Non-shoplifters	Past shoplifters	Recent shoplifters
If I shoplift I will get goods without paying	51%	73%	100%
If I shoplift I will be able to save money	49%	60%	100%
Getting goods without paying is good	5%	22%	78%
Saving money by shoplifting is good	2%	13%	81%

Only 15% of recent shoplifters thought it likely that they would be caught shoplifting, compared to 81% of non-shoplifters, and 56% of past shoplifters, and only 33% of recent shoplifters thought that they would be arrested if they were caught, compared to over 70% of past shoplifters and non-shoplifters. The respondents' perceptions of the risks and costs of being caught will be discussed further in the next two sections; however, they have been included in this section as they illustrate the 'rationality' of shoplifting. The attitudes of recent shoplifters are influenced by their perception that the economic benefits of shoplifting outweigh the risks and costs of being caught, and 78% of this group felt shoplifting to be a rewarding rather than punishing behaviour (compared to 5% of non-shoplifters and 16% of past shoplifters). In addition, 72% of all respondents agreed that people shoplift because they think that the benefits exceed the costs, with 89% of recent shoplifters thinking it likely that people shoplift for this reason, and 45% thinking it extremely likely. The analysis of shoplifting motivations shown in Table 5 provides further support for the rationality of shoplifting. This Table compares the mean scores for the three groups of respondents. The questions were scaled: 7=extremely likely, 1= extremely unlikely.

Table 5. Shoplifting motivations - comparison of means

People shoplift because they	Non-shoplifters	Past shoplifters	Recent shoplifters
can't afford the things they need*	5.1972	5.4000	6.0370
have easy access to goods they want to steal*	5.1793	5.3333	6.2963
think they won't get caught	5.6491	5.4095	6.0741
think they won't be punished if caught*	4.8256	4.2762	5.5185
think shoplifting is exciting*	5.6877	5.7308	6.3704
have psychological problems	4.3439	4.1238	3.8889
are under stress	4.1404	4.2095	3.7778

* Significant differences between groups at $p<.05$

Over 80% of the recent shoplifters though it likely that people shoplift because: they can't afford the things they need, they have easy access to the goods they want to steal, they think they won't get caught, they think they won't be punished if they are caught, and they think shoplifting is exciting. These are all 'rational' motivations for shoplifting; however, there was less support for 'irrational' motivations, with only 48% of recent shoplifters thinking psychological problems a likely reason for shoplifting, and only 37% thinking stress a likely reason. In addition, the recent shoplifters were significantly more likely than the other two groups to agree with the rational motivations and disagree with the irrational motivations. For the recent shoplifters therefore, shoplifting appears to be a rational crime, which suggests that it can be prevented by increasing the risks and costs of being caught.

The risks of being caught

When asked about the risks of being caught shoplifting, 82% of the recent shoplifters agreed that there was little risk of being caught, and this is probably due to their previous experiences of shoplifting and their perceptions of the ineffectiveness of retailers' security measures. For example, 82% of the recent shoplifters had never been caught shoplifting, and only 15% thought it likely that they would be caught in the future. In addition, over 70% of recent shoplifters thought it unlikely that they would be caught by the retailers' security measures, and 89% thought these security measures to be ineffective.

However, the non-shoplifters and past shoplifters had a different view of the risks of being caught, with less than 45% of the respondents in these two groups agreeing with the statement that there is little risk of being caught shoplifting. Although 80% of the non-shoplifters thought that they would be caught by the retailers' security measures, only 56% of the past shoplifters thought this likely, possibly due to fact that over 70% of them had never been caught. Over 45% of both past shoplifters and non-shoplifters agreed that retailers' security measures are ineffective; however, the wording of this question may have influenced the responses (respondents were asked to indicate their degree of agreement or disagreement with the statement 'I think that the security measures used in shops are ineffective').

Do consumers' perceptions about the risks of being caught reflect reality? The 1996 survey by the British Retail Consortium[24] suggests that only just over 30% of shoplifters are apprehended, and this is supported by the experiences of shoplifters in this survey: 71% of the past shoplifters, and 82% of the recent shoplifters had never been caught shoplifting. As already discussed, the recent shoplifters were significantly more likely than the other two groups to view shoplifting as a low-risk crime, and this view is undoubtedly influenced by their own experiences. However, for those who have never shoplifted, their perceptions of the high risk of being caught is an effective deterrent, and possibly contributes to their negative attitude towards shoplifting.

To increase the risks of shoplifting, UK retailers spent nearly £450 million on security and shoplifting prevention measures during 1995/6,[25] yet, as already discussed, the perception of the recent shoplifters in this study is that retailers' security measures are ineffective, and that there is little risk of being caught. To investigate the value of retail security, respondents were asked to evaluate the effectiveness of ten security measures, and were also asked to name the three security measures they felt to be the most effective for both deterring and catching shoplifters.

Table 6 indicates that over 90% of all respondents thought the technological devices of CCTV, electronic tags, and alarms were the most likely to deter shoplifters, and these were also the three measures named by non-shoplifters and past shoplifters as being the most effective in deterring shoplifting. However, although over 85% of recent shoplifters agreed that these three measures were likely to deter shoplifters, they felt the 'human' deterrence measure of uniformed security guards to be more effective than the technological measures, and they also indicated limited support for friendly and helpful staff, perhaps because shoplifters will ultimately find a way to circumvent technology, whereas 'human' security measures are more difficult to bypass. These findings support the research of Butler,[26] which suggests that shoplifters perceive humans to present a greater risk than security devices, and thus are a more effective deterrent to shoplifting.

CCTV was seen as being the most effective measure for catching (as opposed to deterring) shoplifters by 81% of all respondents, and this was the most frequently mentioned measure for all three groups. The second most frequently mentioned measure for both non-shoplifters and past shoplifters was store detectives (58% and 60% respectively); however, for recent shoplifters it was electronic tags (70%), suggesting that although the recent shoplifters viewed the 'human' security measures as being more effective in deterring shoplifting they thought technological measures to be more effective in catching shoplifters.

Table 6. Percentage of respondents thinking it likely that the security measures will deter people from shoplifting

	All respondents	Non-shoplifters	Past shoplifters	Recent shoplifters
CCTV	93.7%	95.4%	91.5%	85.1%
Uniformed security guards	86.8%	88.1%	81.9%	92.5%
Store detectives	81.0%	81.4%	78.2%	88.8%
Electronic tags	92.1%	93.3%	89.5%	88.8%
Ink tags	77.7%	78.3%	73.3%	88.8%
Alarms	92.7%	95.1%	88.5%	85.1%
Friendly and helpful staff	32.6%	32.2%	31.5%	40.7%
Anti-shoplifting notices	18.0%	19.6%	14.3%	14.8%
Mirrors	39.4%	41.8%	32.4%	40.7%
Locked display cases	85.1%	84.1%	86.6%	88.8%

In all, 63% of the non-shoplifters stated that none of the named security measures would make them feel apprehensive, and 91% that retailers' security measures had never prevented them from using a shop. For both past shoplifters and recent shoplifters, the security measure that made them feel the most apprehensive was the security measure that they named as being the most effective deterrent, ie for past shoplifters CCTV, and for recent shoplifters uniformed security guards; 22% of the past shoplifters, and 41% of the recent shoplifters also stated that retailers' security measures had occasionally prevented them from using a shop. These findings suggest that although overall shop security is seen as being poor, there is considerable support for the effectiveness of individual security measures such as CCTV, electronic and ink tags, alarms, locked displays, uniformed security guards and store detectives, and that the presence of these measures is deterring some shoplifters.

The costs of being caught

Being caught will only be an effective deterrent for shoplifters if they think it will result in them being penalised for their criminal behaviour. In fact, 77% of the past shoplifters who had been caught stated that it was likely that being caught would deter them from shoplifting in the future, and this has obviously influenced their decision to refrain from shoplifting. However, only 20% of the recent shoplifters who had been caught said that it would deter them in the future, and 100% of those caught more than once said that being caught would be unlikely to deter them, suggesting that for those motivated to shoplift the current penalties for being caught do not act as a deterrent.

Sixty-four per cent of all respondents agreed that the penalties for shoplifting are not severe, and that people shoplift because they think they won't be punished if they are caught, and 81% of the recent shoplifters agreed with these views. In addition, 63% of recent shoplifters thought it unlikely that they would be arrested if they were caught, with 33% thinking it extremely unlikely. The perception is, therefore, that being apprehended for shoplifting is unlikely to result in serious legal sanctions, and for some of the recent shoplifters this view is undoubtedly a reflection of their own experiences and their beliefs about the inadequacies of the criminal justice process. However, although the majority of non-shoplifters and past shoplifters agreed that the penalties for shoplifting are not severe, over 70% thought it likely that shoplifting would result in being arrested for committing a crime, and that this is a 'bad' outcome of shoplifting behaviour, suggesting that the implications of a criminal record contribute to their negative shoplifting attitude.

To investigate appropriate penalties for shoplifting behaviour, respondents were asked how they thought shoplifters should be dealt with, and one-way analysis of variance was used to compare the views of the three groups. Table 7 shows the mean scores for these questions, which were scaled: 7 = strongly agree to, 1 = strongly disagree.

Table 7. Attitude to the ways of dealing with shoplifters

	All respondents	Non-shoplifters	Past shoplifters	Recent shoplifters
Shoplifters should be treated more severely*	5.9233	6.0912	5.6571	5.1852
Shops should report all shoplifters to police*	5.8201	6.0421	5.5143	4.6667
All shoplifters should be prosecuted*	5.5735	5.7509	5.3173	4.6538
Shoplifters should be dealt with by the shop	3.1058	3.0281	3.3143	3.1154
Shops should be able to fine shoplifters	4.5097	4.4841	4.7238	3.9231
Shoplifters should be banned from shops*	5.2837	5.4175	5.2476	3.9615
Anti-shoplifting campaigns*	3.8317	4.0877	3.3143	3.1154
I would report a shoplifter*	4.8053	5.3368	3.9619	2.3846

* Differences between the three groups significant at p<.01

Although there was substantial support from all respondents for shoplifters being treated more severely, only 7% of recent shoplifters indicated *strong* agreement with this suggestion, compared to 31% of past shoplifters and 41% of non-shoplifters. Over 80% of non-shoplifters agreed that all shoplifters should be reported to the police and subsequently prosecuted, and over 70% of this group thought that shoplifters should be banned from shops. However, although the majority of past shoplifters and recent shoplifters also agreed with these suggestions, their degree of agreement was not as strong as that of the non-shoplifters, suggesting that these two groups felt there may be situations in which shoplifters should be treated more leniently (extreme economic hardship and age of the shoplifter were among two of the extenuating circumstances mentioned in the comments section of the questionnaire). There was little support for the shops dealing with shoplifters themselves, with only 27% of all respondents agreeing with this suggestion; however, there was more support for shops being able to fine the shoplifters they catch, with 60% of respondents overall agreeing that this was a viable method of dealing with shoplifters.

Less than half the respondents felt that anti-shoplifting campaigns in the press and on television would help reduce shoplifting. Non-shoplifters were significantly more likely than the recent shoplifters to agree with this proposition, suggesting that this type of campaign would reinforce the attitudes of those who already think shoplifting is wrong, rather than change the attitudes of shoplifters to shoplifting.

When asked if they would report someone shoplifting to the shop, only 58% of respondents overall agreed that they would and 17% did not answer either way. There were significant differences between the three groups for this question, and, unsurprisingly, 78%, of the recent shoplifters would not report a shoplifter. However, offering incentives for reporting shoplifting behaviour may be a valid approach to reducing shoplifting, or at least to increasing apprehensions.

The recent shoplifters' perceptions that the penalties for shoplifting are not severe, and that there is little risk of being arrested for shoplifting is confirmed by Bamfield's[27] analysis of the 1994/5 BRC *Retail Crime Costs Survey*. Bamfield reports that of the 1,708,649 shoplifters apprehended during 1994/5 only 46% were reported to the police, with only 8% being found guilty by the courts or receiving formal cautions by the police, only 3% being convicted, and only 0.2% being sentenced to prison. In addition, only 18% of the apprehensions for shoplifting were recorded by the police as notifiable theft offences from shops, suggesting that the majority of the apprehended shoplifters were given informal police cautions. Bamfield concludes that shoplifting is 'a low-risk, low-cost crime'.

Implications for retailers

To design effective anti-shoplifting strategies which will increase the risks of shoplifting, retailers and their security managers need to understand how shoplifters view the risks of shoplifting, and how they react to deterrence measures. By investigating consumers' perceptions of shoplifting and shoplifting prevention, this study has attempted to provide some understanding of the factors which influence shoplifting (and non-shoplifting) behaviour. The main findings of the study are summarised below and the implications of these for retail security will then be discussed.

- Shoplifting is a rational crime.
- Shoplifters do not think that they will be caught.
- The current penalties for shoplifting do not deter shoplifters.

- Shoplifting is an 'easy' and 'available' crime.
- CCTV, EAS and security guards are the most effective anti-shoplifting measures.
- Shoplifters do not perceive shoplifting as harmful behaviour.

The majority of consumers perceive shoplifting to be a rational crime: that is, they think it likely that people will shoplift if they think the benefits from shoplifting outweigh the risks of being caught. This suggests that shoplifting will be prevented either by reducing the opportunities for shoplifting or by increasing the risks and costs of being caught, and the results of this study identified several areas where this could be achieved.

One of the major findings of the study is that shoplifters think that there is little risk of being caught despite the investment by retailers in shoplifting prevention and detection measures. Although the figures from the 1996 BRC *Retail Crime Costs Survey*[28] suggest that 32% of shoplifters are apprehended, the shoplifter's perception of the risk of being caught is much lower than this, with 82% of the recent shoplifters in this survey thinking it unlikely they would be caught shoplifting. This indicates that retailers need to publicise the apprehension rate of shoplifters, both nationally and locally, in order to change shoplifters' perceptions of the risks of shoplifting. Encouraging consumers to report shoplifting, possibly by offering financial incentives, may also change perceptions of the risks of being caught, especially if this is well publicised, both in the media and in shops.

Being apprehended for shoplifting will only act as a deterrent if shoplifters perceive that they will be punished for their criminal activity. The majority of the recent shoplifters in this study felt that being caught would not deter them from shoplifting in the future, due to their perception that the punishment for shoplifting is unlikely to be severe (a perception shared by the majority of the consumers surveyed). Consequently, more effective penalties for shoplifting must be devised: obviously, imprisoning more shoplifters would impose a burden on a criminal justice system already stretched to the limit of its resources, and therefore alternative solutions must be considered, for example increasing the practice of banning shoplifters from shops, civil recovery (Bamfield[29]), 'restorative justice' (currently being tested in the UK), or even 'shaming', which is presently being experimented with in the USA.[30] Although there is overwhelming support for more severe penalties for shoplifters, the analysis suggests that the punishment of shoplifters should be dealt with by representatives of the legal system rather than retailers themselves.

Shoplifters think that there are plenty of opportunities for shoplifting and that it is an 'easy' crime, and these perceptions could be changed by communicating the presence and effectiveness of security measures within the store. Uniformed security guards, CCTV and EAS were perceived as being the most effective measures for both deterring and catching shoplifters, and a combination of all three would possibly provide the most effective (and the most costly) anti-shoplifting strategy. As the recent shoplifters felt 'human' security measures to be more effective for deterring shoplifting, this should also be considered. The majority of non-shoplifters agreed that retail security did not make them feel apprehensive, or prevent them from using shops, and, as suggested by one of the respondents, 'honest shoppers have nothing to fear from retailers' security measures.'

This study suggests that non-shoplifters refrain from shoplifting because of their anti-shoplifting attitude, their strong moral views about shoplifting, and the influence of people important to them, most of whom feel that they should avoid shoplifting behaviour. On the other hand, recent shoplifters have a more positive attitude toward shoplifting, and a less moral view of the behaviour, and are little influenced by the opinions of others. Media anti-shoplifting campaigns should therefore aim to change shoplifters' attitudes toward shoplifting, emphasising the moral and harmful aspects of the behaviour, and that shoplifters will be caught and punished. However, as the majority of recent shoplifters felt it unlikely that television and press campaigns would reduce shoplifting, perhaps a more effective approach would be to use this method in conjunction with posters in shops and public places, although the design will have to be improved if they are to be effective.

The consumer behaviour approach has proved to be an effective method of researching shoplifting, which has enabled the investigation of how consumers' attitudes, and their perceptions of the risks and costs of being caught, influence their shoplifting (and non-shoplifting) behaviour. The findings from this study not only suggest areas where the risks of shoplifting can be increased, but also demonstrate the importance of retailers communicating these risks to the consumer in order to change the perception that shoplifting is a low-risk, low-cost crime.

Notes

1   Michele Tonglet is a PhD student at Nene College of Higher Education, Faculty of Management and Business, Park Campus, Boughton Green Road, Northampton NN2 7AL.

2   Cornish, D.B. and Clarke, R.V.G. (eds) (1986) *The Reasoning Criminal: Rational Choice Perspectives on Offending*. New York: Springer Verlag.

3   Beck, A. and Willis, A. (1994) Customer and Staff Perceptions of the Role of Closed Circuit Television in Retail Security. In Gill, M. (ed.) *Crime at Work: Studies in Security and Crime Prevention*. Leicester: Perpetuity Press; Farrington, D.P., Bowen, S., Buckle, A., Burns-Howell, T., Burrows, J. and Speed, M. (1994) An Experiment on the Prevention of Shoplifting. In Clarke, R. (ed.) *Crime Prevention Studies*. Vol. 3. Monsey, NY: Criminal Justice Press.

4   Bamfield, J. (1994) *National Survey of Retail Theft and Security 1994: Final Report*. Northampton: Nene College; Mirrlees-Black, C. and Ross, A. (1995) *Crime Against Retail and Manufacturing Premises: Findings from the 1994 Commercial Victimisation Survey*. Home Office Research Study 146. London: Home Office; Wells, C. and Dryer, A. (1997) *Retail Crime Costs Survey 1995/96*. London: British Retail Consortium.

5   Baumer, T.L. and Rosenbaum, D.P. (1984) *Combating Retail Theft: Programs and Strategies*. Boston: Butterworth; Klemke, L.W. (1992) *The Sociology of Shoplifting: Boosters and Snitches Today*. Westport, Connecticut: Praegar.

6   Sohier, J. (1969) Shoplifting - A Rather Ordinary Crime. *International Criminal Police Review*. Vol. 24, pp 161-166.

7   Moore, R.H. (1984) Shoplifting in Middle America: Patterns and Motivational Correlates. *International Journal of Offender Therapy and Comparative Criminology*. Vol. 28, pp 53-

64; Ray, J. (1987) Every Twelfth Shopper: Who Shoplifts and Why. *Social Casework*. Vol. 68, pp 234-239.

8   For example: Butler, G. (1994) Shoplifters' Views on Security: Lessons for Crime Prevention. In Gill, M. (ed) *Crime at Work*. Vol.1. Leicester: Perpetuity Press; Carroll, J. and Weaver, F. (1986) Shoplifters' Perceptions of Crime Opportunities: A Process-Tracing Study. In Cornish and Clarke, op cit.

9   Cox, A.D., Cox, D., Anderson, R. and Moschis, G.P. (1993) Social Influences on Adolescent Shoplifting — Theory and Implications for the Retail Industry. *Journal of Retailing*. Vol. 69, No. 2, pp 234-246; Kallis, M. and Vanier, D. (1985) Consumer Shoplifting: Orientations and Deterrents. *Journal of Criminal Justice*. Vol. 13, No. 5, pp 459-473; Klemke, L.W. (1982) Exploring Juvenile Shoplifting. *Sociology and Social Research*. Vol. 67, No. 1, pp 59-75.

10   Cowell, D. (1984) *The Marketing of Services*. London: Heinemann.

11   Ajzen, I. (1991) The Theory of Planned Behaviour. *Organisational Behaviour and Human Decision Processes*. Vol. 50, pp 179-211.

12   Ajzen, I. and Driver, B.L. (1992) Application of the Theory of Planned Behaviour to Leisure Choice. *Journal of Leisure Research*. Vol. 24, pp 207-224.

13   Parker, D., Manstead, A.S.R., Strading, S.G., Reason, J.T. and Baxter, J.S. (1992) Intentions to Commit Driving Violations: An Application of the Theory of Planned Behaviour. *Journal of Applied Psychology*. Vol. 77, pp 94-101.

14   East, R. (1993) Investment Decisions and the Theory of Planned Behaviour. *Journal of Economic Psychology*. Vol. 14, pp 337-375.

15   Netemeyer, R.G., Andrews, J.C., and Durvasula, S. (1993) A Comparison of Three Behavioural Intentions Models: The Case of Valentine's Day Gift-giving. *Advances in Consumer Research*. Vol. 20, pp 135-141.

16   Beck, L. and Ajzen, I. (1991) Predicting Honest Actions Using the Theory of Planned Behaviour. *Journal of Research in Personality*. Vol. 25, No. 3, pp 285-301.

17   Beck and Ajzen, op cit.

18   One-way analysis of variance tests the null hypothesis that the mean scores for the three groups are equal (ie there is no difference between the three groups). If the F probability is less than .05, then the null hypothesis is rejected, and the differences between the three groups are statistically significant at the 95% confidence level. Any results that are statistically significant at the 95% confidence level are described as statistically significant within the text.

19   Baumer and Rosenbaum, op cit; Klemke (1992), op cit.

20   Cameron, M.O. (1964) *The Booster and the Snitch*. Glenco, IL: Free Press.

21   Buckle, A. and Farrington, D.P. (1984) An Observational Study of Shoplifting. *British Journal of Criminology*. Vol.24, pp 63-73; Buckle, A. and Farrington, D.P. (1994) Measuring Shoplifting by Systematic Observation. *Psychology, Crime and Law*. Vol.1, No.2, pp 133-141.

22   Multiple regression calculates R^2, the proportion of the variance in the dependent variable accounted for by the independent variables. The statistical significance of this is tested by the f ratio, and the model in this study was significant at the 99% confidence level. The

relative contribution of each of the independent variables to explaining the variance in the dependent variable is determined by the beta weight. Those variables with a t sig of less than .05 are significant at the 95% confidence level. Any results that are statistically significant at the 95% confidence level are described as statistically significant within the text.

23   For example: Grasmick, H.G. and Bursik Jr, R.J. (1990) Conscience, Significant Others and Rational Choice: Extending the Deterrence Model. *Law and Society Review.* Vol.24, pp 837-861; Meier, R., Burkett, S. and Hickman, C. (1984) Sanctions, Peers and Deviance: Preliminary Models of a Social Control Process. *Sociological Quarterly.* Vol.25, pp 203-211.

24   Wells and Dryer, op cit.

25   Ibid.

26   Butler, op cit.

27   Bamfield, J. (1997) *Fighting Retail Crime: How Major Multiples Curb Theft from Stores.* Maidenhead: ICL Retail Systems.

28   Wells and Dryer, op cit.

29   Bamfield, J (1997) *Making Shoplifters Pay: Retail Civil Recovery.* London: Social Market Foundation Paper No. 28.

30   ITV documentary, 'The Big Story'. 18th September 1997

Chapter 9

A Breach of Trust: Employee Collusion and Theft from Major Retailers

Joshua Bamfield[1]

This chapter discusses the extent of shop theft by retail employees of major retailers and the significance of collusion with customer thieves. A survey of retailers responsible for more than 50 per cent of all UK retail trade indicated that theft by staff was thought to have a significant impact on the business, and that the effect was reinforced by staff collusion with customer thieves. 'Staff-related' theft was estimated to represent one half of these firms' theft losses. It is argued that collusion tends to be under-reported by conventional crime surveys and could well be prevalent because it often carries a lower level of risk than direct theft by staff or customers on their own. A survey of 219 staff in ten stores showed that whilst the great majority of staff were thought to be honest and direct theft of cash and goods was rare, collusion was a significant problem and formed part of a social exchange process for many employees. The research finds that motivation and perceived risk may be critical determinants of the level of staff theft. It recommends that retailers spend more time focusing on the risks of detection and punishment by explaining to staff the range of methods used to combat theft by employees and showing that detection does lead to significant punishment.

Introduction

Although much of the work of the retail security department is directed towards containing or reducing theft by customers, theft by shop *staff* has long been regarded as a serious problem. The most recent British Retail Consortium figures indicate that staff theft suffered by retailers in 1995/6 amounted to £386 million.[2] Many of the systems, accounts and procedures used by retailers to control stock and money have had the subsidiary purpose of preventing theft by staff.

Employee, staff, or internal theft is all defined in this research as the theft of goods and merchandise from the employer by a member of the payroll, and diversion of funds from customers. This study does not cover other staff-related crime including computer fraud,

123

payroll fraud, theft in distribution centres, or procurement fraud. Moreover, the current research does not cover the other types of deviant employee behaviour such as absenteeism, poor timekeeping, aggression, truculence, or time-wasting at work.

Method

This chapter is based on two empirical surveys of retail crime. The *security manager* survey is based on a series of lengthy interviews with the chief security managers of 30 large retailers drawn from a representative number of different kinds of business. The total turnover of the companies surveyed was more than one half of total UK retai¹ sales. The *sales staff* survey reports the key results from a survey of 219 staff in four grocery superstores and six clothing stores to ascertain their views about employee theft.

Thirty security managers were interviewed in December 1996-July 1997. They were drawn from a range of businesses, including grocery (2), mixed retailing (9), department stores (2), DIY (2), variety chains (1), pharmacists (1), footwear (1), clothing (2), electrical goods (1), furniture (1), catalogue stores (1), recorded music (1), and bookshops (1). Many, particularly the mixed businesses, traded in several individual types of business including food, clothing, houseware, furniture, and books. The sample was chosen to be fully representative of a range of most kinds of food and non-food business.

The interviews were an attempt to collect qualitative data from retail security managers about the main trends in theft, crime and loss prevention. In some cases this was backed up with reference to internal company reports about crime statistics and accounting and shrinkage data. The businesses chosen were amongst the most successful companies in their field (measured by turnover growth and profitability), with two exceptions chosen to include certain categories of business. The response rate from those selected was 100%. They were promised anonymity.

There was a remarkable amount of consistency between security managers across the entire sector. It must be admitted that the views of 30 security managers may not be fully representative of the views of the entire retail sector. However, these 30 were senior managers able to speak authoritatively for 50 per cent of UK retail sales, who worked for companies well known for having good information systems.

How much employee theft is there in retailing?

Beck and Willis found in four surveys of 1,800 staff between 1991 to 1994 that 45% of all retail staff reported that some colleagues steal money and 57% said that some steal goods.[3] They reported institutionalised dishonesty in serving friends and other deviance. The 1995 London House survey of 2,673 supermarket employees in the USA randomly selected from stores in 29 companies found that 42% admitted some involvement in taking cash or goods, but only 2% admitted stealing cash.[4]

The most authoritative national studies in the UK of the impact of this deviance are the British Retail Consortium's (BRC) annual series of *Retail Crime Costs Surveys,* which provide a valuable resource for researchers and retail managers.[5] The total theft figure (derived from the most recent data for 1995/6) was £1,039 million, of which 37.2% was attributed to staff and 62.8% to customer thieves. Its estimate of staff theft as costing £386 million in 1995/96 was equivalent to £1,322 of pilferage from every retail store. However, the cost of staff theft was thought to be falling (a reduction of 31.1% since 1992/3), whilst the cost of customer theft had apparently *increased* since 1992/3 by 22.3%. In addition to theft by staff and customers, retailers suffered other crimes such as burglary, arson, robbery and criminal damage, costing a further £384 million.

The UK picture, where retail estimates show that customer theft is almost 70% higher than staff theft, can be contrasted with the USA, where staff theft is considered by American retailers to be much more costly than customer theft. Hollinger, Dabney and Lee's 1996 study from the University of Florida is part of an annual series which shows that except in 1992 (when customer and staff theft were thought to be roughly equivalent), estimates of staff theft in the USA have always exceeded customer theft.[6] The 1996 results indicate that employees were responsible for 51.8% of combined US staff/customer fraud compared to the BRC's estimate for the UK of 37%.

All aggregate figures about retail theft are likely to be subject to a considerable degree of error.[7] Only one-quarter of the thefts recorded by the BRC study were witnessed or 'known':[8] the total theft figure cited can only be established following an audit. What proportion of the losses result from administrative error (for example, being invoiced for goods that are not received), wastage, or mistaken pricing is a matter of sheer conjecture for many businesses. Retail inventory shrinkage (measuring the difference between expected and actual inventory levels) may be popularly regarded as a coy euphemism for theft but will usually include a significant level of non-theft losses. Some managers may wish to minimise their declared shrinkage figure to conceal the existence of problems in their department or business, while others may fail to record their true losses owing to inefficient systems or ignorance. Thus, global theft figures may be regarded, at best, as not wholly accurate.

Clarke and Hollinger suggest that virtually anyone can be tempted in the 'right' circumstances[9] and other authors[10] feel that employee crime is so prevalent that employers should keep an eye even on those staff who are apparently the most trustworthy. Ditton felt that theft by employees was regarded as natural and 'fiddling' was supported by the supervisory team in the company he studied.[11] Mars developed a general theory of staff theft, arguing that the type of crime will depend upon how work is organised, *grid* (ie dependence on rule-based or cultural restrictions) and *group* (working in teams, the importance of the group).[12] He argued that a supermarket cashier has limited autonomy: 'fiddling' may simply be a response to the job and may be more pleasurable than the job itself. Retailers generally specify the content of the jobs of sales staff very precisely (Mars calls this 'high grid'), partly to prevent theft by employees. Mars' main focus is the lower-grade worker who steals regularly from his or her employer. Staff theft is not unrestricted excess: most fiddles have boundaries. There has been considerable discussion about the ways in which wrongdoers come to terms with their crime. Ditton and Mars see it as normal behaviour.[13] Another way of understanding how employees can regard staff theft as 'normal' is shown by Hollinger, who applies the concept of 'neutralisation' to employee crime.[14] For example, wrongdoers may argue that employee crimes are a normal part of working life, that everybody is stealing, the impact is slight or negligible, or that the company tolerates theft. Neutralisation may be fostered by supervisors who break company rules themselves or reward certain behaviours by allowing a degree of staff theft.

Hollinger, and Greenberg and Scott have argued that staff theft can be viewed as a form of retaliation against work injustice.[15] Low wages may produce staff crime as some form of compensation (perhaps sanctioned by supervisors). Other important factors are thought to include arbitrary decisions, perceived unfair treatment, poor communications and lack of involvement by managers.[16] Greenberg and Scott refer to a 'cycle of acceptance' involving poor ethical standards at work, a low detection rate of wrongdoers and lack of use of criminal sanctions against those who are apprehended.[17] Employee crime is not necessarily stimulated by monetary reward: Mars argues that employee thieves may get peer recognition and status from stealing as well as money.[18]

Survey of security managers[19]

No security manager interviewed felt that the shrinkage rate was an accurate indicator of the level of theft from shops. Twenty per cent of managers had so little confidence in company data that they established their own computer-based systems which ran alongside the official company shrinkage figures. However, changes in company shrinkage rates were thought to be 'reasonable' indicators of progress, particularly when there were several periods of improved (ie low) shrinkage performance. As noted earlier, this suggests that 'shrinkage' is a crude rule of thumb used by retailers to monitor changes rather than an exact measure of performance.

Four-fifths of the security managers felt that the cost of staff theft to their business was roughly comparable to losses from customer theft. However, they found it difficult to prove or substantiate such strong statements about staff crime. Most retailers surveyed arrested very few employees for theft. BRC figures show that retailers apprehended only 20,000 staff thieves in 1995/6 compared to 31,000 in the previous year (a fall of 35 per cent), but the managers surveyed did not relate this fall to a decline in the level of staff crime. They felt that a retailer's employees handle cash and goods in order to do their work, they know the weaknesses of the company's administrative systems, and they can recognise (and may well be friendly with) supervisors, managers and security staff whose role is to protect the company's assets. They argued that this showed why detecting theft amongst employees was more difficult than finding dishonest customers. It could not be used to demonstrate that staff theft was rare.

The security managers felt that the most common methods used by retail staff to steal from their employers were:[20]

- Direct theft of merchandise by staff which is worn or carried out of the store.
- Bogus refunds to self, perhaps using a customer's discarded till receipt.
- Overcharging customers or giving short change.
- Taking cash from the till.
- Loyalty card fraud based on wrongly allocating a customer's points to the till operator's card.
- Failure to enter a transaction or part of a transaction.
- Misuse of a customer's credit card information to create a false transaction, allowing the employee to take money or goods out of the store.
- Grazing in food stores (snacking or drinking the merchandise).

Till fraud and refund fraud were the most frequently mentioned methods of staff theft.

Collusion between employees and customer thieves

Most surveys of retail crime ask the respondent to break down responsibility for 'unknown losses' or shrinkage into several categories including errors, staff crime and customer crime. This assumes that there is a rigid separation between staff theft and customer theft. The view of four-fifths of the security managers interviewed was that the impact on the business of collusion between certain staff and customers was substantial. Supermarkets, department stores, pharmacies, variety chains, clothing, record shops and DIY believed they were especially susceptible to collusion. Hence the normal practice of calculating staff and customer theft as separate totals may *understate* the involvement of staff in crime. They were asked to estimate what proportion of customer theft was likely to involve collusion. The result, weighted to reflect those retailers who thought there was minimal or no collusion, showed that around 40 per cent of customer theft in their businesses was thought to be linked to staff collusion.

Table 1. Estimated crime costs 1995/6

	Retail costs by cause £	Theft % crime	Total costs %
Customer theft	512 million	49.2	
Staff-related theft			
- collusion	141 million	13.6	
- staff crime	386 million	37.2	
Theft total	1,039 million	100.0	73.0
Other crime	384 million		27.0
Totals	1,423 million		100.0

Source: derived from Wells, C. and Dryer, A. (1997) *Retail Crime Costs Survey 1995/96*, London: British Retail Consortium; also see text.

Table 1 shows the result of reworking the most recent BRC data to take account of collusion.[21] The total of collusion, £141 million, is assumed to be suffered *only* by the major retailers surveyed. Nevertheless, on the basis of this restricted assumption, *staff-related theft* is seen to be £527 million or 50.8 per cent of total retail theft, roughly equivalent to customer theft. This is only a preliminary exercise, but it demonstrates the possible significance of collusion.

The main forms of collusion were thought to be: [22]

• *Refund fraud*: making a fraudulent repayment to an accomplice for goods that have not actually been returned. There may be no goods at all; the merchandise may have been stolen and perhaps has not left the shop; a refund may be given against an article that is dearer than the one returned; or more than one refund may be given against a single item returned.

• *False markdowns*: allowing the customer to obtain a low price.

• *Two for one*: receiving payment for one item but allowing the collaborator to have two or more.

• *Discounts for friends (sweethearting)*: keying in a cheaper product to the cash terminal.

• *Staff discount*: allowing friends and family to use the employee's staff discount card to obtain lower prices.

• *Fitting room fraud*: assisting a customer to steal by such measures as allowing them to take too many goods into the fitting room, or placing extra garments in the fitting room knowing that the thief can wear or carry the extra garments out of the store.

• *Stolen credit cards*: accepting credit cards that are known to be stolen to pay for goods.

• *Identity/delivery fraud*: delivery of goods 'purchased' on credit using bogus identification to a temporary address. Proceeds may be split with the staff member.

Rational expectations about collusion

How likely were these views about the significance of collusion to be true? There are three factors to be taken into account. Firstly, there was a uniformly high level of consistency about the need to recognise the importance of collusion across many different retail sectors coming from experienced senior managers. Secondly, the high market share of respondents indicates that if their perceptions were accurate only for the companies studied then this would itself indicate that there was a large-scale national rate of collusion. Lastly, there is an understanding based on a rational view of the criminal that collusion is likely to be significant because it will normally be safer than shoplifting or staff theft practised as separate autonomous activities. All collusive thefts usually leave an audit trail of some kind. Compared with conventional staff theft the employee will not be found with goods or cash on his or her person. The customer thief in collusive activity will have acted like a normal shopper rather than a shoplifter and will be much less likely to attract the suspicions of supervisors, managers, or security staff. If they are apprehended, the 'customer' will have a receipt and the employee can claim he or she made a stupid mistake. Collusion lowers the risk of being arrested. A higher quality of evidence will be needed for a successful prosecution, which lowers the risk of a serious penalty. However, it may be difficult to use collusion to steal considerable quantities of merchandise or cash, purely because customers who visit the store too frequently may become the subjects of the security department's attention. This apart, as collusion is a lower-risk activity than either staff or customer theft, the rational criminal attempting to optimise gains at low risk would be expected to desire a considerable level of involvement in it.[23]

Apprehending and sanctioning staff thieves

For 80% of the sample of security managers the 'typical' staff thief that they detected was usually someone who had been employed for less than 12 months and was frequently a part-timer, indicating perhaps a lower attachment to the organisation. Detailed interviews that most had carried out with staff thieves showed that thieves usually admitted to starting to steal in the first few weeks of their new job (sometimes being taught to steal by a co-worker) and they would steal for about six months, around which time they might be caught. Someone stealing £40 per week would thus have stolen £1,000 in 25 weeks. Retail businesses have low net profit margins in comparison with other types of company. If a retailer achieved a net profit margin of 3 per cent, the business will need to sell £33,333 more goods in order to replace the £1,000 that has been stolen. If the Company has 30 such thieves, it will need to sell £1 million extra to replace the missing money. This is the reason why few retailers view staff theft as a legitimate perk of the job.

It is possible that the reason why so many new employees were apprehended for theft is that they were not very good at it. A new member of staff may not have learned to overcome the behavioural clues often given off by thieves, he or she may not know the systems well enough to cheat effectively and may not have been accepted by the work group which might otherwise cover up for the thief.

More experienced employees may be continuing to steal for many years. Forty per cent of the sample reported that one quarter or more of their total staff apprehensions were management grade, supervisor, senior administrator or security officer – the very people entrusted with guarding the company's assets. They usually had unsupervised access to most parts of the building at unsociable hours and were able to steal, often in conjunction with associates, over many months or years. Whilst the novice thief would steal between £1,000 and £2,000, they felt that the more experienced and senior employees would probably steal more than £10,000 over a much longer period.

Ninety per cent of retailers surveyed had a policy of referring *all* cases of theft to the police for prosecution. In practice, however, virtually all accepted that there could be reasons why the police might not be involved in every case. The British Retail Consortium figures for 1995/6 showed that only 40% of staff thieves were referred to the police. Although this percentage was a slight increase on the previous year, the proportion of apprehended staff thieves handed over to the police has been falling since 59.2% were referred in 1992/3.[24] The security managers said that in cases of staff theft they would be keen to get the person off the premises to staunch the losses. This often meant that except in highly damaging cases the security investigators or the store management did not spend a considerable period of time collecting volumes of evidence suitable for a court appearance. A suspected thief who was thought to be stealing from the cash till might well be dismissed for a breach of rules, such as having cash on his/her person whilst working on the shop floor. The investigators would not need to prove that the cash belonged to the company in order to sack him/her. The store managers commented that whilst they tried to involve the police as much as possible, this would only be a strict rule where the amount stolen was high, there seemed to be theft over a long period, or several people were involved.

The shop staff analysis

Following the interviews with the security managers of major retailers, a study of 219 shop staff was carried out to investigate their perceptions of staff crime in retail companies. Data were gathered from (a) a short self-report written questionnaire issued in-store and (b) four focus groups of a total of 24 staff. With the agreement (but not the involvement) of senior management, questionnaires were given to 273 staff in 4 grocery supermarkets and 6 clothing and general stores in the West Midlands of England. The survey was restricted to two kinds of business because it was felt that this would produce a statistically more stable sample whilst these two kinds of businesses were both thought to suffer a number of different types of staff theft and collusion. The stores were regarded as being well managed by the retail security managers: the previous year's shrinkage rates were all below the company averages. The number of usable questionnaires returned was 219 (a response rate of 73% in the grocers and 64.8% in the clothing stores). To prevent the validity of the study being vitiated by a low response rate, considerable in-store activity took place to explain the purpose of the questionnaire and to allay any fears that the results might be used as the basis of disciplinary procedures against individuals or groups. No compulsion was put on staff by managers to take part. The salient characteristics of the respondents to the survey can be found in Table 2.

Respondents were asked to complete a separate card to show whether they were prepared to join a focus group. The planned final composition of the focus groups was made up of (a) 50%, from a random sample of those who indicated that they were prepared to attend a group, (b) 25%, who had expressed interest in attending when contacted in the earlier 'publicity' period, and (c) 25%, who were recommended by other people in the 'publicity' period. Not everybody who had promised to attend arrived: one group had only four members. There were two groups in clothing and two in grocery. In grocery, one group consisted of 18-26 year olds and the other a more mature group.

Staff were not asked directly whether they stole, but were asked about the attitudes and practices of other employees.

Table 2. Characteristics of the sample survey of retail shop staff

	Grocery	Clothing/general
Number of stores	4	6
Male	30.6%	19.9%
Female	69.4%	80.1%
Full-time	32.3%	22.1%
Part-time	67.7%	77.9%
Roles		
Management grade	7.3%	4.8%
Supervisory grade	7.3%	6.1%
Sales/operations staff	53.5%	51.7%
Security staff	4.8%	2.0%
Nil return	27.1%	35.4%
Total	100.0%	100.0%
Number of staff	124	95
Survey response rate	72.9%	64.6%

How important is theft?

Most staff felt that theft was an important problem for their company: more than 80 per cent of the sample said that theft was 'quite serious' or 'extremely serious'. Staff in all four grocery stores and one clothing store had received a thorough grounding during induction in the perils for them of stealing from the store. Focus group opinion was that the message at induction was very powerful and would dismay many potential thieves. Several part-time staff had not been well inducted, however: this was particularly true of staff who worked less than 12 hours per week.

More than 85 per cent of staff felt that the primary responsibility in preventing theft was their own. This came over very strongly in the focus groups, although in two stores staff thought that the security operation (now equipped with CCTV) had little involvement with sales personnel, who felt increasingly alienated from it.

There was evidence that all the stores in the study attempted to communicate the need to control losses and show staff how to do this. However, whilst 37.1% of grocery staff and 31.6% of clothing/general stores had been told within the last four weeks how to curb losses, the majority of staff had not been present at these briefings. One in twenty (5.6%) of grocery staff had last been told about curbing losses between 6 months and 12 months earlier. Most of these were part-timers.

Witnessed acts of staff theft

Staff were asked whether they had witnessed any acts of theft in the previous 12 months by other staff.

Table 3. Proportion of staff respondents who witnessed one or more acts of staff theft in the previous 12 months

Number of questionnaires	Grocery		Clothing/general	
	Witnessed (n=124)	No reply	Witnessed (n=95)	No reply
Theft of goods	15.3%*	18.6%	17.9%*	12.6%
- number of respondents	(19)	(23)	(17)	(12)
Theft of cash	4.0%	14.5%	13.6%	14.7%
- number of respondents	(5)	(18)	(13)	(14)
Credit card fraud	0.9%	14.5%	0.0%	17.85%
- number of respondents	(1)	(18)	(0)	(17)

* Significant at .95 level

Table 3 shows that around one in six clothing/general staff or one in seven grocery staff witnessed another worker stealing merchandise, whilst only 4.0% of grocery staff saw theft of cash, compared to 13.6% of the clothing/general staff who witnessed a till fraud. The results for staff theft of merchandise were significant at the .95 level (ie there was a one in twenty chance that these results would be generated in error). The difference between the theft of cash in grocery and clothing/general stores may be that grocery cashiers work in isolation and are unlikely to be observed by others, whilst the clothing/general environment involved tills grouped in threes at sales positions and staff using different techniques to speed customer flow including team-working and changing between tills as soon as one became free. Thus the clothing/general staff were more likely to see a case of cash fraud than a grocery worker.

These figures are much lower than those reported by Beck and Willis, who found that 45% of those questioned knew that some staff stole money and 57% knew that goods were stolen.[25] Whilst the Beck and Willis survey is evidence of a corrupt culture, the survey of grocers and clothing/general stores asked staff whether they had *witnessed* an act of theft rather than whether they 'knew' it was taking place. Thus both pieces of research are consistent with each other.

Ease of theft and perceived sanctions against staff theft and collusion?

Staff believed that internal theft was relatively easy, with 45.2% of grocery staff and 57.9% of clothing/general staff answering that most staff felt that staff theft was 'very easy' or 'quite easy'. The focus groups showed that the difference between grocery and clothing/general was caused by the virtual absence of searches and greater tolerance towards infringements of rules in the clothing/general stores. Employee working patterns at the tills in clothing/general stores were also supportive of staff theft and collusion. The results were significant at the .95 level.

Table 4. How easily can staff steal?

Which of these statements reflects the views of most staff here about stealing from this store?

	Grocery		Clothing/general	
	Number	Per cent	Number	Per cent
Number of questionnaires	124		95	
Theft by staff is very easy	11*	8.9	3	3.2
Theft by staff is quite easy	45*	36.3	52*	54.7
Theft by staff is neither hard nor easy	17	13.7	13	13.7
Theft by staff is quite hard	21*	16.9	12*	12.6
Theft by staff is very hard	16	12.9	4	4.2
No reply	14	11.3	11	11.6

* Significant at .95 level

Do staff feel that the business is prepared to tolerate staff theft within acceptable limits? Eighty-five per cent of grocery staff believed that the retailer was very antagonistic to staff stealing, as did 74.7% of clothing/general staff. The grocery staff pointed to very harsh rules prohibiting eating waste food or fruit that dropped on the floor as evidence of this, and a culture of threats and disciplinary action taken against people who had apparently infringed these rules. Seventeen per cent of grocery staff knew of a member of staff who had been dismissed for theft in the previous 12 months but only two people (1.6%) were aware of exactly what punishment had actually occurred. No clothing/general staff were aware of anyone dismissed for theft in 12 months, although a supervisor had been asked to resign for stealing within this period.

All focus groups felt that although theft by staff was a crime, employers would condone it. They would be unlikely to call the police because it was felt this could reflect badly upon the company. The most likely punishment would be for the individual to be sacked or asked to leave.

The extent of different kinds of theft

Staff were asked in the focus groups about the prevalence of different kinds of theft. Employees were not asked directly whether they had stolen anything in the recent past because it was assumed that in front of their peers many people would lie (including those who might claim to be more dishonest than they actually were). Staff were asked about the behaviour of other employees in order to discover something of the types of behaviour used and how widespread these were thought to be. Neutral phrases or euphemisms (such as 'taking things home', 'not putting everything through the till', or 'running a business on the side') were used wherever possible instead of 'theft' or 'crime' to avoid biasing the responses.

It was felt that occasional theft of cash and goods was widespread, with perhaps one third of people being tempted at some time when they thought no one was looking or they would not be caught. However, continual theft from work was believed to be less common: fewer than one in twenty were thought to be regularly adding to their earnings by stealing, although the accuracy of this figure is impossible to verify. In the grocery store people might take items from cases that had been damaged or had already been opened. Goods might be left in the waste bins and put outside for later collection. The direct theft of goods was not an easy option: care would have to be taken about personal searches and knowing which security guards were on duty.

Theft of cash from the till was thought to be more prevalent in the clothing/general store because there were fewer controls: staff would use any one of several tills and there would be a common cash float, whilst the grocery store used the grocery standard of staff responsibility, individual tray inserts, and the use of a single till with a full audit trail available. Nevertheless, till frauds involving bogus receipts, overcharging customers, and failing to enter all items correctly could create till surpluses which could later be removed from the cash drawer without creating a cash deficit. It was felt that it was easier for staff to steal a large quantity of cash every week without being discovered than to steal goods every week.

Three of the four groups were aware of people 'in the past' who had been running elaborate cashpoint fiddles in conjunction with several 'customers' and were known to be given their 50 per cent share of the proceeds once per week. This was not thought to be very common. The groups felt that a moderately experienced member of staff who put through seven false refunds in five days could have produced between £350 and £1,000 in this time. This would probably attract attention and would only be rational behaviour to adopt shortly before leaving the company's employment.

Helping out 'friends' and relatives by giving discounts or not ringing everything through the till was thought to be well established. The amounts involved in each transaction were rarely large, but the system was a recognition of a common bond. Examples quoted included a sister-in-law using someone's staff discount card, pricing the favourite alcoholic drink of a friend's mother as lemonade, and only charging a schoolfriend for one skirt when two were taken from the store. The motive was not seen as financial gain, but as duty or 'helping them out'. However, not everybody was thought to be a willing accomplice in this: one girl who had been sacked from the store was thought to have been intimidated by her father into underpricing articles for his brothers.

Several people knew of crime barter schemes: for example, a hairdresser would be given a 'free' CD every time she visited the shop and the shop assistant (male) would get a free haircut. One female assistant was known to be helpful to a car mechanic about the price of shirts, and in return he serviced her car. A pub barmaid would expect to pay less than the value of the goods she had bought to people whom she undercharged in the pub. It was known that when some staff made new acquaintances, they could ground this relationship by inviting them to come to the store when they were on duty so they could be given a 'discount'. It was thought that important life events such as marriages, the birth of a child, or retirement might be the occasion of significant collusion to reduce the costs of celebration ('Come in on Tuesday between 10 and 12 and I'm sure we can do something for you') or to provide gifts at the company's expense.

Much collusion was therefore a social exchange activity, an exchange of obligations rather than a significant source of income or a means of getting back at the business. Low wages, disciplinary problems or poor management were only raised by one of the focus groups to excuse or explain staff theft. The other groups (including people of suspect ethical standards) felt that the company needed to be much more robust in detecting and punishing wrongdoers.

Hollinger has argued that the level of staff theft is regulated by social controls. This seemed to be true for the collusive activity studied here. Collusion (or demands for collusion) thought to be excessive would be rejected. Euphemisms were used by almost everyone to describe 'acceptable' collusion with friends and family: only people who objected to the practices described it as 'theft' or 'stealing'. This research is only small-scale and is not a test of the different academic approaches used to analyse staff deviance, but the results are more compatible with social exchange and neutralisation viewpoints than with work injustices.

Staff theft impact: commitment grid

The discussions with store employees in the focus groups and the security managers of major multiples showed that staff, typically, were involved with theft in several different ways. In Figure 1 I have mapped out the engagement of staff with theft against a four-cell construct. The horizontal scale measures the *level of commitment to theft* of members of staff, varying from those who never steal (0) to those who steal regularly (1). The vertical scale measures the *relative impact of staff theft* on the business: those who steal nothing or who pilfer only low value items have little unfavourable business impact (0), whilst those who steal regularly by themselves or in collusion with others have a major effect on the business (1, or 'high cost'). This grid is the *impact: commitment grid*. This will now be discussed.

Figure 1. Staff theft impact: commitment grid

0 ——————— Level of commitment to theft ——————— 1

Angels Opposed to all staff theft (0,0)	**Jackdaws** Occasional or frequent pilferage of goods or money for self or family (0,0)
Baboons Collusive help for friends (0,1)	**Crocodiles** Semi-professional frauds and collusion (1,1)

Relative impact of staff theft (vertical axis, 0 to 1)

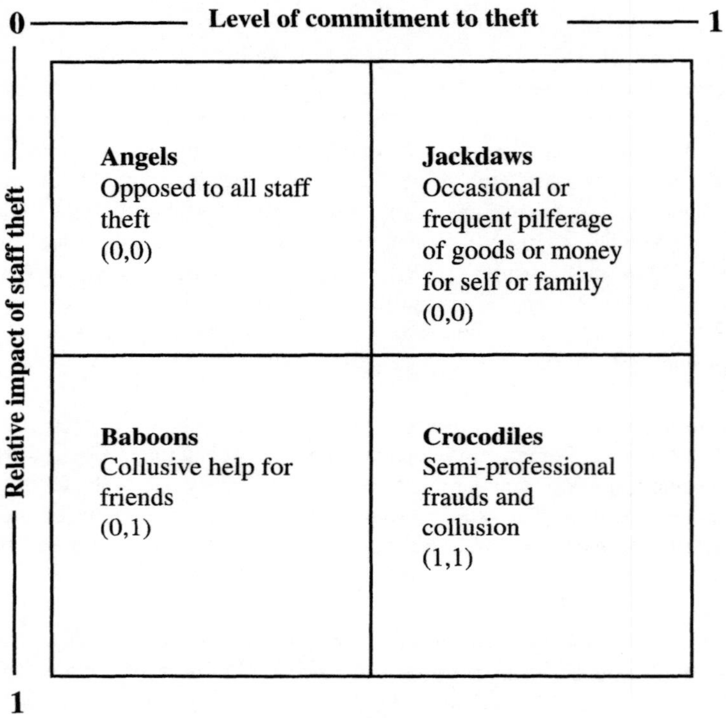

Staff are classified at any point of time in one of four categories depending on their commitment to staff theft and its relative impact. Staff can be allocated, using this grid, to a cell. Staff are categorised as *angels, jackdaws, baboons, or crocodiles*. The explanation of every cell is as follows:

• *Angels:* These are staff, usually the great majority, who commit no crime at all. They regard stealing from shops as wholly wrong, lacking in moral integrity. Many of them come from poor backgrounds and may be single parents. They regard it as essential to live within their means even if their lifestyle is restricted. They are bitterly opposed to justifications of staff theft on the grounds of low wages, poverty, or family needs. For them, honesty, integrity and decency are central to the way they view themselves. Several of them had been involved in petty larceny when young, and had typically undergone a personal struggle to become what they would describe as 'honest, decent people'. Honesty was not simply a behavioural choice – it was how they defined themselves. Angels have zero commitment to theft and zero impact upon the business. The way staff who are *angels* think about theft and crime is completely dissimilar from the way others do so. This is why staff who are not angels are classed as members of the animal kingdom: baboons, jackdaws or crocodiles.

• *Baboons:* Like baboons, these are friendly social beings who fulfil assumed obligations to friends and family using collusive methods. They are often young persons and tend not to regard their behaviour as fraudulent but 'what everybody does'. They do not feel their actions are opposed to the company because they give away only small amounts at a time. They do not necessarily profit from theft: they create or acknowledge obligations, they obtain status, or they buy (or try to buy) friendship. Middle-aged people may respond charitably to a particular situation. Collusive activity can be limited by what is socially acceptable. However, success can breed overconfidence and the amounts stolen can increase week by week, particularly when the staff member lacks the social skills to control the other people with whom he or she is colluding. The risks they run are small if they are careful, although security staff are trained to watch for fleeting expressions of triumph which may indicate collusion. Baboons can have a serious impact on the business because frequent collusive thefts even of small amounts rapidly become significant: a checkout operator giving discounts to three people every week may cost the business an average of between £2,000 and £4,000 in a calendar year.

• *Jackdaws:* These are attracted by a range of merchandise and cash for themselves and the use of their families, rarely using collusive methods. The motive is personal use gain, and encompasses, at one extreme, the individual who helps himself to some cans of drink and, at the other, the person who regularly takes home cash or goods because he can get away with it. This is not viewed as theft but a perk of the job. Some jackdaws regard staff theft as part of being a good provider for the family and will inform others of the fortunate position they are in as a 'trusted' employee. The occasional theft may not have a major impact upon the business, but some jackdaws may be so diligent that they operate virtually as semi-professional criminals.

• *Crocodiles:* These may be regarded as semi-professional thieves in terms of their commitment to theft and their impact upon the business. They may work singly, as part of a team, or in collusion with customers. They gravitate to this position through starting off as a jackdaw or a baboon, see the possibilities of much greater rewards, and find it impossible to stop stealing because their expenditure has increased. In practice, they may be very good employees. The commercial acumen that makes them quick-witted crooks can make them good salespeople or effective administrators. Consequently, they may be trusted more, and not subject to so many controls because their performance is so good. If a crocodile gets into a senior position which allows him or her to steal, then the individual is unlikely to leave, and in the opinion of security managers these may cost the retailer £10,000 per year until or unless the person is caught.

Obviously, these four categories represent a very generalised method of assessing different types of shopworker. Classifying individuals may be difficult, and there may be a large number of workers gathered around the interstices of the grid. An individual may change over time and move from being a jackdaw to a crocodile. The security message tends to be sent to all employees as a group. A more focused approached, based on the different perceptions and types of infraction shown in the *impact: commitment grid* may give greater benefits. Only the crocodiles recognise that their behaviour is crime. Ultimately it may be possible to use angels to police baboons, and baboons to police the crocodiles and jackdaws.

Conclusions and actions

This is not a national study and caution should be used in interpreting the results. Nevertheless, a large group of chief security managers from major retailers has been interviewed with consistent results across a range of different vertical markets. The sample of shop staff provided a statistically acceptable response rate and the key percentages were statistically significant. But it must be admitted that there is a possibility that the results may not be typical of other kinds of business or other areas of the country. This is a preliminary study and further research may support or contradict these results.

Making full allowance for the above reservations about the difficulties of generalising from these results, there are several conclusions which may be drawn from this study.

• *Employee theft* may well have a greater impact on losses than national and company indicators suggest. This is likely to mean some change in the traditional emphasis of security departments to focus more upon staff deviance.

• *Collusion between staff and customers* may well form a large part of staff-related theft. Further investigation is needed to assess this hypothesis. An important argument about why this might be so is to do with the ability of staff to relate risks to rewards: the same (or greater) reward is possible at lower risk for staff who adopt collusive behaviour. Rational staff will adopt collusive approaches to theft to limit their risks of detection.

Recommended actions
The research reported here suggests that two factors, *motivation* and *perceived risk,* are critical determinants of the level of staff theft.

• *Motivation to steal* may be addressed by accepting that most staff are honest, but that there may be substantial levels of ambiguity about collusion. Programmes based on using angels to create a climate of honesty in the stores may be more effective that those which operate by hectoring everyone to refrain from crime. Store security committees and team-briefing approaches may be ways of doing this. The fact that part-time members of staff may not be fully involved in this activity needs careful attention.

• *Perceived risks* may be divided into an employee's perception of the risks of detection and the perception of the risks of punishment.

The risks of detection are seen as low. Staff crime is viewed as easy and staff collusion as carrying low risks. Employees were not fully aware that a proportion of discrepancies were thoroughly investigated every week and that this might lead to the detection of staff who seemed otherwise to have developed a foolproof method of theft. Companies were anxious not to give possibly fraudulent staff insights into their investigation processes, but this created the widespread view that thieves who were careful and not too greedy could succeed indefinitely.

Retailers should re-emphasise policies such as the use of spot checks and staff searches to increase the risks of detection. The growing use of CCTV/electronic point of sale systems with associated exception software will increase the chances of detection and improve the *quality* and accessibility of *evidence,* thus increasing perceived risk for the member of staff. The logic of this chapter suggests that shop staff should be shown how these work rather than it being kept secret.

The perceived risks of punishment were seen as low. Only a proportion of those who were caught were handed over to the police, and many of these were not prosecuted. Because store management was embarrassed about staff theft and concerned about seeming to slander someone who might be found innocent by a court, there was no policy of keeping other shop staff informed about what was happening in particular cases. Thus the policy was seen to be more lenient than it actually was. The long period of time a thief had spent waiting on bail before he appeared in court had given the impression that nothing was to happen.

Store policy should be directed towards increasing the perceived risk of punishment. Thus stores should clarify with store staff what exactly is to happen to apprehended thieves. Every staff thief should receive a civil demand to repay a significant sum of money (say, £400 or more) to the employer in addition to being reported to the police.[26] Civil recovery would be additionally useful because the sum could be demanded within a few days of arrest. As well as increasing the perceived risks and costs of punishment, it will make other staff aware both that the company is serious about punishing wrongdoers and that part of the sanction can be applied very quickly.

Theft by staff is an acknowledged, although unfortunate, feature of retail employment. Businesses need to have a much clearer idea of the various types of staff theft, including collusive activity, which are occurring, and to attempt to reduce the impact by changing the motivation of staff and increasing the perceived risks of detection and risks of punishment resulting from staff theft.

Notes

1   Professor Joshua Bamfield is Director of the Centre for Retail Research, Mapperley Place, 476 Mansfield Road, Sherwood, Nottingham NG5 2EL, Telephone/fax: 0115 962 3717 (email: retailing@compuserve.com website http://www.emnet/retailresearch).

2   Wells, C. and Dryer, A. (1997) *Retail Crime Costs Survey 1995/96*. London: British Retail
         Consortium.

3   Beck, A. and Willis, A. (1995) The Enemy Within. *Security Management Today*. Vol. 4,
         No.9, February.

4   Boye, M.W., Jones, J.W., Martin, S.L. and Beck, R.P. (1995) *5th Annual Report of Super-
         market Employee Behaviour.* Rosemont, Illinois: London House and Food Marketing In-
         stitute.

5   Wells and Dryer, op cit.

6   Hollinger, R.C., Dabney, D.A. and Lee, G. (1996) *1996 National Retail Security Survey:
         Final Report*. Gainesville, Florida: University of Florida. Some security implications are
         discussed in Bamfield, J. and Hollinger, R. (1996). *Managing Losses in the Retail Store: A
         Comparison of Loss Prevention Activity in the United States and Great Britain*. Security
         Journal. Vol. 7, pp 61-70.

7   Note the figures provided in Tonglet, M. and Bamfield, J. (1997) Controlling Shop Crime
         in Britain: Costs and Trends, *International Journal of Retail and Distributive Manage-
         ment,* Vol. 25, 8, No. 9, pp 293-300.

8   Wells and Dryer, op cit.

9   Clarke, J. and Hollinger, R. (1983) *Theft by Employees in Work Organizations*. Lexington,
         Mass.: Lexington Books.

10   Baumer, T. and Rosenbaum, D. (1984) *Combating Retail Theft: Programs and Strategies*.
         Stoneham, Mass.: Butterworth; Snyder, N. H., Broome, O. W., Kehoe, W. T., McIntyre, J.
         T. and Blair, K. E. (1991) *Reducing Employee Theft: A Guide to Financial and Organiza-
         tional Control*. New York: Quorum Books.

11   Ditton, J. (1977) *Part-Time Crime: An Ethnography of Fiddling and Pilferage*. London:
         Macmillan. See also Zeitlin, L.R. (1977) Stimulus/response: a Little Larceny Can Do a
         Lot for Employee Morale. *Psychology Today*. Vol. 5, pp 22-64.

12   Mars, G. (1982) *Cheats at Work: Anthropology of Workplace Crime*. London: Unwin.

13   Ditton, op cit; Mars, op cit.

14   Hollinger, R. (1991) Neutralising in the Workplace: an Empirical Analysis of Property
         Theft and Production Deviance. *Deviant Behaviour: An Interdisciplinary Journal*. Vol. 12,
         pp 169-202.

15   Hollinger, op cit; Greenberg, J. and Scott, K.S. (1996) Why Do Workers Bite the Hands
         that Feed Them? Employee Theft as a Social Exchange Process. *Research into Organiza-
         tional Behaviour.* Vol. 1, pp 111-156.

16   Merriam, D. (1977) Employee Theft. *Criminal Justice Abstracts*. Vol. 9, pp 380-386;
         Gottfredson, M. and Hirschi, T. (1990) *General Theory of Crime*. Stanford, California:
         Stanford University Press; Hirschi, T. (1969) *Causes of Delinquency*. Berkley, California:
         University of California Press.

17   Greenberg and Scott, op cit.

18   Mars, op cit.

19   A report of these interviews was published by ICL Retail Systems Ltd, who funded the study, as Bamfield, J. (1997) *Fighting Retail Crime: How Major Multiples Curb Theft from Shops,* London: ICL Retail Systems.

20   Ibid.

21   Wells and Dryer, op cit. The Table 1 figures provided here are based on a more recent edition of the British Retail Consortium's crime cost figures and hence differ from those given in Bamfield, ibid.

22   Discussed more extensively in Bamfield, ibid, pp 17-23.

23   The utility-maximising criminal is discussed in Cornish, D. and Clarke, R. (eds) (1986) *The Reasoning Criminal: Rational Choice Perspectives on Offending.* New York: Springer-Verlag. Repeat offending can also be considered as a risk-reduction strategy.

24   Wells and Dryer, op cit.

25   Beck and Willis, op cit.

26   Bamfield, J. (1997) *Making the Shoplifter Pay: Retail Civil Recovery.* Social Market Foundation: London, Paper No. 28. Also Bamfield, J. (1998) Retail Civil Recovery: Filling a Deficit in the Criminal Justice System? *International Journal of Risk, Security and Crime Prevention.* Vol. 3, No. 4, pp 257-267.

Chapter 10

Repeat Robbers: Are They Different?

Martin Gill and Ken Pease[1]

The last decade has seen an increase in the study of repeat offending against the same target. Recognition of the facts of repeat victimisation provides much scope for prevention. Despite this, little study of offenders' perspectives in targeting the same person or place has been undertaken. This paper reports interviews with robbers, in particular their replies to questions about repeat offending against the same targets. Some robbers are moved to rob premises when they are aware, from personal experience or indirectly, that a previous raid proved easy and successful. The findings are discussed in the context of the attempts to increase the risks to robbers.

Introduction

In recent years attention has been focused on the extent to which crime victimisation is concentrated upon the same areas and the same individuals, households and businesses within those areas. It seems that areas experience high levels of crime in substantial measure because of the levels of concentration on particular victims.[2] Recognition of this fact encourages the allocation of crime prevention resources and interest to recently victimised places and people. This approach is currently in vogue and has been employed in prevention projects with varying degrees of success.[3] The basic facts seem to be that repetition becomes increasingly likely as the extent of prior victimisation increases,[4] revictimisation tends to occur quickly,[5] and revictimisation across crime types is more likely than would be the case were these independent events.[6]

Two rival (or complementary) accounts of the phenomenon of repeat victimisation have been offered, referred to as 'risk heterogeneity' and 'event dependence' in the criminological literature, more simply known as *flag* and *boost* accounts respectively. Risk heterogeneity accounts for repeat victimisation by stressing that people and places vary in their continuing vulnerability to crime. In one way or another, they *flag* their vulnerability. Any passing offender would recognise this vulnerability and offend accordingly. Event dependence suggests that prior events *boost* the probability of victimisation. It does not require that the same perpetrator is involved on each occasion, and the extent to which event dependence occurs through the sharing of information between offenders has been considered.[7] Numerous undetected or unpunished instances of staff dishonesty in the past will make perpetrators more confident and may thereby make future theft more likely. Put simply, a successful offence makes its own repetition more likely. When no extra (or insufficient and ineffective) security is installed after a robbery, future robberies may become more likely. A well-known example of a boost account is the 'broken windows' hypothesis, whereby the non-repair of initial damage is a sign of lack of care for the building, and invites further damage to the same building and the area in which it is located.[8]

Flag and boost explanations are conceptually separate, but practically intertwined. For instance, divorced women are more likely than others to receive obscene calls. Is a woman's divorce a factor which increases her vulnerability (boost) or does her continuing state of lone living underpin a level of hazard (flag)?[9] There are some offence types, however, which should clearly be thought of in terms of boost explanations. Domestic violence is one such, where the repeated offences are known to be the work of the same perpetrator. Substantial research[10] underlines the important role which event dependence (boost) plays in repeat victimisation.

The choice between boost and flag explanations has consequences. They suggest different approaches to crime prevention. In particular, the boost account proposes that the perpetrators of repeated offences against the same person or premises are the same people (or their associates). Thus *detection* of a repeated offence will lead to the identification of someone who has committed a series of crimes. A focus on detecting the perpetrators of offences will lead to a demonstrable increase in risk for the perpetrator. Action flowing from flag accounts will focus on *deflection* of the offender, by manipulating social and situational factors, such as the installation of surveillance equipment or the appointment of security guards, to reduce the chances of a robbery being successfully undertaken. This may or may not increase the likelihood of failure. It is primarily directed at the offender's *perception* of increased risk.

Research already done, as well as common-sense understanding, makes it abundantly clear that some offenders do repeatedly offend against the same victim.[11] Everson, in work as yet unpublished, suggests that those who do commit repeat offences against the same target tend also to be the most prolific offenders.[12] If Everson is right (and research on burglars by Julie Ashton and others suggests that he may well be),[13] the implications are enormous. Offender targeting as now practised by the police is contentious, because those chosen for targeting are a product of the imperfect process which police apply in identifying the most prolific offenders. That imperfection means that some prolific offenders will not be targeted, and some of those targeted will not be prolific offenders. It will not take many tabloid stories of police harassment of the (relatively) innocent to reactivate civil liberty concerns which have been largely dormant in recent years.

If repetition of an offence against a target is a characteristic of the prolific offender, then the detection of repeats is an elegant way of targeting prolific offenders without raising difficult civil rights issues. Nonetheless, we should not rush to judgement. Even basic facts about the intersection of criminal and victim careers are not yet known. The patterns may vary by offence type, age of offender, circumstances of offence, and the like. In any event, there is a stunning lack of research that makes this kind of connection, and much more needs to be done before links can be made with confidence.

This chapter reports evidence derived from a study of robbers. Elsewhere the research has been discussed in much more detail.[14] Here the results from questions which addressed repeat offences are analysed. While robbery, an offence which involves theft under force or the threat of force, includes both street robbery (or 'mugging') and robberies of premises, this study focuses on the latter, specifically robberies of businesses. Robbery is a serious offence, and those convicted are almost invariably sent to prison. Robbers often use weapons, not infrequently firearms. Much money is invested by commerce to prevent the offence or to generate evidence (for example CCTV pictures) to help catch those responsible. Significant police resources are devoted to tackling robbery. Yet there is relatively little research which attempts to evaluate the behaviour patterns of robbers.

The study consisted of interviews with 341 robbers in prison.[15] Each interviewee admitted to being involved in at least one robbery. Robbers were asked about how they planned offences, their motivations, the way they chose their target, their methods of carrying out their robberies and their views of the police, criminal justice and security, and more general questions about their perspectives on their crimes. A key part of the undertaking was to collect data on how robbers choose their target. Such choice is not a simple matter.[16] Certainly, commercial robbers are attracted by premises that look easy, although many do not take much time to make a judgement, and their interpretation of what is 'easy' varies. For example, robbers generally expect to encounter security measures, but some robbers avoid premises that have either cameras or security screens. Similarly, when asked whether they considered being able to see inside the premises from the street an advantage or disadvantage, opinions varied. Some felt that being able to see inside enabled them to check the premises more easily (the level of security, the numbers of staff and customers, the layout) before the raid. Others felt that where the interior was invisible from the street there was less danger that passers-by would notice a robbery in progress and raise the alarm.

While clear differences in views and behaviour were distinguishable, developing a classification system for robbers is fraught with problems. In the fuller discussion of these overall findings Gill argues that while, in theory, it is possible to identify 'professionals' (characterised by being organised, which includes planning the offence) and 'amateurs' (who are much less discerning in their choice of target and plan less), in practice the distinction is less clear. Indeed, the notion of the amateur as someone acting for the intrinsic love of an activity rather than the expectation of profit is surely a misnomer when applied to robbers! If 'professionals' and 'amateurs' are viewed as opposite poles of a continuum then very few robbers will be at either end; most will be somewhere in the middle. Thus Gill suggests that if classifications are going to be useful for crime prevention purposes then one way forward might be to develop an awareness of the type of decisions, and the emphasis placed upon them by offenders in the commission of their offences. He terms these 'rationality indicators'. The object would be to find out the points at which offenders make decisions and to influence those decisions in such a way that a crime is seen as less desirable or undesirable.

In the meantime, the words 'professional' and 'amateur' provide the poles of a crude continuum (and the words reflect different levels of organisation and planning). It is quite clear that robbers' choice of target is influenced by the perceived ease with which it can be robbed, although professionals take more steps to ensure that (often more difficult) targets are made easier to rob. In this paper we explore one aspect to this, namely the extent to which knowledge or conduct of previous raids informs judgements of target suitability. The findings derive primarily from answers to three questions which robbers were asked about repeat offending, and the association between these answers and a robber's criminal record and robbery tactics. The three key questions concerned whether the interviewee had ever robbed the *same premises* more than once; whether he had ever robbed premises he knew had been robbed by *someone else*; and whether the target of his *last trobbery* had been robbed before. This chapter will consider each of these questions in turn.

Robbing premises on more than one occasion

Robbers were asked whether they had ever robbed the same premises more than once; of the 341 respondents, 65 (19.1 per cent) said that they had done so. Many of them mentioned the fact that robbing the premises in question had been easy the first time, and that having robbed the place before, they knew what to expect. Thus there was support here for boost interpretations of repeat victimisation. Being able to exercise control over the environment is a key concern for robbers, and knowing what to expect reduces the chances that they will meet an unwelcome obstacle. Some typical comments on why they said they returned to premises included:

> Because it was easy.

> Three times. First one was easy, second one was easy, and the third one I thought would be the same.

> It was easy the first time so I thought I'd try it again.

> It was so easy I went back ten days later.

> A factory and shop twice. It is easy, it's about 25 minutes before the alarm goes off, and the shop didn't have one. They didn't learn.

> Fun, for the crack, bizz. It was an easy target; guaranteed money.

> I thought it was an easy touch.

> Nobody had been arrested there before.

> I knew what to expect.

> If you get a good result, you go back a second time.

A few robbers had undertaken a robbery, in part at least, because they were colluding with a member of staff. This gave them confidence and was a reason why at least one robber returned to the scene to carry out a second raid:

> It was easy. I knew the woman, and she helped me, so I did it twice.

There were other views. Indeed, it is slightly ironic that the effectiveness of situational measures are dependent on a rational robber, and yet some robberies do not take place because a robber had anticipated a rational reaction by the victim, even when such a reaction has not taken place. For example, one rather thoughtful if perhaps naive robber noted:

> I would never rob a place more than once because the security is going to be better.
> They may be more vigilant.

Further analysis indicated that in comparison with other robbers, those who had robbed specific premises more than once *were* distinct: they were more professional and determined, even violent in the way they carried out their robberies. This determination was evidenced by the fact that in comparison with other robbers, they were less likely to say they would have given up if somehow prevented from robbing the intended target of their last offence[17] - only 14% responded in this way, compared to 31% of other respondents. In addition, they were more likely to have carried a gun and significantly more likely to have carried a loaded gun (eight in ten did so, compared to six in ten of those who had not robbed the same premises on more than one occasion), and more likely to have committed a robbery where someone was injured (approaching a half said that this was the case, compared to a quarter of others).

There is also some support for saying that Everson's findings that repeaters are more prolific offenders applies to robbers: repeat robbers were significantly more likely to have been in prison before, and significantly more likely to have spent five years or more in prison in total. They were significantly more likely to have expected a sentence of more than five years prior to being sentenced for their last robbery. Their expectation was significantly more likely to have been realised - 79% received such a sentence, compared to just 56% of others.

Robbers who repeatedly targeted a single premises appeared to be more professional in their approach to planning their robberies and in discerning cues of time, place and personal identifiability relevant to target choice. Asked about their most recent robbery, they were significantly more likely both to have worn a disguise and to have chosen the time of the robbery specifically. In addition they were significantly more likely both to have robbed a target that was on a corner and to say that this was relevant to why it was chosen. Similarly, they were significantly more likely to say the fact that the inside of the target was visible from the street was one reason why it was chosen. Altogether this suggests a greater degree of forethought and preparation.

Finally, it should be noted that those who had robbed a particular premises on more than one occasion were significantly more likely than those who had not to say that they had also robbed premises that they knew had been robbed before by someone else. Nearly a third (31%) responded in this way, compared to just over one sixth (18%) of others.

Robbing any premises known to have been robbed by someone else

A second question relating to repeat victimisation which was asked of respondents was whether they had ever robbed premises which they knew had previously been robbed by someone else. Of the 341 in the sample, 63 (18.5 per cent) admitted that they had, and once again, most of this group said that the fact that the premises in question had been robbed before gave them the idea that the offence would be easy to commit, or went towards confirming this notion in their mind. Sometimes the information they needed was provided by the media. Some typical comments here were:

> I knew it could be done.

> Easy target, because I knew the staff wouldn't make it difficult by refusing money.

> Because I was told how easy it was.

> It was in the paper, a complete amateur got £150 and the women there were frightened and compliant.

> I knew it had been done successfully before.

Sometimes the inspiration was not so much the belief that it would be easy, but in order to prove a point:

> The Post Office, because I heard about a chap getting caught and I wanted to prove a point that it could be done.

To some, however, the fact that premises had been robbed before was an irrelevance. Some of the respondents to this question, admittedly a minority, found out after they had raided it that the premises had been robbed before. There may perhaps be support for flag factors (risk heterogeneity) as an explanation for repeat offending here: robbers identified a place to rob that others, independently, had also chosen as a suitable target for robbery. Some typical comments included:

> I only found out afterwards that it had been robbed two weeks before.

> I didn't know it had been robbed the same week twice. Poor girl. I didn't know. Talk about bad luck. It was everyone's favourite target.

> All the Post Offices in my manor had been robbed at some point.

One respondent, however, said that he would avoid a target which he knew had been robbed on a previous occasion:

> If it had been done more than once it would have been dangerous.

When compared with the other robbers in the sample, those who had robbed premises which they knew had previously been robbed by someone else were found to be characteristic in numerous ways. This group of offenders appeared to be more professional and organised in their approach to the planning and carrying out of their robberies. In relation to their last offence, they were significantly more likely to have planned for a period of more than one day — 56% did so, compared to 39% of others, and significantly more likely to have kept the target under surveillance before the robbery, both personally (66% did, compared to 46% of others), and through an associate (49% had done so compared to 30% of others). They were also significantly more likely to have done the following: worn a disguise, and to have been accompanied by associates who wore disguises, and to have worn special clothes. In more general terms, they were significantly more likely both to have considered the threat of police Rapid Response Units and to have monitored police activity at some stage in their criminal careers.

Respondents who had robbed premises that they knew had been targeted previously appeared to be more likely to use violence: in relation to their last robbery, they were especially (and significantly more) likely to have carried a real gun (84% did so, compared to 60% of other robbers) and significantly more likely to say that someone was injured in the last robbery (around a third responded in this way, compared to just under one sixth of others), and they were significantly more likely to have been involved in a robbery at some other point where someone was injured (more than four in ten had, compared to a quarter of others). In a different way, they were less likely to have any sympathy with the employees of the establishments they had robbed; this too was statistically significant.

Finally, respondents who had robbed premises which they knew had been robbed before by someone else were significantly more likely than others to say they had carried out repeat robberies (nearly one third responded in this way, compared to less than a fifth of others), and in relation to their last robbery, they were both significantly more likely to say the target had been robbed before and to say that the question of whether it had been robbed before was relevant (one in five said it was relevant, compared to just over one in fourteen of others).

Robbing the last premises: the influence of it having been robbed by someone else

The third question concerning repeat victimisation related more closely to the last robbery committed by respondents. They were asked whether the target of their last robbery had been robbed before. Of the 341 in the sample, 52 (15.2 per cent) said that this had been the case, and although this group were less distinct than those who had answered in the affirmative to the first two questions, they still shared characteristics with those offenders.

Once again, this class of respondents showed signs of being better prepared and more professional than others (although not to the same extent as the other respondents discussed up to this point). In relation to their last offence they were more prepared: while they were slightly more likely to say that they kept the target under surveillance before the robbery (53% compared to 47%), they were significantly more likely to say that an associate kept the target under surveillance before the robbery (46% compared to 28%), and significantly more likely to have known how many teller units there were in the target before entering (83% compared to 63%). In common with those respondents who answered in the affirmative to the first two repeat victimisation-related questions, this group appeared to be more prone (than others) to the use of violence. While they were only slightly more likely to have carried a gun in their last robbery (62% compared to 55%) and to have been in a robbery where someone was injured (38% compared to 32%), they were significantly more likely to say that someone was injured in their last robbery (33% compared to 18%).

Finally, approaching a third claimed that the fact that the target had been robbed before was relevant to why they chose it. They were also significantly more likely to say they had robbed premises which they knew had been robbed before by someone else (47% compared to 16%).

Discussion

While a minority reoffend against the same premises, it is a significant minority, and these findings are not especially surprising given the previous research on this issue.[18] It suggests that asking offenders about their attitudes to repeat victimisation will prove a useful exercise. If these are indeed more prolific robbers, they will be responsible for a higher proportion of all robberies than their numbers may lead one to suppose. Insofar as they are more professional and violent, they will be responsible for a high proportion of losses and anguish to staff.

One major reason why some premises are victims of robbery on more than one occasion is because the same robber, having been successful, returns to the scene. The reasons for doing so revealed in this research are wholly rational, and chime well with those of the repeat burglars interviewed by Julie Ashton:[19]

> The house would be targeted again a few weeks later when the stuff had been replaced and because the first time had been easy.

> It was a chance to get things which you had seen the first time and now had a buyer for.

> Once you have been into a place it is easier to burgle because you are then familiar with the layout, and you can get out much quicker.

> Keys to the door were usually hanging round, either on a shelf or the top of furniture near to the door in empty houses, so they used the keys to unlock the doors to get out and to use for the next time they broke in.

In addition to repetition by the same offender, word about good targets circulates, sometimes directly from one robber looking for a target to another one with knowledge, other times more generally via gossip and networks or via the press and media. It has been suggested that the more thoughtful robbers, the more professional and determined (and this includes a greater preparedness to be more violent) were the most likely to rob premises more than once or return somewhere they knew had been robbed before. It was precisely because they thought about identifying easy targets that a victimised premises, already shown to be vulnerable, proved attractive; it was the realisation that someone else had been successful that encouraged them to believe they could be too. And since robbers need to exercise control over the environment, to maximise the chances of getting the money and making good their escape, robbing a place that is known to them, either personally or vicariously, had much to commend it.

Implicit in the finding that robbers identify easy targets because someone else is known to have succeeded is an assumption that victims will not install preventive measures to stop them. The collective wisdom of these offenders, based on experience, is that businesses do not act, or do not act sufficiently quickly or with adequate measures to put them off undertaking another raid. While the present research did not address the point, previous work uniformly shows that the first weeks and months after an offence carries the highest risk of repetition. Robbers look for easy targets, and at least one measure of ease is a previous successful raid. While such a finding is not earth-shattering in itself, it is left unheeded at a victim's peril. The lessons have too often remained unrecognised or unheeded by crime victims in the business world and amongst those charged with advising on or installing security in the commercial sector.

The evidence reported here has touched only the surface of what is a far more complex and increasingly crucial issue for security and crime prevention. Businesses must be encouraged to act after the first offence, because both victims and offenders agree that there is a good chance it will happen again. Change does not necessarily have to be massive, but it does have to be prompt. If it were obvious that security had been effectively improved, the discerning robber is more likely to refrain from carrying out a repeat raid. If society collectively were to generate an awareness that a victimisation was a basis for increased security perhaps some would be wary of raiding again. Perhaps if the media in reporting that a raid had been successful for robbers also added that security was being increased, the chances of offenders risking their liberty would go down. At this stage we can only speculate, but repeat victimisation offers important opportunities for increasing the risk of capture and preventing raids from taking place, as the interviewed robbers said. Within the sample were a fairly professional group of robbers who chose previously victimised premises because they were known to be vulnerable.

The potential for detecting the most serious and prolific offenders by focusing attention on clearing repeat crimes against the same target, thereby avoiding charges of police harassment, seems confirmed by this research. The study adds to the advantages of the approach by demonstrating that the perpetrators of repeats are more serious offenders *even when they did not commit the earlier offence(s)*. Moreover, both *flag* and *boost* accounts of repeat victimisation have been shown to be operative and provide valid areas of further research, at least as far as robbers are concerned. The role of deflecting and detecting repeat crime provides an intriguing and promising avenue for investigation. As a means of increasing actual hazard and perceived risk of being caught, it seems to focus on the right perpetrator group without the inefficiency and breach of civil liberties which more conventional offender-targeting approaches entail.

Notes

1   Dr Martin Gill is based at the Scarman Centre, University of Leicester, The Friars, 154 Upper New Walk, Leicester, LE1 7QA (email: mg26@le.ac.uk); Professor Ken Pease is based at the School of Human and Health Sciences, University of Huddersfield, Queensgate, Huddersfield, West Yorkshire, HD1 3DH (email: ken_pease@compuserve.com).

2   Trickett, A., Osborn, D., Seymour, J., Pease, K. (1992) What Is Different About High Crime Areas? *British Journal of Criminology*. Vol. 32, pp 81-9.

3   Wood, J., Wheelwright, G., Burrows, J. (1997) *Crime Against Small Business: Facing the Challenge*. Leicester: Small Business and Crime Initiative; Pease, K. (1998) *Repeat Victimisation Research: What We Know, Why It Matters, and What Happens Next*. Crime Prevention and Detection Paper (forthcoming). London: Home Office; see also Taylor, G. (forthcoming) Using Repeat Victimisation to Counter Commercial Burglary: the Leicester Experience. *International Journal of Risk, Security and Crime Prevention*.

4   Ellingworth D., Farrell, G., Pease, K. (1995) A Victim is a Victim is a Victim: Chronic Victimisation in Four Sweeps of the British Crime Survey *British Journal of Criminology*. Vol. 35, pp 360-365; Gill, M. (1999) The Victimisation of Business: Indicators of Risk and the Direction of Future Research. *International Review of Victimology*. Forthcoming.

5   Polvi N., Looman, T., Humphries, C. and Pease, K. (1990) Repeat Break and Enter Victimisation: Time Course and Crime Prevention Opportunity. *Journal of Police Science and Administration*. Vol. 17, pp 8-11; Spelman W. (1995) Once Bitten, Then What? Cross-sectional and Time-course Explanations of Repeat Victimisation. *British Journal of Criminology*. Vol. 32, pp 81-89.

6   Fienberg, S.E. (1980) Statistical Modelling in the Analysis of Repeat Victimisation. In Fienberg, S. E., and Reiss, A. J. (eds) *Indicators of Crime and Criminal Justice: Quantitative Studies*. Washington DC: Bureau of Justice Statistics.

7   Bennett, T. (1995) Identifying, Explaining and Targeting Burglary Hot Spots. *European Journal of Criminal Policy and Research*. Vol. 3, pp 113-123.

8   Kelling, G. and Coles, C.M. (1996) *Fixing Broken Windows*. New York: Free Press.

9   Tseloni, A. and Pease, K. (1998) Nuisance Phone Calls to Women in England and Wales. *European Journal of Criminal Policy and Research*. Forthcoming.

10   Chenery, S., Ellingworth, D., Tseloni, A. and Pease, K. (1996) Crimes Which Repeat: Undigested Evidence from the British Crime Survey 1992. *International Journal of Risk, Security and Crime Prevention*. Vol. 1, No. 3. pp 207-216; Lauritsen, J.L. and Davis Quinet, K.F. (1995) Repeat Victimisation among Adolescents and Young Adults. *Journal of Quantitative Criminology*. Vol. 11, pp 143-166.

11   Gill, M. and Matthews, R. (1994) Robbers on Robbery: Offenders' Perspectives. In Gill, M. (ed.) *Crime at Work.* Vol. I. Leicester: Perpetuity Press.

12   Everson, S. (1998) *Prolific Offenders and Repeat Victims.* PhD thesis in preparation, University of Huddersfield.

13   Ashton J., Brown, I., Senior, B. and Pease, K. (1998) Repeat Victimisation: Offender Accounts *International Journal of Risk, Security and Crime Prevention.* Forthcoming.

14   Gill, M. (forthcoming) *Robbers on Robbery: Offenders' Perspectives on Security and Crime Prevention.*

15   For a discussion of the methodology, please see ibid.

16   Ibid.

17   In the text we have used the term 'significantly' to indicate a statistical significance, p< 0.05. We have refrained form using the term 'significant' in making comparisons where the relationship was not statistically significant at this level.

18   Conklin, J. (1972) *Robbery and the Offender Justice System.* Philadelphia: Lippincott.

19   Ashton et al, op cit.

Chapter 11

The Craft of the Long-Firm Fraudster: Criminal Skills and Commercial Responses

Michael Levi[1]

This chapter sets out to explain the techniques of bankruptcy fraud and the way that they both reflect and adapt to the measures of commercial (and, to a lesser extent, criminal justice) control. Some fraudsters already possess an existing business and exploit the credit rating that they have built up (whether or not for the initial purpose of fraud); others buy new or existing firms to generate a credit rating and then use pretexts to explain their need for enhanced credit. Provided that suppliers request credit references from bureaux, the latter can build up a pattern of suspicious trading that fits the long-firm fraud model, and, in any case, can use technology to check the fit between references and their existing databases, and look for mutual referencing between undisclosed interconnected companies. Police action against fraudsters enhances risks both for criminal professionals and professional criminals, but it is only when fraud levels rise across the board that serious credit control efforts are made against such frauds, which anyway are inherently difficult to differentiate from respectable business.

Introduction

During the past 40 years, since the end of the first phase of the 'professional crime' and 'white-collar crime' traditions Sutherland tried to stimulate in his books *The Professional Thief* [2] and *White-Collar Crime*,[3] 'crime at work' has been a largely neglected part of the criminological enterprise.[4] The reasons for this are not obvious, but they include the fact that many criminologists have been heavily engaged in the drugs, policing and corrections debates — where most of the research money is — and the fact that sophisticated adult offenders for gain are less readily accessible and less touched by the populist politics of law and order than are juveniles or petty persistent offenders or violent criminals. There are many types of offender for gain and many types of fraudster, but I have chosen here to revisit the craft of the long-firm fraudster — someone who establishes or purchases a company in order to defraud creditors — within the context of the socio-economic organisation of commerce and the attempts of (a) commercial credit controllers and (b) the police and insolvency examiners to regulate misconduct and crime. In other words, this article is looking at the organisation of crime from a perspective that is the reverse of that usually adopted in crime prevention studies, though 'rational offender' approaches have implicit or explicit models of offender decision-making which may even include motivational elements such as culture and shaming.[5] Looking from an 'appreciative' perspective at the offenders' ways of looking at 'their' problems — which latter will include the activities of most readers of this book — may be treated either as a route to more scientific planning of prevention and criminal justice interventions, or as a scientific *verstehen* enterprise worthwhile for its own sake, albeit an 'amoral' approach no longer fashionable.

Although most of the fieldwork for this article was done during the 1970s and was published earlier in *The Phantom Capitalists*,[6] the earlier material has been reworked modestly in the light of contemporary changes in criminal organisation and commercial controls, and is intended to introduce readers to the principle that where a form of behaviour is considered to present 'acceptable risks' and is hard and expensive to eliminate without impacting hard on the core marketing functions of commercial organisations, it will be tolerated, however much companies may prefer to do without it. In other words, 'increasing the risks for offenders' might not always be possible cost-effectively, and — in the absence of any strong governmental/police interest in reducing opportunities to defraud — companies are seldom interested in reducing crime for its own sake or even in reducing the risks for their competitors: an approach exacerbated by the tendency towards separate cost-centres within companies. Improvements in the professionalism of credit controllers, in the speed and breadth of commercial credit, and in computer modelling of credit risks have reduced the opportunities for fast 'get credit and run' tactics that were so popular during the 1960s, but — as with other sorts of fraud such as plastic fraud[7] — the skills to defraud are omnipresent and, if and when commercial controls are relaxed, they are likely to re-emerge, if not to the same extent. Moreover, it is never possible to eliminate the 'slippery-slope' fraudster who simply carries on trading at the risk of his or her creditors, hoping — like Dickens' Mr. Micawber — that 'something will turn up', the something being large insolvency: there is no evidence that liability (often present anyway in the form of personal guarantees to the banks) or the risk of director disqualification has had any significant effect on people who are either endemically optimistic or fixated more on the loss of the source of their money and prestige than on more abstract costs to others. Displacement effects are always difficult to determine in an area such as this where the definition of a 'failed company' as a 'bankruptcy fraud' is so problematic in practice and even in principle: one of the fraudster's skills is to persuade us to define 'what might have been crime' as either wholly legitimate or as excusable, and even when we find it inexcusable, it may not seem like good business to 'throw good money after bad' by pursuing proof.

The organisation of long-firm fraud (and many other types of crime for gain) requires the following components:

- finance;

- persons willing to participate in the crime;

- victims, or *in*capable guardians, who have assets that can be obtained;

- skill levels appropriate to the complexity of the crime and victim guardianship levels;

- the ability to escape conviction or a long term of imprisonment.

Changes in any of these components will affect the level of fraud, as will the relative attractiveness of other methods of obtaining money, legal and illegal, that are within the perceived reach of potential offenders. The top-class fraudster is able to obtain goods on credit *and* avoid imprisonment; the middle-range fraudster succeeds on the first but not the second count; and the incompetent fraudster fails on both counts.

Financing and setting up long-firm fraud

By contrast with credit card fraud, the establishment or purchase of a firm that will obtain large quantities of goods on credit requires some start-up capital for the business and for initial purchases, as well as sufficient funds for maintenance of lifestyle before the fraud comes to fruition. Success at obtaining goods on credit may be attained in a number of ways, to be discussed later in this chapter, but there are two essential components to this process: first, the provision of a confidence-inspiring front for the fraud; and second, the negotiation of credit within the framework provided by this front.

From the fraudster's perspective, the ideal long-firm fraud is one that does not require the manufacture of a 'front': for example, a company with a good established credit rating. For if this is the case, then the fraudster can allow the reputation of the company to provide him (or, very rarely, even during the 1990s, and almost not at all in the 1960s and 1970s, her) with credit without his having to do anything further in the way of specific confidence trickery. Some long-firm fraudsters are fortunate enough to be generously financed, sometimes by means of tax-evaded funds from professional people in search of profitable activities that beat inflation, perhaps even stimulated by contact with the illicit (at least until they are defrauded in turn!); others must work on shoestring budgets.

During the early and mid-1960s, when credit control was unsophisticated because levels of credit fraud had been low, the most common technique of long-firm fraud was the setting up of a number of apparently independent, but actually linked, companies. These companies might all be trading companies, or some might exist solely on paper: for the price of £25, any number of companies could be bought 'off the shelf'— 'no questions asked'— from agencies specialising in company formation. By 1998, the price had risen in line with inflation to £250 or more, rising to several thousands of pounds: the price is a function of the level of secrecy from the authorities offered by the 'offshore financial centre' (sometimes described as 'tax haven'), and — subject to possible future changes driven by anti-money laundering legislation — they can still be bought, few or no questions asked from firms advertising weekly in *The Economist*, the *International Herald Tribune*, in airline magazines, and on the Internet.

Establishing credit: the arts of deception

In the simpler type of operation, the 'front man' — recruited from underworld or commercial contacts — would be installed in rented or leased accommodation and would order goods from lists of suppliers who advertise in trade directories or from those mentioned by other fraudsters as a 'good touch'. If asked for a reference regarding his creditworthiness, he would refer a supplier to his own 'paper' companies.

These 'paper' companies might be real trading companies — perhaps indeed other frauds in the same group — or they might exist purely on paper, operating from accommodation addresses, such as (then) newsagents or (now) offices, sometimes with fancy addresses, or rooms rented by fraudsters as 'mail drops'. The mail would be collected and brought to the main premises, and the trader would write out the references himself. One small firm with a paid-up capital of £2 — still the legal minimum — at the beginning of the 1960s was provided with the following 'in-house' reference: 'Have dealt with this firm for five years, and have always found them very prompt payers and very reliable. I would consider them good for credit up to £5,000.' This very crude effort was often successful at that time, because few firms had any sophisticated form of credit control or were sensitised to the possibility of their being defrauded. However, even then, a credit inquiry agency might well have picked up the similarity in the typeface used in the references, checked the dates of registration of the companies involved, and checked the places of work of the referees. In these circumstances, the 'front' would prove inadequate to withstand the most superficial checks, and there would be clear evidence of deception if the fraudsters were caught. However, they would generally use false names, and fingerprinting was not at that time standard in police investigations of fraud. Consequently, unless the police were alerted during the operation of the fraud, the chances of escaping unidentified were quite high, though some professional fraudsters were targeted and taken out of circulation.

The more subtle operator, again within this basic technique, would use different typewriters, have headed notepaper printed for each firm by a different printer, and give a more sensible estimate of the creditworthiness of his trading firm than the one quoted above. In this way he would hope to pass the superficial scrutiny of investigators, and since he often obtained the typewriters and printing on credit, he would have to pay out little more than the crude fraudster. Even now, though large commercial credit bureaux such as Experian and Equifax have large, computerised databases which can quickly cross-correlate references and check whether the telephone number corresponds to the firm and/or the location given (mobile phone numbers being suspect because they are not tied to any particular area), such deceptions remain possible, though harder. Moreover, the advent of multi-font computers has made the detection of self-referencing much harder, provided that the offenders are disciplined: forensic laboratories might be able to pick up the similarities, but this is of little use to commercial creditors, who have to make rapid decisions and would seldom be willing to pay a substantial sum for such technical advice, when the ratio of frauds to genuine trades is so low.

If the fraudster was part of, or had access to, a wider circle of villains, he might extend this technique of self-reference-writing to a number of *actual* trading firms. The organiser or organisers would buy anything up to six 'off the peg' companies (or, if the price was right, existing trading companies). Each company would write to or telephone creditors, giving the other companies as referees, and in this way, a chain of long-firm frauds could be created. Although this method had the advantage over the cruder ones that the integrity of the would-be debtor could not be falsified simply by physical examination of the business premises of the referees, it had the disadvantage that it provided clear evidence of conspiracy to defraud if the police were able to detect the perpetrators (and if the crime was perceived and reported as such).

In order to surmount these 'little legal difficulties', the more subtle operators adopted two refinements. First, they would carry out 'dummy' transactions between the companies, so that there would be a record of trading to which they could refer the police for 'authentication' of the references. All of these transactions would be purely paper ones: they would not relate to any actual transfer of goods which such payments would normally represent, but this fact could not be established unless the police or some other body were conducting contemporaneous surveillance or could get an insider to turn Queen's Evidence against the other conspirators. Secondly, operators would give slightly more ambiguous references, such as 'I have done business with the owner of this firm for a number of years, and I feel sure that he would not enter into any transaction which he would be unable to fulfil.' References such as this might make it difficult to prove a substantive deception.

In the early 1960s, a large number of such cross-referenced frauds were operated by people connected with the Kray and Richardson gangs, both inside and outside London, and most of the fraud organisers were eventually imprisoned, after continuing to defraud after they were released in exchange for giving evidence against the gangsters. Their normal practice was to set up the companies in mid or late summer, pay the first few bills in cash, and gradually to increase orders 'for the Christmas trade', thus mirroring the patterns of trading of legitimate businesses. Then, as Christmas approached, there would be a large increase in orders, the goods would be sold virtually overnight, and the premises closed down. The timing of the frauds was done in this way because it provided a 'normal' context in which large orders could be justified and goods could easily be resold as part of the pre-Christmas spending spree. This technique continues to the present day, since its underlying logic remains: the more enthusiastic the supplier to maximise sales or the more desperate the victim is to unload the stock — particularly in a depressed retailing climate — the less likely they are to look carefully at the 'borrower', since the opportunity cost of rejecting the 'sale' — or unwitting donation! — rises under such circumstances.

The cross-referencing technique is normally used for relatively small operations, but is sometimes used in the larger ones. In 1967 a fraud was organised which involved six companies and some twenty fraudsters in an interlocking series of long-firm frauds in England. In this conspiracy the principal organisers even had the nerve to issue a fictitious debenture by one company to another, thereby ensuring that the recipient would be a preferential creditor in the liquidation. However, the main difficulty in attempting cross-referenced long-firm frauds within a time span longer than two or three months is that the chain is only as strong as its weakest link. As one organiser stated to me:

> Cross-referencing by l.f.s [long-firm frauds] is not a good idea, because if one of
> them crashes for some reason, and another has used it as a reference, that other may
> find that the suppliers are wary of delivering. In that way, you can lose very large
> orders. It is also very difficult to get the timing of the fraud right, and there is a much
> greater risk of police observation. So I would never try it unless I was so short of cash
> that I could not finance the payment of the first few orders to suppliers.

These types of fraud tend to be the largest long firms, those which obtain over £250,000. They may be operated in two basic forms: first, the owner of the business builds it up and then extends his credit in the classic long-firm manner; and second, the organiser of the fraud builds up his business 'as if' it were legitimate, resigns as director in favour of his 'front man', and gets the long firm to 'take off' under his *covert* control. The objective here is for the organiser to disclaim culpability, given that his or her involvement in the firm is unlikely to be known to the police (without informant leaks) or, even if the police become aware, prior business and criminal records will not be communicated to the jury.

Where they have bought a legitimate business, the organisers usually attempt to conceal from the suppliers the fact that there has been a change in control. Sometimes they are able to persuade the vendor to stay on in an advisory capacity, 'to help them find their way around the business'. Sometimes they put in their own 'front man' with the same name as the vendor, who claims to be a relative. In most cases, to give the impression of continuity, they keep on existing staff in all departments save that of accounts. They usually find ways of getting the vendor to delay informing Companies House of the change in ownership, while tying in the previous owner to help to make the firm 'a success'. As McIntosh[8] argues generally, society creates the venue for its own victimisation: in this instance, trade newspapers advertising businesses for sale provide the opportunity, and when their owners are trying to get out, they tend not to be 'capable guardians'. The fraudster is literally a 'phantom capitalist', for his capital is wholly illusory, an entity woven into the imagination of his suppliers.

The final category of 'fronts' comprises firms which are run for a period of time in a respectable fashion before their owners turn them into long firms. These may have been wholly straight firms, part-time 'fences' of long-firm goods which can be merged into their normal stock, or may have been built up from the start with the intention of being turned into long firms. Whatever the case, the credit rating will have been generated by earlier trading experiences with the long firm itself in its legitimate or pseudo-legitimate phase, and the fraudster makes use of the unwillingness of creditors to suspect people whom they know. For example, when businessmen seek to delay payment, their creditors will question them about their reasons for delay in such a manner that one feels that they seek reassurance rather than conflict. The depressing tales of 'phoenix' companies where different firms rise from the ashes of the old, with the same owners, are regularly imparted as 'sad tales' on consumer programmes such as *The Cook Report* or Radio 4's *Face the Facts*, reflecting the anonymity offered to traders in a larger-scale urban society in late modernity.[9]

In one variant, the proprietors were ageing and wanted to make their exit from the long-firm scene, in which they were long-time buyers of goods. After obtaining hundreds of thousands of pounds' worth of goods — immediately re-sold for cash to their existing customers — they sold part of their premises, 'cut price', to another team of fraudsters. Although this particular firm had traded in a superficially respectable fashion for almost a decade before it went 'bent', this length of time is not necessary for this particular technique. For example, again in the early 1970s, an enterprising organiser set up two 'front men' in a wholesale fruit, vegetable and grocery business in Covent Garden, London. They were given substantial financial backing, and they gradually built up the level of their orders over a year, paying well and inducing confidence. Then, at the planned end of the firm, orders were given for approximately £750,000 worth of goods, including £250,000 of fresh fruit and vegetables which were obtained on the normal trade terms of seven days' credit. Virtually overnight these goods were disposed of, and the 'front men' disappeared. Again, what is necessary here to raise the risks for fraudsters is for a substantial number of firms to make credit-rating requests (for a cost) to the same bureaux and for the bureaux to spot a pattern of unusual trading for which an explanation is required from the debtor. To the extent that this does not happen, frauds can be successful today as they were then.

Another aspect of the fraudster's technique lies in his use of banks. Though defamation and other legal risks have made bankers' references less useful by the end of the 1990s, a bank can make a very useful referee, or can stop the fraud in its tracks by commenting neutrally or negatively upon the business's potential. Moreover, bank managers can be helpful, for example, by allowing a firm to pay out money against uncleared cheques that have been paid into it, or unhelpful, by forbidding this and 'bouncing' cheques. For this reason, most fraudsters attempt to keep their banks 'sweet'. This may involve actual corruption or image manipulation. One way in which sophisticates attempt to generate a good image of their business turnover is by the use of 'accommodation cheques' on a large scale: this is sometimes called 'cheque kiting' and is used by many small businesspeople to create a good impression for less nefarious purposes. One such operation is described thus by a great 'cheque artist' of the 1970s:

> What you need is at least three people, and you get number 1 to give a cheque to number 2, who gives another one to number 3, and so on, in a circle, with, say, number 3 giving a cheque to number 1. You know how long cheques take to be processed and you time it so that each cheque can be fed in at the time when the debit is coming through the account. In this way, you can build up a large turnover of money going through your account without needing to have a great deal of money in the first place. The object is to impress your bank with what a lot of business you are doing, because he gives you an overdraft on the basis of your turnover. Naturally, the more people you have giving you cheques, the better it looks, because the manager might be a little suspicious ... Also you would be amazed at the number of people who will exchange cheques for you for a small percentage. My friends and some of the people I used to meet at the Club would exchange cheques for me at between one and five per cent of their face value, and I had four drivers and four cars permanently stationed at my command, all the time running around to pay in the cash to meet the cheques as they fell due. If you exchange your cheques for cash in this way, you

don't run the risk of being caught by a manager refusing to pay out against un-cleared effects. But the strain of doing this is terrible ... Not many people could do this with the accommodation cheques, for few people had the connections and could be trusted, and few people had the knowledge of the banking system that I had. For example, at that time, cheques drawn on and paid into Barclays Bank took one day less than the other banks. Sometimes, I would ask the bank manager to hold up the payment of a cheque until 11.30 the following morning, which I was quite entitled to do. In another case, I was introduced to this bank manager as a man of ability by a big client of his. I didn't pay him anything — he was just trying to help me. He couldn't give me an overdraft of more than £1,500, because that was his limit from his Head Office. But every day, I would arrive at the Bank before it opened, and we would spread out all the cheques that the company had to pay on the table, and sort them into groups. Some went for immediate payment, others were less urgent and were sent back 'effects not cleared', some with 'words and figures don't match', and still others we would tear slightly and send back 'cheque mutilated'. However, we always made sure that the cheques were paid the next time that they were presented, and in this way, we were never technically in default.

Bankers — especially in headquarters fraud and security departments — are very wary during the 1990s of kiting and of 'funny money' scams generally — partly as a conse-quence of regulations regarding money-laundering[10] — but these understandings may not be transmitted perfectly throughout the banking system to local managers, even though in the current competitive climate, managers who 'screw up' may find themselves in the redundancy queue. As banking has been depersonalised by the widespread use of credit scoring and tighter loan limits, corrupt or misled discretion by managers has been re-duced, but there is still some scope in the area of business lending and, if the fraudsters do not want to borrow money from the bank, the scope for deception remains. In still more sophisticated instances, stolen shares and bonds are used as collateral on bank loans, since not all banks always check the standing of such certificates, but more commonly may be made to create an illusion of affluence by the customer by him/her *not* using them as collateral, thereby reducing the risk of exposure to the bank and of their reporting the matter to the police: banker awareness has increased substantially during the 1990s, not least because false collateral may be used by the customer to inveigle the bank into unwit-tingly providing legitimacy for 'advance fee fraud' on other customers. Foreign banks can be used to delay payments, since they are outside the clearing system, but by the late 1990s, harmonisation of regulatory controls and anti-laundering provisions made it harder to start up or buy crooked banks in Western Europe: in the UK, for example, the Bank of England has been very rigorous in vetting the fitness and propriety of bank directors, though the European Banking Directive makes the system only as strong as its weakest link.

However, these developments in financial services regulation trouble the long-firm fraudster very little, since there is almost no control of who may set up in business and transfer liability to the company. All s/he must do is to tell a good story, and this is done both to banks and to trade victims in a way that has witnessed few changes in the past 30 years, as each new set of potential victims seeks to make its sales and in turn is lured into false optimism. For example, in the late 1960s, a man with an American accent arrived at a South Wales coastal resort and announced that he represented an American syndicate (sic!) which wished to purchase a leisure and amusement arcade in the town. He offered a generous price, which was accepted gratefully by the owners. Unfortunately, however, there was a small snag preventing immediate completion: the money was temporarily tied up. However, he asked the owners if, pending completion of the sale, they would allow him to order goods for the coming season; this request was acceded to, the owners even going so far as to give him their headed notepaper to use in ordering. He wrote off to a number of suppliers as if he already owned the arcades and obtained some £350,000 worth of fancy goods, toiletries and groceries on credit. One night all of these goods were covertly taken away, and the man disappeared for good. His identity remains unknown to this day.

Less audacious long firms, however, require a little more subtlety. Here is one from the early 1970s:

> I used to do this really good double act with Blank. I would be the baddie and he would be the goodie. A rep would come in from one of the suppliers and Blank would say that his stuff was fantastic, but I would say it was rubbish and I didn't want any of it. Blank would pretend to try to persuade me to take it, but I would storm out of the office, saying 'I don't want it, but if you do, you buy it. As far as I'm concerned, it's your responsibility'. I would switch on the intercom in the other room to hear what went on after I left, and on many occasions, the rep would actually bribe Blank to take the stuff.

Another organiser, who used to front his own frauds, made the following observations:

> The psychology of l.f.s is very important. I know that credit controllers and these trade protection societies are wise to the straight l.f. pattern of ever-increasing orders. So what I would do was to gradually increase orders at first, paying promptly, make one large order, pay, and then order little or nothing for a couple of visits by the rep. This would get him nice and worried, because he would think that maybe I'd found a better and cheaper line from a competitor ... Then, after a few gaps in my orders, I would put in a really big one coupled with a good excuse, like a half-page advert in the local paper, which I would show to the reps and tell them that my business was going like a bomb. Which it was, only they didn't realise that it was them who were going to be blown up ... You have to be a good judge of the right tactics to adopt with suppliers. Things don't always work out though. There was one case where I owed Schweppes £11,000, paid them, and put in an order for £25,000, but they stopped my credit. I could have screamed. Things have changed a lot, though, and gone are the days when you could set up your own grocery store, print letter headings, and coin the money. The suppliers have got too cute.

In order to be successful, the fraudster has to adapt his technique to the methods of control: he has to simulate the style of the sharp businessman and yet obtain large quantities of goods. Some trade representatives, however commission-hungry they may be, will not sell goods to people who appear to them to order recklessly, for this is a sign that payment is not intended; others are not so particular. In many cases, representatives do not seem to question why a firm should want such large quantities of their products, and believe that they have 'pulled a fast one' on the purchasers. This 'kidology' is part of the long-firm fraudster's tradecraft.

A further crucial aspect of his skill is the way the long-firm merchant organises the 'fronting' of his fraud. Some prefer their 'front men' to use their own names, because this gives a better impression if the business is investigated and court proceedings ensue. In other cases, however, particularly when the 'front man' has a criminal record, elaborate measures are taken to build up a false identity which will withstand all but the most thorough scrutiny by the police and by credit inquiry agencies. The aim here is twofold: to generate a respectable image for the 'front man' and to make it difficult for him to be traced after the fraud has been carried out. One organiser obtains a copy birth certificate from Somerset House, for preference selecting a child born to an unmarried domestic servant or barmaid from a high-mobility area. Thus, it will be very difficult for anyone to prove that the 'front man' is not the person he purports to be. The 'front man' then obtains accommodation in his false name near to the proposed area of business, and writes from that address to obtain a provisional driving licence. He (or a skilled driver using his name) then takes a driving test, thereby obtaining a driving licence in his new name and address. He may then buy a car, which will also have his new name and address on it. Consequently, anyone checking up on his background is likely to believe that everything is as it appears to be: everything about him fits together.

If the 'front man' does not possess previous business experience, he requires some training before he can 'pass' and deal with 'screamers', as angry creditors are called. In preparation for a vast *coup* of over one million pounds (at current prices), the 'front man' was given simulated situations in which he had to learn what to say to 'reps', when to say it, how to haggle with them so that it would appear that he was a sharp businessman, thereby allaying any suspicions that they might have. All this was done before he was introduced into the business, which had been built up in preparation for the fraud.

Another organiser would find people who were prepared to front a fraud in their own names, start up a business and train them *in situ*. He would place a tape recorder in the office and get them to record every single conversation that they had, whether on the telephone or in person. At the end of the day the 'front man', making sure that he was not followed, would bring over the tapes and they would go over them in detail, pointing out mistakes and making suggestions for improvements in technique. The length of these evening classes depended upon the ability and experience of the 'front man'. In general, however, there is some coaching with regard to the market for the goods, trade jargon and other allied matters: the 'front man' has to appear to be a principal.

Banks, tradespeople and credit inquiry agents may ask the 'front man' about his previous business experience, so he may have to put on a very convincing cover story, though modern developments of electronic databases and computer searches make the generation of false fronts that will withstand examination substantially harder in the 1990s than in previous times. Where such cover is not readily available, there may have to be a false explanation for his taking up business, such as 'I have just come back from South Africa/ Zimbabwe: there's no future there any more for us whites.' However well he builds up a false identity, though, he cannot be proof against chance contingencies which may penetrate his cover. It is the ability to withstand tests of cool and of character such as this which distinguishes classes of long-firm fraudster. It is a major element in their status system, as well as a source of considerable personal satisfaction.

Strategies to avoid arrest and conviction

'Front men' are usually expendable, though managing their expectations requires skill, lest they 'grass' the organisers to the police. Organisers may generate bogus transactions which are difficult to prove fraudulent. For example, the organiser may get a long firm going by operating 'upfront' for a while before appearing to sell the business, in the manner described earlier in this chapter. Even if he is seen on the premises *after* the transfer of ownership, he can claim that he was conned by the 'diabolical villains' into quite innocently helping them out in the running of his former business. Other bogus transactions are designed to protect those who 'fence' the long firm's goods. In some cases the purchasers are genuinely innocent of the fraudulent nature of the vendor of the goods. Henry[11] points out in his study of the resale of goods stolen from work that:

> Typically, then, goods are sold by ambiguous presentation; that is, the sale is accomplished by a gloss which relies on the fact that the purchaser will supply his own explanation of their origin ... With goods presented in this way, a person may feel morally free to go ahead and make a purchase.

This ambiguous presentation is far easier to carry out in the case of long-firm frauds than in more traditional types of property crime because the vendor has an apparently genuine trading concern and has a genuine title to the goods that he is selling. Even if goods are offered at below cost price, there are many circumstances in which traders do this quite lawfully, for example to get rid of unwanted stock when their cash flow is tight. In many cases, however, the goods are sold to people who do know that they are buying from a long firm. Here, there are two principal ways of protecting the 'fence' from subsequent prosecution.

- The fraudster may issue the 'fence' with an invoice marked up to the full market value of the goods. However, this is not the price actually paid, for the fraudster is paid a sum in cash that is agreed between him and the 'fence'. When the goods have been delivered and resold by the 'fence', the invoice is destroyed and there is nothing to link the fraudster to the 'fence', unless the police have been carrying out covert observational work or unless the fence and fraudster are 'grassed up' (which, especially if they are operating outside the criminal milieu, is unlikely).

- The fraudster may issue the 'fence' with an invoice marked up to the full value of the goods. In this case, however, instead of paying cash, the 'fence' pays the full amount by cheque, thus giving him hard evidence of bona fide purchase should an account be demanded of him subsequently by the police or the courts. In reality, the fraudster gives him a kickback in cash to make up the difference between the agreed and the phoney price.

These techniques help to protect the 'fence' considerably. The second method tends to be preferred, since although it exposes the identity of the purchaser, at least until all documentation is destroyed before the fraudsters abscond, it provides the semblance of a normal trading relationship and is proof against undercover police surveillance of the long firm. Furthermore, by helping the 'fence', they also provide security to the organisers, by removing a major incentive for 'fences' to 'grass', that is, the 'fence's' need to trade off the organisers in exchange for his own non-prosecution.

In many countries, throughout the century, a false or genuine burglary, robbery or a fire is sometimes used as a means of hiding the true nature of the fraudulent enterprise: in Northern Ireland, it might be put down to terrorist attacks, though this might attract unwelcome police interest. Burglary and truck hijacking have the advantage over arson that they require no capital outlay on the goods to be burned, but they can generate greater police suspicion than arson, particularly if the police are unable to pick up any trace of the allegedly stolen goods.

The final technique for avoiding conviction to be discussed here is the use of the voluntary liquidation to 'con' creditors. This is used only by the more sophisticated long-firm merchants, and was particularly popular during the 1950s and after the mid-1970s, when it gradually came to be replaced by the Individual Voluntary Agreement. A businessman may obtain, say, £100,000 worth of goods on credit. He sells them for about £70,000 cash, pockets £50,000 and leaves the remaining £20,000 in the business in the form of cash and goods. For some £5,000 he will buy approximately £30,000 of bankrupt stock from another trader, and get his accountant to write the value of these goods into his books of account as £50-60,000. With £15,000 in cash, and what appears to be £60,000 worth of goods, the businessman will try to get his creditors to agree to a voluntary liquidation. The deficiency will be explained by 'bad debts': he may arrange to receive cheques from a dummy company or even another long firm which conveniently bounce and remain unpaid. He may claim that a 'trusted employee' has disappeared with his funds or stock, or put the losses down to 'stock pilferage'. Finally, he may provide a rationale in the form of a fire or burglary, as mentioned in the previous section. Carried out with nerve and panache, and sometimes aided by corrupt accountants and provisional liquidators, this can be a highly profitable and risk-free technique. Much later the creditors will find out that the stock is not worth the book value, but after all, valuation is a difficult matter and values change! Mostly, creditors will 'put it down to experience', unless the police intervene on their own initiative on the basis of information received elsewhere. Even if the police try to do something about the suspected fraud, they may be unable to find a complainant. The voluntary liquidation long firm requires the ability to handle creditors and others 'upfront' and the acceptance of a lower *percentage* profit than the cruder 'bust-out' techniques. However, as the hypothetical example above demonstrates, it can combine profitability with relative safety to a degree that other modi operandi cannot.

This type of operation can be and is carried out in many areas of trade, but in the late 1970s it was particularly popular in the record business, where companies going 'bust' might sell their perfect stock for a good price in cash and replace them with almost worthless 'deletions' which they bought for a very low price. They then claim to the liquidator that these deleted records are their normal stock, if he takes the trouble to ask them. After the 1990s, the integrity and experience controls on who is able to obtain a licence as an Insolvency Practitioner will eventually weed out most of the crooks who used either to inspire or conspire with fraudsters: but the logic remains unchanged whereby insolvency practitioners have to ask permission from the creditors, who are reluctant to throw good money after bad and may even be suspicious of the liquidator's motives in asking for more money for themselves.

In order to become a top-class long-firm fraudster, the skills described in this chapter have to be refined until they become almost 'second nature' to the person concerned. Top-class fraudsters can judge within moments the strengths and weaknesses of the people with whom they are dealing, can sense when one of their partners is trying to 'con' them, and can adjust their public persona to the environment in which they operate. They will have had to improvise schemes and stories for the benefit of creditors, backers, partners and 'front men': social skills for the human jungle. The skills that he or she must have vary according to the routines of social and economic control — for example, credit scoring has reduced discretion and therefore certain forms of fraud that depend on interpersonal skills — but the amount of pain caused by long-firm fraudsters to any one victim (however 'multiple') is usually modest, and this conditions overall industry and police responses. In particular, the replacement of gangster-connected fraudsters — which attracted police interest — by businesspeople with no previous convictions for serious crime, combined with cutbacks in fraud squad strength, has reduced the likely down-side risk from the criminal justice system, placing more of a burden upon the commercial sector. Unlike shop thieves, long-firm fraudsters' pictures are seldom captured on CCTV, and they are more varied in their choice of victims and geographical areas of operation, so they are not amenable so readily to 'hot spots' prevention strategies. In the final analysis, their social skills also make raising the stakes harder, except where the estimated probability of being defrauded leads victim companies to make sufficiently frequent credit-rating requests to trigger industry-wide judgements of suspiciousness. The chances of this happening are inhibited by the lack of long-term memory in most corporate credit divisions, leading to a cyclical pattern in which the lessons of the past have periodically to be relearned, since *unless one does happen to be defrauded*, credit status requests will always be more expensive than making judgements internally, and the system needs larger patterns of data to be better at making judgements of bankruptcy fraud. Contemporary long-firm frauds require more money and sophistication for build-ups than was the case before the 1980s, but there will always be scope for those who are bored by the routines of ordinary business struggles and prefer to defraud, and for those who — faced with ruination of their dreams and lifestyle anyway — figure that they might as well try to 'save a few pennies for my wife and children' (or, in his case, over £1 million at current prices). They can always change their identities afterwards and do the same thing again in any of our names.

Notes

1   Michael Levi is Professor of Criminology at Cardiff University, 50 Park Place, Cardiff CF1 3AT.

2   Sutherland, E. (1937) *The Professional Thief: by a Professional Thief*. Chicago: University of Chicago Press.

3   Sutherland, E. (1949) *White Collar Crime*. New York: Holt, Rinehart and Winston.

4   For a recent attempt to pull some contemporary work together in this area, see Gill, M. (ed.) (1994) *Crime at Work*. Vol. I. Leicester: Perpetuity Press.

5   For a recent elaboration of the situational fraud prevention theories, see Clarke, R. and Homel, R. (1997) A Revised Classification of Situational Crime Prevention Techniques. In Labb, S. (ed.) *Crime Prevention at a Crossroads*. Cincinnati: Anderson; Clarke, R. (1997) Introduction. In Clarke, R. (ed.) *Situational Crime Prevention: Successful Case Studies*. New York: Harrow and Heston.

6   Levi, M. (1981) *The Phantom Capitalists*. London: Heinemann.

7   Levi, M., Bissell, P. and Richardson, T. (1991) *The Prevention of Cheque and Credit Card Fraud*. Crime Prevention Paper 26. London: Home Office; and Levi, M. and Handley, J. (1998) *The Prevention of Plastic and Cheque Fraud Revisited*. Research Study 182. London: Home Office.

8   McIntosh, M. (1975) *The Organisation of Crime*. London: Macmillan.

9   See Levi, M. and Pithouse, A. (forthcoming) *White-Collar Crime and its Victims: the Media and Social Construction of Business Fraud*. Oxford: Clarendon Press.

10   See Gold, M. and Levi, M. (1994) *Money-Laundering in the UK: an Appraisal of Suspicion-based Reporting*. London: Police Foundation.

11   Henry, S. (1978) *The Hidden Economy*. Oxford: Martin Robertson, p 57. For an excellent development of the stolen goods market and its implications, see Sutton, M. (1996) Supply by Theft. *British Journal of Criminology*. Vol. 35, No.3, pp 400-416.

Chapter 12

Drugs and Doors: Improving Door Security and Tackling Drug Dealing in Clubs and Pubs

Sheridan Morris[1]

Clubs and pubs which cater for young adults, especially those which are popular dance venues, face the risk of drug dealing taking place on their premises. Evidence suggests that door staff may be involved in such dealing in the premises they are employed to protect. The pressure is on for venue management to tackle such problems, or face investigations from their licensing authorities. This paper discusses models of door staff involvement in drug dealing, including associations with organised crime groups and drug dealers. Measures are discussed to ensure a 'clean' security team and to disrupt and deter drug dealing at venues.

Introduction

Drug taking and criminal doormen[2] have long been a source of concern for the police, local authorities, venue managers and customers themselves. A number of ongoing government initiatives aimed at tackling such problems, whilst good for many parties concerned, may require venues to change their security arrangements, and increase the risk of closure if they are found to be the focus of drug dealing. The *Public Entertainment Licences (Drug Misuse) Act 1997* has strengthened the police's ability to have night clubs closed by revoking or preventing the renewal of a venue's Public Entertainment Licence, as well as requiring a club to remain closed whilst it appeals against such a decision. In support of this act, the Home Office is developing guidelines for 'the health and safety of young people at dance venues' including the management of doormen and drug taking. It is essential, therefore, that organisations take measures to disrupt and deter drug dealing on their premises by increasing the chances of dealers and consumers being caught and arrested. In attempting to increase the risks to such offenders, managers will need to consider both their security procedures and staff. As this paper will show, the issue of staff selection is highly relevant to increasing the risk to criminals, being pertinent also to a Home Office review of the private security industry. This review will include the statutory regulation of doormen, and possibly the owners and managers of the companies that supply them. This paper will seek to illustrate the nature of the problems behind these initiatives and show managers and owners how to start addressing such concerns.

Drugs and clubs
Many businesses such as pubs, nightclubs and other entertainment venues frequented by a young adult customer segment face problems with drug consumption on their premises. The use of doormen is an established feature in such enterprises, in the belief that, as well as coping with troublemakers, they will help prevent the threat of drug dealing. In contrast, this paper will examine how door staff can be linked with drug dealing and organised crime groups, and the role they may play in facilitating drug dealing in the venues they are charged to protect. This paper does not seek to suggest that all doormen are involved in drug dealing; indeed, a good practice case study is presented, Club A in London, to illustrate effective security procedures and staff recruitment practices and the results a 'clean' security team can produce in tackling the presence of dealers in clubs. What this research does seek to show is how a legitimate enterprise — the protection of business premises and customers — can facilitate illegitimate activity — drug dealing — and can also itself be corrupted by criminal elements.

The involvement of door supervisors in drug dealing in venues was examined in a number of ways.[3] First, a review of police data identified drug-related operations against pub and club venues over a two-year period in the Merseyside and Northumbria police areas. Second, police records were reviewed to consider the extent of door supervisor involvement in drug dealing, violence and other offending. Third, interviews were held with police officers from a number of departments, including central crime teams, force intelligence officers and licensing units. Finally, a small number of club managers were interviewed. The limits of such, often anecdotal, information are acknowledged, but it is believed that the combined data sources provide a valuable insight into the complex and hidden world of the doors and drug trade.

The market that the criminal groups in this chapter are targeting developed during the mid-1980s with the emergence of the 'dance drug' scene amongst popular youth culture, representing a new front for both criminals and enforcement agencies, as well as problems for the owners and managers of clubs and pubs. The term 'venue' has been used to cover a variety of premises, including large warehouses, nightclubs and pubs or bars, especially those which feature music and a dance floor. In discussing the link between dance venues and drugs, the early term 'rave', frequently used to describe this type of leisure/musical milieu, is now misleading. The venue for this scene has grown extensively, the illegal warehouse parties of the 1980s giving way to permanent, legal locations. The combination of drug use with a strong dance orientation can now be found amongst attendees of high street nightclubs and disco bars.

A recent survey[4] provides some insight into this drug market. Ninety-seven per cent of those surveyed attending dance venues had taken an illegal drug at a dance venue. This is twice the level of drug use amongst 16-29 year olds found by the 1996 *British Crime Survey* (BCS).[5] These individuals were nine times more likely to have taken ecstasy (81%) and five times more likely to have taken amphetamines (81%) compared to the wider

BCS sample. In looking at drug use at the dance venues on the evening of the interview, four key drugs were identified: cannabis (59%), ecstasy (53%), amphetamines (39%) and LSD (16%). Ninety per cent of those who had ever taken a drug intended to do so that evening, suggesting that most were current users. Sixty-eight per cent named ecstasy as their favourite 'dance' drug, although the most popular 'general purpose' drug was cannabis (64%). Forty-six per cent of respondents generally bought from 'a dealer who sells regularly'. Whether such dealers were present inside venues was not reported by the survey, though numerous anecdotal reports and the results of police operations clearly indicate that dealers operate close to consumers inside the venues themselves. Of the remaining respondents, 50% bought drugs from 'a friend who did not sell regularly', though of course such friends have in turn to obtain the drugs from another source, possibly a dealer. Whatever the source, the picture is one of a high level of drug use amongst the type of customers attracted to night clubs found in every high street, not just specialist venues.

Doormen

A door supervisor has been defined by the Home Office as 'a person employed on premises which have a music and dancing licence [Public Entertainment Licence - PEL] in operation with authority from the owner or landlord, exclusively or mainly, to decide upon the suitability of customers to be allowed on those premises; and/or to maintain order on those premises'.[6] Exceptions to this are doormen who operate in non-PEL premises such as pubs. An important distinction amongst door supervisors, whatever their level of organisation, is between those registered with a local authority-run scheme and those who are not. Many local authorities in England and Wales now administer schemes which require individuals who wish to work as door security staff to meet certain standards with regard to training, the wearing of identity cards and the submission of any criminal conviction details. The granting of a Public Entertainment Licence by the issuing authority to venues such as nightclubs is conditional upon the employment of only approved registered door staff. Pub-type premises holding a publican licence, are generally outside this scheme as their 'liquor' licence is granted by local magistrates, who have not sought to attach such conditions to the granting of licences.[7]

Extensive discussions with detectives, uniformed officers and club managers, and consideration of police intelligence during the course of the research, led to the identification, detailed in Figure 1, of varying levels of organisation in the provision of door staff to licensed premises. Such models are to be found with both registered and unregistered doormen provision.

Links between clubs, drugs and doormen

The research identified varying degrees of door staff involvement in the availability of drugs — if not directly dealing themselves — within the premises they were charged with overseeing. The least 'active' role is that of turning a blind eye to drug-dealing activity, sometimes as a result of intimidation from drug dealers. A more involved role is played by door supervisors who, whilst not actually involved in the supply of drugs, receive payment — in cash or drugs — from dealers for allowing them to trade. This role may involve the removal of competing dealers not part of the organised protection. The most active, but perhaps least frequent, role played by door supervisors is that of a primary dealer, holding drugs for the floor dealers who actually sell the drugs to the customers. Once the floor dealer has sold his or her stock they will obtain further drugs from the door supervisor acting in a wholesaler role. The doorman may or may not hold enough merchandise for the whole evening, possibly having himself to obtain further supplies from a main drug dealer.

Figure 1: Levels of organisation in doormen provision

Individual employment. A venue may employ staff on a purely personal basis. Staff may be employed on a contract or non-contractual basis, individuals frequently being paid cash-in-hand on a nightly basis.

'Team' employment. A frequent form of organised security, a 'team' is retained to provide an agreed number of door staff at certain times at a specified venue. Such a team will normally, though not always, have a name and often a presence in two or more venues. Such a grouping will not be a legally registered company. A team's reputation and survival generally depend on the credibility of the key individual(s) who 'front' it and the relationships they have with other head door supervisors. Such teams tend to be employed on entertainment premises.

Security company employment. The most organised form of door supervision, with a level of management expertise beyond a 'head doorman' figurehead and registered company status. Such firms will generally control more venues than a team outfit, often the result of an aggressive drive for expansion, leading to inevitable clashes with smaller door security providers. Such firms may also be involved in other non-entertainment security provision such as construction sites and retail areas.

To illustrate the criminal nature of certain doormen, the backgrounds of 87 door supervisors[8] known to the police from previous and ongoing operations in the Merseyside and Northumbria force areas were examined. In relation to drug offences, six had been found guilty of possessing drugs; two of them twice, three others with further charges pending. Four others had received cautions for possession. One individual had been convicted of drug production, another of drug supply and another of conspiracy to supply; the doorman convicted of drug production had been a director of a security company (discussed below), whilst the individual charged with conspiracy to supply had been the head doorman of a nightclub in Liverpool. Eleven other individuals carried drug possession 'flags' on their files, indicating they were considered to be potentially in possession of drugs. In relation to other offences, these 87 individuals at the time of writing had between them 72 convictions for violence[9] and 27 more pending, including 3 murders, 3 attempted murders and 1 case of manslaughter. One had been convicted of witness intimidation, with another charge pending. Three individuals held firearm-related convictions, whilst six had been found guilty of offences relating to offensive weapons. Other convictions included arson, threats to kill, kidnap and false imprisonment, possessing counterfeiting equipment, possession of counterfeit currency, handling stolen property, selling CS canisters and illegal beer importation. Thirteen individuals carried warning 'flags' relating to violence, three to firearms and fifteen to the possession of weapons (other than firearms).

Whilst it is not suggested that these individuals represent 'typical' doormen, these profiles illustrate the scope of offending and capacity for violence that many criminal doormen possess, and it is these factors which make them a threat to legitimate enterprise.

Drugs in clubs
Criminal doormen, as individuals or part of a team or company, operate in venues run by the owners or professional managers. Discussions with police officers and club managers identified a number of scenarios regarding venue management involvement in drug dealing within premises they own, manage or are hiring as promoters. Managers may be:

•   unaware of drug dealing;
•   aware but not involved, and unable/unwilling, due to intimidation, to prevent drug dealing;
•   aware but not involved, happy to turn a blind eye to drug dealing; and
•   aware and involved in drug dealing.

A final scenario is one of club management aware of drug dealing within the premises, but committed to tackling it. An example of such good practice will be discussed later, after further examination of links between doormen and drug dealing.

To illustrate the nature of the problem in certain venues, police records were examined to identify the response of two large forces. During the two-year period from January 1995 to December 1996, around 32 drug-oriented operations, including surveillance-only jobs, were undertaken against pubs and nightclubs in the Merseyside and Northumbria areas. Eighteen such operations involved raids on premises, all resulting in numerous arrests. Ten of the raids were against nightclubs, the rest being pubs, hotels and an entertainment complex. Examples are given in Table 1.

If a venue becomes the focus for drug dealing, these examples illustrate the scale and impact of police operations targetted against them. Such raids generate a lot of bad publicity, often facilitated by the police, for a venue and its owners and such clubs may not re-open unless under new management or ownership.

Having illustrated the nature of the problem faced by the police and many managers in terms of drug dealing in dance venues and the criminal nature of many security providers, the following case studies detail two examples of the form that links between door security and drug dealing may take and how they are shaped by local factors.

Table 1: Drug operations against venues in Merseyside and Northumbria 1995-96

Operation 1(1996): Ten weekends of observations and test purchases were made to identify dealers in a club. External video surveillance assisted in identifying target individuals. On the night, undercover officers detained dealers inside the club as 120 uniformed officers executed the raid. Thirteen individuals were arrested for drug possession and supply. Four have been convicted as of September 1997.

Operation 2 (1996): A four-month operation led to a raid and 11 arrests for drug possession and supply. Eleven door supervisors were charged with violent disorder. £2,000 worth of drugs were recovered.

Operation 3 (1995): A nine-month operation identified 20 floor dealers, overseen by door supervisors. Twenty-two individuals, one of whom was the head of security, were charged with drug-related offences including intent and conspiracy to supply. Thirteen individuals were found guilty, including one door supervisor. Charges against the remaining door staff are pending.

Operation 4 (1995): A three-month operation identified an ecstasy factory above a public house. Five individuals were convicted for conspiracy to supply, with prison sentences of up to 14 years.

Operation 5 (1995): Test purchases were made every weekend for three months in one club. On the night of the raid, 30 undercover officers were inside the premises to detain 10 targetted dealers. Seventeen arrests led to 15 convictions for the supply of ecstasy and amphetamine, with prison sentences of 3-5 years.

'Control the doors, control the floors': two case studies

Merseyside
In December 1993 Merseyside Serious Crime Squad began a major operation against a highly organised 'drugs and doors' crime group. An established guarding outfit, Company A, had been taking over the provision of door security at numerous entertainment venues in Liverpool city centre and the surrounding area. A registered company, known as a provider of security in the local construction and retail sectors, it had not previously come to the attention of the police. Its swift displacement of existing door security firms was engineered by making a cash payment to key incumbent door supervisors to secure their services — physical intimidation and violence was meted out to those who refused.

Licensees who refused to accept their services were threatened with disturbances on their premises. The company appeared to be run by two key directors, one of whom was known to the police. This individual — brother one — was considered, along with two brothers (two and three), to be involved in drug dealing and club security. The other director was the original owner of the firm. Information received from an informant indicated that the company's door supervisors either sold drugs in the premises they regulated or otherwise vetted and took a cut from — 'taxed' — other dealers operating within 'their' premises. The philosophy of this approach is given in the expression 'control the doors, control the floors'.

The scale of the drug dealing overseen by Company A, with its large share of the club and pub door supervision, and the contacts it had in the region's drug supply fraternity made the organisation unusual in that it controlled access to a significant drug market, as well as being largely responsible for supplying that market. During eight months of surveillance little was initially gained as the suspects were very surveillance-conscious. However, a number of incidents contributed to the disruption and termination of Company A's activities. For example, following informant intelligence, brother one (a director of the company) was arrested after making a major drugs purchase from an associate in Sunderland. The transaction was observed and the offender was later stopped by a motorway traffic unit, who found 250 ecstasy tablets in the car. Whilst on bail for this offence, informant intelligence again enabled the observation of another drugs purchase by brother one, some months later. Once more, the strike was undertaken by a team other than the surveillance officers, so as to avoid alerting the targets to the police surveillance operation. This time, a search of the vehicle found 2,000 ecstasy tablets, whilst another 1,000 were found in a search of his home, along with an amount of cocaine and heroin. Brother one received eight years after pleading guilty to conspiracy to supply drugs, thus fortunately avoiding any disclosure of the police surveillance operations. The Sunderland associate who supplied the drugs received four years for possession and the supply of drugs. Finally, in January 1995, police arrested a number of individuals in a day of raids in the Merseyside area and charged them with a number of drug-related offences. Charges were also brought for arson, relating to the destruction of the company's offices in an attempt to disrupt an ongoing tax investigation by Her Majesty's Customs and Excise. Brother two and two doormen were sentenced to three years for arson. Following the discovery of £12,000 in his loft, brother three, who had acted primarily as a drugs courier for the company, received nine months after pleading guilty to the concealment of drug trafficking money. His car and the money were also confiscated under the 1986 Drug Trafficking Offences Act. Another director is still awaiting trial for the £250,000 VAT fraud.

With the removal of Company A, a void was created in the door security and drug dealing markets. As expected, there was an increase in inter-door supervisor rivalry, with numerous teams vying to take up the opportunities in the market place. Within 12-15 months of the cessation of Company A, Company B emerged as a major force in door security in Merseyside, Warrington, Manchester and Southport. The catalyst for this rapid expansion was the need for door supervisors in pubs during the summer of 'Euro 96', when inordinately large numbers of customers presented potential public order problems for licensees. Three key figures involved in the running of Company B's door operations were identified as being former head supervisors under Company A. Again, this organisation is a registered company, although the focus is purely on entertainment venues. During 1997 a number of incidents occurred as door supervisors from Company B clashed with those of other teams, including the non-fatal shooting of a number of prominent door supervisors at work and drive-by shootings of their homes. The partner of one security firm which resisted the loss of one of its contracts to Company B was subsequently stabbed, allegedly, according to various doormen, by door supervisors from Company B. The fallout from these tensions and the proactive approach by Merseyside Police has led to a second operation, ongoing at the time of writing.

Newcastle-upon-Tyne
Door security was found to be less organised than in Merseyside, doormen operating predominantly as individuals or relatively informal 'teams'. There was little evidence of general door provision by registered companies other than at the largest of clubs, nor was there evidence that any single provider of doormen had a dominant control of the door business — drug related or otherwise — within the force area, although a handful of individuals were considered key players. In the absence of a dominant security team, the link between doormen and drug dealing did exist, but was more indirect and on a smaller scale than that found in Merseyside. The picture that has emerged is one of drug-based criminal[10] groups providing relatively few door supervisors directly themselves but forcing existing door supervisors, through intimidation and extreme violence, to allow 'approved' drug dealers to operate in the premises under their supervision, sometimes even requiring the doormen to pay them a 'tax' for running a door. One estimate by local officers was that no more than 10% of door supervisors were selling drugs themselves, working for drug dealers as door supervisors or actually receiving a tax from dealing within venues they controlled.

This situation may be seen as a product of various local factors, including the absence of a criminal grouping with the inclination, and commercial and management acumen, to develop a significant door security operation. Another factor was the introduction of a door supervisor registration scheme by Newcastle City Council in 1990, which prohibited a number of key criminals from continuing as door supervisors in the city area. This had led to what the police identify as two distinct categories of door supervisors, registered and unregistered, the latter maintaining an influence in the city centre by intimidating the former, sometimes acting as the 'hidden hand' behind teams of registered doormen. The loose nature of such teams and the lack of registered company details, allows organised criminals and violent individuals to remain involved in 'legitimate' door supervision in this manner.

An example of good practice

Club A (fictitious name) is one of the major dance clubs in London. Despite its prominence in the UK dance music scene, its owner has consistently sought to tackle the drug consumption associated with large dance clubs. The risk to offenders has been increased by the adoption of a partnership approach with the local police and vigorous action by the club itself. The club has a reputation amongst dealers and drug users as a venue which is anti-drugs, in contrast to the more tolerant atmosphere of many similar venues, although the management freely admit that the dealing within its premises can never be fully prevented. The basis of the partnership approach between the club management and the police is a code of practice, established in 1995, for dealing with drug offences. The code increases the risk to dealers through encouraging security staff to arrest and detain those in possession of drugs. The security staff and management are assisted in making such arrests by police training on common drug offences and the powers of citizen's arrest, and an agreement that the police will respond quickly to a request for assistance following a citizen's arrest. Despite the code, the real basis of co-operation between both parties are informal meetings, which occur at least once a month between the local police inspector and the club's management.

The club employs a security team to secure the club entrance and search customers as they enter, whilst another floor team patrols the interior of the venue. All security staff are linked by radio and individuals rotate positions throughout the evening. As well as responding to any problems within the club such as fights, the internal security team is charged with actively searching out floor dealers who have escaped the body search by the door team. When such an offender is identified the security team will make a citizen's arrest and inform the police. The police have provided basic training in evidential requirements to the security staff, covering issues such as hearsay and continuity of evidence. Occasionally, the security staff will patrol the streets in the vicinity of the club, especially if there have been any problems, or at the informal request of the police. Concerns are drug dealing, disorderly or disruptive behaviour by clubbers and thefts from the cars of clubbers who park nearby. Security staff report any suspicious behaviour to the police.

To undermine possible links between the door staff and local drug dealers, half the door team, including the head of security, is brought in weekly from the West Midlands. The club adopted this approach after problems with their original, locally recruited, door team. The club management monitors the performance of the security staff by indicators such as the number of citizen's arrests made within the club. Finally, the club uses the occasional 'mystery clubber' approach to test security procedures and the level of general service within the club.

As well as handing over suspected drug dealers to the police on a regular basis, the club is keen to work with the police when it suspects problems which are beyond its resources. During the summer of 1997, the police undertook a number of test purchase operations, at the club's request, against dealers in the club who it was believed were part of an oriental drugs group. When such operations strike, the club is keen to publicise its support and co-operation with the police. As well as seeking to prevent the tarnishing of the club's reputation with local magistrates and the police, they wish also to deter other potential dealers.

By the entrance to the club, where individuals are searched, is a secure letterbox-type facility (the 'amnesty' box) where suspicious items seized from individuals — such as a pill — are disposed of on a no-questions-asked basis. The box is emptied about once a month by the police, the contents being recorded and then destroyed. Figure 2 details items recovered by the police from the box.

Figure 2: Seizures from the Club A amnesty box, 1 June - 21 August 1997 (number)

22	capsules of brown powder	3	reefers
15	wraps of white powder	2	bags of herbal cannabis
61	white pills	1	piece of cannabis resin
17	coloured pills	6	bags of white powder
21	shaped tablets	4	bags of brown powder
2	'pebble' - type pills	1	tear-gas canister

If an individual is found with a more significant amount of suspected drugs on their person or in their bag, or is spotted dealing in the club, they will be arrested and detained by the club security. During an 18-month period, from June 1995 to November 1996, 46 incidents were recorded by the club, involving a total of 67 arrests for possession of drugs. Of those arrested, eight were women, eight individuals were described as working as pairs and two 'teams' of three or more dealers were arrested. Among the 40 arrests where the amount seized was given, 18 individuals were found to be in possession of 20 tablets or more, the largest amount being 84 tablets. Records indicate the seizure of over 761 tablets, 7 wraps containing white powder, 1 bag of white powder and 7 bags of suspected herbal cannabis. Twenty-seven arrests also led to the recovery of additional unspecified amounts of drugs.

Lessons on increasing the risk to offenders

As the activity of organised criminal groups and dealers occurs on a number of levels — by doormen, against doormen, within venues — so measures to tackle them must also be multifaceted and seek to increase the risk to those involved at each level of offending. There are three foci.

(i)   The drug market: A number of venue-based measures can help disrupt the selling of drugs within venues. Such disruption of the market increases the risk to dealers and their associates, including doormen.

(ii)   Door supervisors and venue management: Venue-based measures and the regulatory actions of police and local authorities can be brought to bear on the standards of security staff and club managers. Such measures can help to prevent or restrict the actions of those overseeing and facilitating dealing in venues.

(iii)   Door security provision and organised crime: Longer-term police operations are

needed to challenge the corrupting influence of drug dealing on the legitimate function of door supervision. The groups behind door teams, and their relationship to
the drug trade, can best be identified by drawing upon intelligence from a number
of police resources, and information from venue managers and owners.

Measures should deter criminal behaviour by doormen and drug dealers, (affiliated to the
security team or not) by not only increasing the risk of detection, but also by disrupting
and reducing their opportunities for crime.

Increasing the risk to criminal doormen
An essential first step is to employ only registered doormen where possible. Although
they are rarely required for non-PEL venues such as pubs, such premises undoubtedly
experience problems with doormen and drug dealing. As well as employing staff with
basic professional training, a PEL venue is generally required to record the names of all
door staff working each night.[11] Such a measure prevents staff from claiming not to have
worked a particular night if an incident takes place, a frequent occurrence when the police
attempt to investigate problems. Even registered staff should preferably be employed from
a registered security company. As a 'genuine' commercial operation, such companies may
be considered less inclined towards criminal involvement and are easier for police to
investigate if required. Good firms may also rotate security staff among venues (preventing local involvement) and maintain discipline amongst the door staff, something venue
managers may find difficult.

The need for a greater scrutiny of both doormen and their suppliers may increase as a
result of possible changes to the regulation of the security industry. If such regulation
occurs, then any venue which employs individuals in a door supervisor capacity may
require them to be trained and registered with a formal body. Security company directors
or managers may also be required to meet certain conditions regarding an absence of
defined criminal convictions. Whilst customers are not yet in a position to confirm the
honesty of their security suppliers, checking with other customers and the police may
provide an informal indicator of any problems or concerns, until the new regulatory structure is in place. Although many security firms may be considered 'respectable', unwitting
involvement with a criminal firm could lead to major problems. Whilst the predominant
role in investigating and tackling criminal doormen, especially those involved in larger
organised criminal groups, lies with the police, an awareness of the broader concerns will
inform corporate in-house security teams and venue managers and owners. Managers,
especially those with multiple outlets, should maintain a watching brief on organisations
providing security. Areas to watch for are significant changes in door contracts and large-
scale door provision by a single individual, team or company. Given the territorial and
volatile nature of much door security, ousted teams or individuals may retaliate against
the new doormen or venue management. As a criminal firm expands its share of the
market so it is able to increase its control. The implications of such control are its ability
to:

- intimidate other doormen;
- intimidate venue managers; and

• control and develop drug selling within venues.

As with Company A in Merseyside, the sheer number of door staff the company was able to call upon enabled it to intimidate and neutralise other door providers. Venue managers then had little choice over who to choose for their door security, leading to a further strengthening of the organisation's position. As well as remaining informed of who is working where, security managers should try and be aware of any criminal figure(s) behind a door team; as was found in Northumbria, there exists the possibility of registered door teams being controlled by unregistered individuals, barred from registration. Registered companies are required to register their directors and the information easily obtainable from Companies House in Cardiff.

Another factor to consider when choosing a door security supplier is their ability to provide doormen that reside outside the area where they are to be deployed. It is less likely that non-local security staff will be involved in the drug dealing scene due to lack of contacts, and they are less susceptible to intimidation as they live outside the area. There are, however, benefits in employing some local door staff as their knowledge of individuals can be valuable in identifying local criminals. A split team also prevents any single team from establishing a dominant grip on the venue. Each team may act as check on the actions of the other and represent a resource for management if a problem arises with doormen from the other security crew. It should not be assumed from the occasional arrest or seizure by door security that they are not involved in drug dealing within the premises. Such incidents often serve to mislead the police by merely offering up the odd unprotected dealer, whilst countering the competing dealers.

Organisations should review their own management structure and training, especially in larger clubs. Venue managers should be supported by at least one managerial assistant. A strong management team permits a greater presence in the club and provides mutual support in overseeing the door team. The potential for intimidation of managers should not be underestimated. As was found with one brewery/leisure organisation, inexperienced managers or licensees should receive basic training on drugs awareness and how to manage door staff.

Increasing the risk to drug dealers inside premises
Venue management need to be aware of the techniques employed by dealers, their associates and criminal doormen, so as to increase the chances of intercepting them. In larger venues, dealing teams may number as many as 10-12 individuals, often with defined roles eg primary dealer, floor dealer, referrer, spotter/protection. A few points to consider are:

• Females are reported as increasingly bringing drugs into clubs (due to the absence of, or cursory, searching) and may also work the floor, referring customers to a dealer in a fixed, less exposed location.

• Any organised dealing operation will invariably feature floor dealers holding only a small amount of drugs. These individuals will restock from a primary dealer who will also generally adopt a fixed, less exposed location. The drugs may not be kept on the individual in case of his/her interception by security staff.[12]

- Dealing teams may also separate the holding of cash and drugs, minimising the loss if one individual is identified.

- Solitary or floor dealers may adopt a certain 'trade mark' to identify themselves as dealers. Such signals are not obvious to the uninformed and constantly evolve. Previous examples include the blowing of a whistle or the flourishing of a fan when 'open for business'.

Once a secure door team is in place, an effective anti-drugs policy requires a considered strategy and tactics for them to follow. Such a policy should preferably be drawn up in consultation with the local licensing authority and the police (as with Club A). Management should define and communicate to all security staff clear guidelines on searching and carrying out citizens' arrests and how to record incidents. In drawing up guidelines for staff, organisations should seek to engender a relationship with the local police, a liaison which may be formalised with a mutually agreed code of practice, as with Club A. Contact allows management concerns regarding door staff, drug dealing or other matters to be communicated to the police. Also, the effectiveness of citizens' arrests by venue security and managers can be greatly aided by basic police training regarding evidential issues and the recording of statements. Such training sessions may also be a two-way process, where officers learn from the door supervisors the latest dealing methods.

Where appropriate, everyone entering the event should be liable to a search of outer clothing, pockets and bags, carried out by a door supervisor of the same sex. Ideally, searches should be complemented by the use of metal detectors to deter the carrying of weapons, and to reassure customers. Door staff do not have the right to insist on performing a body search, and consent must be established, possibly by a prominent notice at the entrance. Seized drugs or offensive weapons must be immediately handed over to the licensee for secure storage until they are handed over to the police. Seizures should be witnessed by the management and recorded in an incident book. Although door staff may only occasionally seize drugs from club-goers or dealers entering venues — though a deterrent effect will be generated — further interception is possible by patrolling the club floor. Seizures and arrests made at Club A indicate what can be done. Such incidents should be recorded and possibly looked upon as an indicator of security staff's vigilance. Where no attendant is present, toilets should be regularly patrolled by security, with guidelines formulated for when it is appropriate for staff to try to enter a cubicle and when assistance should be sought.

A venue's anti-drugs stance, with its policy on searching visitors and arresting dealers should be strategically and prominently placed at the entrance. Notices should tell customers that the police will be informed in the event of individuals being found in possession of controlled substances or offensive weapons. Any policy on non-entry and ejection should be on display to reduce the likelihood of arguments with staff.

Two specific techniques which may have a deterrent impact are the installation of CCTV and the use of private sniffer drug dogs. CCTV can be particularly useful for the surveillance of the entrance to a venue, though its effectiveness within the darkened confines of a club is severely limited. Taped material may confirm the presence of individuals on a given night and may record the associates of suspects. A relatively new initiative in club security is the provision by private security firms of sniffer dogs. Such dogs are deployed to inspect queuing club-goers and even inside the venue. Again, although their final effectiveness has yet to be proven, they may constitute a highly visual deterrent.

Conclusion

Many of the points made here embody basic security management principles, adding not only security to an enterprise but also efficiency and effectiveness to its overall operations. Registered doormen will invariably be better trained than unregistered ones, better at customer relations and invaluable in a basic medical incident. The logging of incidents, documented policies and a stronger management team will help improve the overall management of a venue and encourage the establishment of basic administrative systems for other aspects of the enterprise. The threat of drug dealing and criminal doormen is significant and will represent an increasing risk to the type of venues discussed here, as the local and central government statutory measures are implemented. Effective managers will start to consider the concerns highlighted in this paper now, or run the risk of a possible encounter with their licensing magistrates, local authority, police, or worst of all, the criminal elements discussed above.

Notes

1   This paper is based on research conducted by the author during 1997 (Morris, forthcoming), whilst a Research Officer at the Police Research Group, Home Office, Queen Anne's Gate, London E3 2UT.

2   The term 'doormen' has been adopted in this research. Although female door staff do exist, they are infrequent and found predominantly in larger premises where they are required to search women.

3   A particularly detailed, albeit anecdotal, insight into these links can be found in O'Mahoney (1997) *So This is Ecstasy?*, Edinburgh and London: Mainstream Publishing.

4   Release (1997) *Release Drugs and Dance Survey: An Insight into the Culture*. Release: London.

5   Home Office (1997) *Drug Misuse Declared in 1996: Key Results from the British Crime Survey*. Research Findings No. 56. London: Home Office.

6   Home Office (1995) *Home Office Circular 60/1995 (Registration Schemes for Doormen)*. London: Home Office.

7   At least one exception (from February 1997) being Manchester Licensing Justices, who, at the request of the police, attach to all new liquor licences a requirement for only regis-

tered door supervisors to be engaged where door security is required.

8   These individuals, thus, do not represent a randomised representative sample of registered door supervisors.

9   Offences included assault, ABH, GBH, wounding, violent disorder and affray.

10   Such criminals were known also to be involved in armed robbery and other offences to fund their drug-dealing operations.

11   The specific requirements attached to a PEL vary with each issuing local authority. Examples of the requirement to record periods of duty (when worked) were found in the licensing conditions of St Helens, Wigan and Newcastle City Council. The author was informed by local officials that such a requirement is common to all PELs granted by authorities with doormen registration schemes.

12   In one incident the primary dealer took up position sitting on a giant speaker cabinet. After his removal by security, his 'stash' was found inside the speaker cabinet, but could not be conclusively linked to him.

Chapter 13

Bad Goods: Product Counterfeiting and Enforcement Strategies

Jon Vagg and Justine Harris[1]

Product counterfeiting has grown in scope, scale and complexity in the last two decades, and now affects almost every area of manufacturing and retailing. However, the problems and issues posed by counterfeits vary greatly across different industrial sectors. This chapter illustrates the complexity of the current situation with special reference to videos and the fashion industry, and argues that the nature of the problem in each industry depends on the structure of that industry itself. Moreover, the diversity of these problems means that the enforcement of trading standards has become a complex business. Drawing on interviews with trading standards officers and others, the chapter concludes with an overview of the prospects for anti-counterfeiting enforcement strategies.

Introduction

The figures are unreliable, but every source concerned with the issue of counterfeit products contends that the scope and scale of counterfeiting has grown enormously since the mid-1970s. Twenty years ago the problem in the UK, for example, existed primarily in relation to fashion accessories and perfumes, where poor-quality fakes were typically sold on street markets or by hawkers. In other manufacturing and retail sectors, such as car spares and toys, there were sporadic flurries of concern — often, in the case of toys, in the run-up to Christmas each year — but few people perceived counterfeiting as a pervasive and long-term threat. By the 1990s, the problem had mushroomed. Counterfeit videos, a major problem for the film industry in the 1980s, had peaked and begun to decline, yet this had been offset by increasing problems across the whole range of retail goods, including, in particular, the fashion industry.

The first part of this chapter deals with the problem of numbers. It outlines the available sources of information on counterfeiting and the difficulties of interpreting the figures they produce. It argues, nonetheless, that there remain good grounds for believing that levels of counterfeiting have increased. The second section argues that the nature of the problem varies between different industrial sectors and suggests that the reason for this may lie with the differing structures of those industries. The final part of the chapter considers problems of law enforcement and concludes, rather gloomily, that these are extensive and unlikely to be solved in the near future.[2]

The counterfeiting problem: laws and numbers

Product counterfeiting is not a new problem. The oldest documented cases of goods bearing manufacturers' marks come from Roman and Greek archaeological sites,[3] and though documented cases of goods being falsely marked are of much more recent origin, they nonetheless indicate that counterfeiting has a long history.[4]

The basic issue in product counterfeiting is simple, even if the law enforcement problems can quickly become complex. In broad terms, a counterfeit is an item that in its appearance, packaging, labelling or in any other way appears to be made by or with the permission of a company that in reality has no connection with it. In legal terms, the counterfeiter has illegally appropriated another company's copyright (eg in the case of videos), design (eg in the case of fabrics), patent (where an item of process has been patented), or trade mark (the brand name or logo). This is so even if there is no 'genuine' item on the market, as might be the case where a pop group's record company has not licensed the use of the group's logo on particular kinds of fashion items. The specific legal provisions for these categories of intellectual property vary in different countries, but in the UK the primary pieces of legislation are the Trade Descriptions Act 1968, the Copyright, Designs and Patents Act 1988, and the Trade Marks Act 1994.

The Trade Marks Act 1994 was the result of lobbying at a national level for stronger sanctions against counterfeits, and the need to incorporate some European directives and international conventions on trade marks and intellectual property into domestic law. Its civil provisions, actionable by individual companies, enable trade mark owners to apply to a court for infringing goods to be seized and destroyed (SS.14-16 and 19). Criminal offences defined in the Act include the unauthorised use of trade marks or marks likely to be mistaken for them, along with the sale, hire, possession, or control of infringing items in the course of business (S.92). The maximum penalty on summary conviction is six months' imprisonment and/or a fine. On indictment, it is ten years' imprisonment and/or a fine.[5]

The Copyright, Designs and Patents Act 1988 contains civil remedies and criminal offences in relation to copyright and patents. These include making infringing material for sale or hire, or exhibiting or distributing it (S.107). This is a summary offence subject to a maximum penalty of six months' imprisonment and/or a fine.[6] The civil procedures (SS.96-103) provide copyright owners and exclusive licensees with rights to damages, injunctions, court orders for the confiscation of infringing material, and the right to seize infringing items 'exposed or otherwise immediately available for sale or hire'.

The Trade Descriptions Act 1968 has been to some extent superseded by these two Acts. It was originally intended to prevent the use of misleading advertising and sales material, and the main offence it creates relates to the application of a false description to any goods, or the supply of falsely-described goods (S.1). A false description in the terms of this Act includes any misleading statement about the product's size, composition, fitness for use, conformity with standards, etc. Hence the Trade Descriptions Act was used for some years as a way of dealing with counterfeits, though there was a loophole by which the sale of counterfeit goods explicitly labelled 'fakes' or 'copies' could not be seen as misdescription.

In summary, the 1988 and 1994 Acts toughened the legal regime pertaining to intellectual property. They created new offences, increased the penalties available for counterfeiting, and provided companies with more extensive rights to investigate counterfeiting of their products, have infringing goods seized and destroyed, and claim compensation. Nor has the UK been alone in following this path: international agreements — most notably TRIPS — commit all member countries to develop their trade mark protection regimes.[7]

Much of this legislative activity has been fuelled by a sense that counterfeiting has become a significant component of domestic commerce in many countries, and indeed of world trade. However, it is almost impossible to put reliable figures on the level of counterfeiting activity for much the same reason that it is impossible to make accurate estimates for trafficking in drugs: our knowledge is based largely on estimates derived from known cases that constitute an unknown proportion of all cases.

Table 1 illustrates the level of discrepancy between different estimates. Counterfeiting may cost US companies anything between US$ 60 and 200 billion per year, though the same upper and lower figures are also often cited in relation to world-wide losses. These figures for 'losses' are suspect in the first instance because they tend to assume that a legitimate item would have been sold in place of each counterfeit actually sold. Equally if not more seriously, most of these estimates are based on assumptions about the percentage of counterfeit goods in US and world trade export markets. The IACC figure appears to have been based on a guess that it accounted for 4% of the world trade export market, itself thought in 1995 to be worth about US$ 5,000 billion. The Counterfeiting Intelligence Bureau (CIB), a specialised division of the International Chamber of Commerce, has meanwhile argued that counterfeits have accounted for an increasing percentage of world trade, from 3% in 1992 to 5-7% in 1997[8] — and if we apply the higher percentage to the US$ 5,000 billion figure for world trade we would have an estimate for world-wide losses due to counterfeiting of US$ 350 billion. One cause of discrepancy, however, may be to do with subsequent misinterpretations of the IACC figure. When John Bliss, President of the IACC, quoted his figure for losses to 'legitimate businesses', some commentators seem to have assumed that it related only to American companies and others that it covered businesses world-wide.[9]

However, whatever disagreements authors have as to the scale of counterfeiting, they all agree that it has been increasing and is continuing to do so. To be sure, this agreement is based largely on the perceptions of Trading Standards officers, trade associations and alliances, and company executives — but everyone we have so far interviewed has been unanimous and, moreover, base their perceptions on quite different sources of information, from street markets to analyses of company sales figures.

Table 1. Estimates of losses due to counterfeiting

Year	Basis for estimate	Annual loss (US $)	Source and remarks
1982	US	5.5 billion	Wittenburg and Overend[10]
1988	US	24 billion	Cordell et al, reporting figures from US International Trade Commission[11]
1991	US	60 billion	*Fortune* magazine, 27 May 1996
1995	Legitimate businesses	200 billion	International Anti-Counterfeiting Coalition (IACC) testimony to US Senate hearing.
1995/6	US	200 billion	Weinburger,[12] Wittenburg and Overend[13]
1995/6	World-wide	200 billion	Counterfeiting Intelligence Bureau[14]
1996/7	US	60 billion	National Law Centre for Inter-American Free Trade[15]

Patterns of counterfeiting

Anything that can be made can be copied, and in principle the only attribute a product needs to be considered fair game for counterfeiters is attractiveness to consumers.[16] Most consumers tend to be aware that counterfeit clothing, watches, and perfumes are available in the market place. These categories were mentioned by approximately two-thirds of those questioned in a recent public survey.[17] However, Trading Standards officers in the UK have seized counterfeit items ranging from clothes and watches to alcohol, toys, car parts, and beer-making equipment. A review by the Counterfeit Intelligence Bureau in 1997 used information from a variety of reported cases of counterfeit seizures across the world to suggest a hierarchy of the most commonly counterfeited articles, of which the top three categories were computer software, audio-visual material (audio and video tapes and CDs), and toys. Surprisingly, fashion items were not included as a category, though information from Trading Standards officers indicates that this is probably now the most common type of counterfeit item they encounter. Finally, we should bear in mind that counterfeits have been discovered even in such unlikely areas as detergents and pesticides.

Although counterfeiting is clearly widespread, the major categories of commonly counterfeited products do exhibit their own distinct patterns. Indeed, the practices of the counterfeiters and their consumers appear to vary depending on the organisation and the structure of the vulnerable industry. The comments below illustrate this point with reference to two industries that appear to be polar opposites in most significant respects: motion pictures and fashion.

Facing FACT: counterfeiting in the motion picture industry

The idea of the 'motion picture' does not adequately convey the complexity of this industry. Films are made and shown in cinemas, but then distributed to video rental shops and are ultimately sold to the public, and also to terrestrial, satellite and cable TV companies.

Most industry and Trading Standards sources are agreed that product piracy became common in the video sector of the market in the early 1980s, as the proportion of homes with video recorders rose quickly. Early pirate tapes were often of technically poor quality and came without packaging of any kind. They were sold from market stalls and mobile shops, hawked around pubs, and sold or rented out from 'under the counter' in video rental shops. Indeed, since they did not purport to be genuine, they probably cannot be described as 'counterfeit' in the true meaning of the term. One Trading Standards officer we interviewed pointed out that there was a sense, in those days, that video companies were inadvertently encouraging copyright piracy by video rental shops because most films had a limited 'shelf life'; distributors were not necessarily quick at delivering new titles; and in any case video shops pay a great deal more per copy than high street outlets charge the public. In short, it made economic sense for rental outlets to keep one or two 'unofficial' copies of popular films to meet demand. However, within the space of a few years many of these problems had been addressed, while the problem had moved from pirate copies to 'real counterfeits', that is goods that appeared to be genuine, including the simulation of some security devices on video labels and packaging and the inclusion of the anti-piracy advertising that distributors began to put at the beginning of their tapes. This shift was possible because the quality of copies improved greatly due to the increased availability of professional high-speed tape copying equipment, while newly-available colour photocopiers could be used to create packaging.

Increasingly, the manufacture of counterfeits, while still a 'cottage industry' in the sense that a rack of copying machines could easily be accommodated in a small room in a house or flat, was on a scale that made it economic to have labels and packaging professionally printed. In addition, it became common for counterfeit tapes to be on the market before the legitimate product and in some cases even before the film had opened in UK cinemas, thus damaging cinema receipts.[18] As the market grew through the 1980s, however, three other issues emerged. One was that unscrupulous counterfeiters would simply print the packaging and insert blank tapes. Another was that since the producers of counterfeits were often also involved in the distribution of pornographic videos, mix-ups occasionally came to light where, for example, tapes labelled and sold as children's cartoons actually contained pornography (presumably the reverse also occurred from time to time, but without any public outcry). And the third was that in Northern Ireland, some paramilitary groups became involved in video counterfeiting as one of the ways in which they raised funds.

The motion picture industry did, however, have one good defence against counterfeiting. For many years it had been used to industry-wide co-operation and pooling of data on issues such as cinema attendances and box-office receipts, which were and are published in trade journals; and trade alliances such as the Motion Picture Association had existed since the 1940s. The major companies were by no means averse to the joint funding of an agency with a specific remit to prevent counterfeiting. Hence FACT, the Federation Against Copyright Theft, was formed in 1983.

FACT had and has a number of important advantages in dealing with counterfeiting issues. Most of its staff are ex-police officers. It has the technical expertise (and staff are technically trained) to identify fake products, using for example cues such as switch-head marks on the picture.[19] Motion picture companies accredit FACT staff as expert witnesses in determining the authenticity of tapes, so that FACT does not have to send tapes away for examination and can produce its own staff in court as expert witnesses. The organisation is geared to providing continuity in the chain of evidence because what happens to seized tapes can be fully documented in-house. And since FACT itself is able to lay information before magistrates, and mounts prosecutions in co-operation with a small number of law firms, it relies very little on local Trading Standards offices and the police, who do little more than accompany FACT staff on raids. This obviates the need for any more than minimal inter-agency co-ordination and co-operation.

All these points have helped FACT achieve a record of substantial success against video counterfeiters. In 1991 FACT carried out 748 searches of premises and seized 170 video recorders and 48,386 pirate tapes; in 1995 it carried out 1,420 searches and seized 1,407 recorders and 140,379 tapes. The peak year for seizures was in fact 1994, but nonetheless over the period 1995-97, FACT was able to prosecute (and thus effectively close down) many of the largest producers of counterfeits in the UK. Its success is confirmed by all the Trading Standards officers we have interviewed. Basing their judgement on complaints from the public and their own market surveillance, they unanimously agreed that apart from a small handful of special cases surrounding particularly popular films, the number of counterfeit videos in circulation by 1997 was negligible.

On this basis it might be thought that FACT will become a victim of its own success. Looking to the future, however, one has to consider the possible impact of new recording formats such as DVD,[20] and new methods of distribution such as the Internet. These technologies enable film and other entertainment media such as computer games to be stored and used alongside each other in a flexible way, and it is highly likely that they will open up new possibilities for counterfeiting, just as video recorders did in the 1980s. In addition, as the following section shows, any slackening of anti-counterfeiting efforts is likely to result in a very rapid increase in the availability of counterfeits and pirate copies in the market.

Getting shirty, but skirting the issue? Fashion's response to counterfeits

Counterfeiting in the fashion industry is an intriguing mix. The industry covers a myriad of intertwining styles including high street fashions, sportswear, and luxury labels, and a range of enterprises from independent designers to large fashion houses and 'sweatshops' who may produce goods for several different retail companies. Counterfeiting and analogous issues can emerge in a variety of ways that shadow these market and production structures.

Although there is a certain amount of tolerance of ideas from the haute couture collections and catwalks making their way into high street fashion, the fashion houses get distinctly 'shirty' when they discover their own labels being copied. In the mass leisure clothing market, jeans, shirts, knitwear, footwear, sportswear and football strip (which is sold legitimately only by arrangement with particular clubs, or only in their own stores) are all frequent targets for counterfeiting. Less obviously, problems of design infringement may also occur. For example young designers seeking to sell designs to larger fashion houses may be turned away, but subsequently find their ideas copied by those who have seen them.

The Trading Standards officers we have interviewed unanimously indicated that there was a large upturn in the counterfeit clothing market in the UK in 1996-7. However, there are several wrinkles in the picture that make it an interesting one.

First, there is some diversity among consumers as to whether or not they intend to buy counterfeits or indeed know whether items are fake. Cordell et al[21] found that consumers were more likely knowingly to buy counterfeit clothing than, for example, a camera because of the 'performance risk' associated with the latter, ie that it may not work properly and would be impossible to have fixed. Some consumers knowingly buy counterfeit clothing because they cannot afford the originals, though there also appears to be a 'crossover' market in which some purchasers for whom the brand name is not important buy counterfeits purely on the grounds of cheapness. On the other hand, some consumers who can easily afford the genuine products may buy fakes because 'like a *trompe l'oeil* painting, [a fake] can be amusing to someone who has everything' (Jay Lane, a New York costume jeweller, quoted in *Fortune*, 27 May 1996). And at the other end of the spectrum, young working-class people in the UK appear to avoid buying fakes because part of their social identity is built around consumerist culture and knowledge of the detailing and design of the original products.[22]

Second, the marketing of brand-name clothing has become a hugely important part of consumer culture since the 1970s, and in particular to younger consumers. Bea Campbell, in her discussion of youth culture, noted that:[23]

> All over peripheral estates across Britain teenagers were wearing designer casuals that signified their refusal to be peripheral ... Vital to all this was the label, the mark of money ... young people exercised a consuming passion for clothes cults ...

She continues:

> The necessity of labels — Berghaus, Gore-Tex sportswear, and Chevignon flying jackets are obsessively labelled — suggests a serious shift in the way that youth subcultures are making their mark.

Campbell's interpretation of this trend towards high-prestige brand-name goods by the young is that it represents an attempt to acquire the 'insignia of privilege', and an attack on the demarcations of function and money that clothes represent.[24]

Third, not all the counterfeit garments are of poor quality. Poor quality certainly exists: some of the logos attached to garments wash out or become detached very easily.[25] However, as some Trading Standards officers were quick to point out, poor quality is not necessarily a feature only of fakes.[26] Some counterfeit garments are of comparable quality to the originals, and many are not of a significantly poorer quality. That they are sold at a fraction of the price of the genuine item through car boot sales, on street markets, or mixed with other stock on discount racks in otherwise legitimate shops testifies to the per-item profit made by the legitimate producers on the basis of the brand name alone.

Meanwhile, and despite the undoubted upturn in counterfeiting in this area in the last couple of years, not all garments claimed to be counterfeit actually are. A Trading Standards officer related to us the following story. One retailer held an exclusive licence from a jeans manufacturer — in essence he had purchased a licence to sell the jeans, in exchange for which the manufacturer would not distribute to any other shop in the area. However, a nearby shop began selling a line of jeans from the same manufacturer. The retailer sent a private detective to the other shop to make a test purchase, concluded that the jeans were counterfeit, and complained to Trading Standards, who made their own test purchase and investigation. At this point the jeans company was contacted. Their representative inspected the test purchases and confirmed that they were counterfeit, noting various design differences between them and articles legitimately on sale in the UK. It turned out, however, that the shop that had been complained about and investigated was selling parallel imports — in this case, jeans destined for sale in the Far East but diverted to the UK. The jeans company representative was simply not aware of the design changes incorporated into his company's export products because he would never normally have any dealings with that side of the business. Although the parallel import argument is very often raised spuriously as a defence in counterfeiting cases (but is relatively easy to crack if no paperwork chain is there to support it), there is a large and growing market in such products and Trading Standards officers have become increasingly aware in recent years that they cannot always rely on the manufacturers for accurate identification of counterfeits, making their job a great deal harder. It also left some officers concerned about whether accusations of counterfeiting were being made by some traders to 'spike the opposition'.

Fourth, and still on the topic of detecting counterfeits, many Trading Standards officers complained about the ways in which manufacturers handled queries about counterfeits. Manufacturers typically expected seized items or test purchases to be forwarded to them for inspection, but would not process queries quickly. Understandably, long delays at this point in the case could lead to prosecutions being discontinued, which Trading Standards officers found frustrating.

Having noted some features of the market in counterfeit clothing, two key questions remain: why has it suddenly grown in size, and who is doing the counterfeiting?

It seems significant that the fake clothing market expanded quite quickly in 1996/7, more or less as the market in fake videos declined so dramatically. It is over-simple to assume that those who had been making videos were displaced, due to FACT's enforcement activities, into a market sector that has comparatively little by way of deterrent. For one thing there is little commonality, in terms of the necessary equipment, contacts, and technical expertise between the two industrial sectors. It is true that in 1997 it emerged that Lancashire counterfeit jeans manufacturers were trading goods with counterfeit video manufacturers in South Wales, so that each was taking on and selling part of the other's output. Yet while this indicates the existence of a social network of counterfeiters, it underlines the point that counterfeiters cannot readily move from one kind of production to another as enforcement patterns change (though they may move between production and retail activities).

Perhaps the more important point, though, is that while individual companies make efforts to prevent counterfeiting, the fashion industry as a whole does not. Some companies have their own staff detailed to inspect contractor factories and retail outlets, and some employ private detectives for these purposes. However, where companies build security and authentication devices into labels, packaging and swing-tags, they are typically rudimentary yet not easily checkable by the general public. And there is no industry-specific association with a mandate to address the counterfeiting problem. Hence, while companies make efforts to counter fakes, the industry as a whole is still skirting the issue of counterfeits. Indeed, we could even say that garment counterfeiting was to a large extent a problem waiting to happen, because so few efforts had been made at an industry-wide level to prevent it.

In short, and in contrast to the video industry, the counterfeiting of garments has been able to grow quickly because the market for brand-name garments has been growing in importance but also because it is characterised by disunity among manufacturers and a lack of collective anti-counterfeiting measures.

Other industries

The two industries discussed above differ greatly in their organisation and structure. One comprises a relatively small number of large producers and distributors who have been used to the exchange of data and the existence of industry-wide associations for many years. As a result they were able to act collectively against counterfeiting, with a great deal of success. The other is a diversified industry with many producers of differing sizes, a great deal of competition, and no track record of industry-wide co-operation. It has found counterfeiting very difficult to combat.

Other industrial sectors fall between these two poles. The software industry, for example, is comparatively young but nonetheless large and has been a major target for counterfeiting. Some sources estimate that one third of the copies of programs used in North America, half the copies in use in Europe, and almost all software used in some Asian countries is illegally copied. Counterfeiting and piracy have been aided by the rapid dissemination of equipment hitherto used only within the industry itself, such as 'gold' (read and write) CDs, enabling large numbers of programs to be distributed quickly and efficiently. It has also been assisted by the ambivalent and cynical attitudes of many consumers — the pages of computer magazines, for example, often carry letters and opinion pieces about whether the prices of software have more to do with the high development and marketing costs for programs or the desire of software companies to generate large profits.

However, the software industry has begun to operate in a collaborative manner, with the setting up of several trade associations dealing with counterfeiting and piracy including the Business Software Alliance (BSA), the Federation Against Software Theft (FAST), and the European Leisure Software Publishers Association (ELSPA). As yet, these associations have mainly confined their work to monitoring the situation and raising public awareness of the problem. Nonetheless, the publicity they have generated has probably changed attitudes towards counterfeits, at least for business users, who may be vulnerable to quite severe sanctions if discovered using counterfeit software.

The spare parts industry, meanwhile, has a problem that may be more hidden but is nonetheless likely to be more difficult to eradicate. The two main industries affected are the car and the aviation industries. Part of the problem within the car industry is that many parts are made by subcontractors, and different components, albeit with similar specifications, may be used in the same type of car. It is not uncommon to find that an item sold as a spare part looks different to the original part that it replaces. Meanwhile, some parts companies have created strong brand names; products alleging to be sourced from those companies can command high prices, thus creating a market for counterfeits. Although this is more of a problem in third world countries than developed economies, relatively little has been done on an industry-wide basis to address the issue.

The aviation industry has even more of a problem. Components in the aviation industry are made by a large number of small companies. Many of the parts are hugely expensive — we were, for example, told of toilet door locks costing about £18 each in the 1980s even though they came from a producer who made similar items for high street stores for a few pence each. However, much of this cost is related to quality control: if a production run was destined for aircraft use, the inspection, testing, and approval of the parts was very comprehensive, including, for example, checks that they would not break under high G-forces. The primary problem was thus not so much one of counterfeit parts, but of unapproved parts — which may be exactly the same as approved parts in every respect except the lack of testing and thus lack of assurance that they would work under high stress loads. Moreover, it is possible to buy reconditioned second or even third-hand products (though presumably not toilet door locks) which are subject to a confusing array of validation procedures. Although the supply chain is in theory strictly controlled, the US transportation department has recently experienced an explosion in the number of indictments in connection with what is suspected to be a blossoming trade in unapproved parts, including fake validation tags and manufacturer data plates. The net result is that a mix of unapproved parts with false documentation, second-hand parts with false records of their history, and 'genuine counterfeits' percolate through the industry. The new director general of the US Transportation Department has promised to try to formulate a workable strategy pertaining to spare parts whereby all manner of parts can be given authority and later identified if necessary.

Enforcement activities and strategies

Enforcement activities against counterfeiters come in various guises. First, individual companies may make attempts to prevent their own products being copied. Second, trade associations may take initiatives on behalf of many or all producers in a particular industry. These may be directed at public education and market intelligence, with individual companies largely left to undertake their own prosecutions (as is the case in the software industry), or at detection and prosecution of offenders on behalf of the industry as a whole, as is the case in the video market. Third, official agencies such as (in the UK) local authority Trading Standards offices monitor the local situation and investigate complaints brought by the public. And fourth, governments have introduced safety standards and procedures for many industries — for example for aircraft parts — but rely on maintenance companies and end-users as the 'front line' of detection for counterfeits and indeed other problems.

The first style of enforcement — companies undertaking it themselves — is the predominant pattern in the fashion industry. Larger companies have their own representatives in the field, checking on both subcontractors and retail outlets; increasingly they have intellectual property departments with a remit to ensure that trade marks and designs are properly registered and to scrutinise reports from company representatives and agents. Some employ private detective agencies to do this kind of work; and others have become members of specialist agencies, such as the International Chamber of Commerce's Counterfeiting Intelligence Bureau, and use their services as and when necessary. These are not necessarily ineffective strategies, and they may be the best alternative in cases such as the fashion industry where there is no trade alliance to pursue the collective interest in counterfeit prevention. Nonetheless, where a trade alliance exists (the second strategy mentioned above) it can be much more effective in preventing counterfeits and detecting counterfeiters — if, of course, its members are prepared to support such 'policing'. The best example is FACT, and its success seems to be based not only on its support by the industry but also on its internal organisation. By having staff accredited by the major companies as capable of identifying fakes, and maintaining tight control over the chain of evidence and prosecution, it has been able to streamline the processes of investigation and prosecute large numbers of cases.

Local authority Trading Standards offices have three roles — to protect consumers, uphold a range of legislation on trading, and protect industry investment in its products.[27] These three broad roles can be unpacked into a wide range of specific tasks, and in consequence only a small proportion of their time, in most cases only about 5-10 per cent, is spent dealing with the detection or investigation of counterfeit products and trade mark infringements.[28] The most recent survey of counterfeiting for Trading Standards confirms that although counterfeiting is perceived to be a growing market, enforcement remains patchy.[29]

The decentralised and fragmented nature of the Trading Standards service, and the fact that it is a function of local government, has two implications for anti-counterfeiting work. One is that the responsibility for determining organisational goals is carried out in conjunction with local councillors and council officials. Greater efforts against counterfeiting, then, tend to be made when the local council is prepared to support them. In some cases councillors see the publicity generated by seizures, arrests, and prosecutions as positive, and regard anti-counterfeiting work as a high priority. In many cases, though, councils have different priorities. The second implication of the localised nature of Trading Standards is that, in the way of small agencies, the degree to which individual offices are involved in anti-counterfeiting work depends to a large extent on the energies and interests of individual officers. Anti-counterfeiting is a specialised area of work that requires a significant amount of groundwork if it is to be successful. Officers need to build networks of contacts amongst companies, trade associations, local people, and other Trading Standards authorities. These contacts help provide the information to start and carry through an investigation and are therefore vital for effective and efficient enforcement practices. The importance of these factors is often realised only when one link in the chain is lost or an individual officer — and hence the contacts and information-base he or she has built up — moves or retires. In practice, it seems, there are small circles of officers who share a common interest and who are responsible for the lion's share of all enforcement activities, seizures and prosecutions relating to counterfeiting. These officers may spend more time with colleagues in other authorities, and in contact with anti-counterfeiting staff from other agencies such as FACT, than they do with others in their own agency. In effect they form a tight-knit community within the Trading Standards world.

Anti-counterfeiting is still, however, for many officers, a frustrating area of work. Much of the work they undertake is made more difficult than necessary. For example, officers often cite cases where trade mark holders have not responded promptly — or even at all — to enquiries about suspected counterfeit goods. Furthermore, situations like that detailed above, where authentication techniques provided by the companies themselves fail, can leave Trading Standards offices vulnerable to prosecutions and compensation claims from wronged vendors. Other difficulties such as the lack of secure storage space provided by local authorities in which to store counterfeit goods until trial, and acceptable ways to dispose of such items after the case has been closed, also place restrictions on the level of cases an authority can undertake.

Finally, Trading Standards officers are often aware that their role can be seen in an equivocal light. Their primary duty is to the consumer, but trade mark protection and anti-counterfeiting work can often be perceived as acting in the interests of big business. Officers rationalise the balance of responsibility in different ways — for example, by arguing that although the actions of Trading Standards officers can be said to be safeguarding commercial profits, they are also protecting consumers against unscrupulous criminals who do not care that counterfeit products may ultimately endanger the life of consumers. As one officer pointed out, it is like protecting the public from themselves — although to many counterfeiting is a victimless crime, causing no immediate harm, in the long term it can be one of the most destructive, economically debilitating activities in which the public participates.

Conclusion

Counterfeiting is a growing enterprise and poses a more serious threat to industry, commerce, and consumers than is often appreciated. However, it appears to be more prevalent in industries that take little or no collective action against it. While organisations such as Trading Standards offices do a great deal, they cannot operate effectively without co-operation from individual companies, which is not infrequently lacking; and they have other equally pressing tasks. In consequence, their effectiveness is patchy both geographically and across different retail sectors.

The most effective form of anti-counterfeiting action, in terms of increasing the risks to offenders, seems to be through trade associations that operate in the collective interests of an industry. It is true that FACT have experienced fewer problems than most industrial sectors would pose, because the product they deal with is uniform and some authentication techniques, such as the detection of switch-head marks, will work with any item and cannot easily be challenged. However, a large part of their success is due to the structure of the motion picture industry, where companies have been prepared to jointly fund a dedicated anti-counterfeiting agency and delegate to its staff the authority to determine the authenticity of products and decisions to initiate prosecutions. It is this streamlining of anti-counterfeiting work that has increased the risks to offenders and reduced the extent of infringement in the market place.

It is worth noting that some anti-counterfeiting efforts are also made on a cross-industry, national basis. The best example of an agency undertaking such efforts at the present is the Anti-Counterfeiting Group (ACG), an umbrella organisation which offers advice and a forum for debate industry-wide. However, since the nature and scope of the counterfeiting problem varies substantially across different manufacturing and retail sectors, it has to be accepted that the ACG and other bodies like it will be most effective when they work at a high level of generality, for example lobbying Parliament for legal changes (as the ACG in fact did in relation to the Trade Marks Act 1994).

None of this is intended to suggest that efforts by individual companies, including their use of private specialists, consultants, or investigators is ineffective. Indeed, in many industrial, commercial and retail sectors such efforts will be the only available strategies for some time to come. However, given the scope and size of the counterfeiting problem, including the alleged entry of professional and organised crime groups into the counterfeiting area, progress is unlikely to be easy or smooth. Moreover, continuing budgetary pressures on publicly-funded enforcement agencies, coupled with their already wide range of responsibilities, may very well prevent them from taking a larger role in anti-counterfeiting work than they presently do. That said, were more companies prepared to handle queries concerning the authenticity of products speedily, and by sending representatives out to inspect items, Trading Standards investigations would become much more efficient. Finally, and despite the diversity of the counterfeiting problem across different economic sectors, better channels of communication between all those concerned with the problem and a larger flow of information into the public domain would provide a stronger basis for developing and implementing anti-counterfeiting strategies in future.

Notes

1   Dr Jon Vagg is a Senior Lecturer in Criminology and Justine Harris a researcher at the Midlands Centre for Criminology and Criminal Justice, University of Loughborough, Loughborough, Leics. LE11 3TU. The project on which this paper is based is funded by the Leverhulme Trust. The authors would like to thank all those individuals and agencies interviewed who have made the project possible. Views expressed in the paper are the authors' own and do not necessarily represent those of the funding agency. The authors may be contacted by phone (01509 223878) or email (J.J.Vagg@lboro.ac.uk).

2   Much of the information used in this chapter was gathered from a variety of interviews with Trading Standards officers, trade organisations, retailers, private investigation companies, and manufacturers.

3   See Jennings, J. (1989) Trademark Counterfeiting: An Unpunished Crime. *Journal of Criminal Law and Criminology*. Vol. 80, No. 3, pp. 805-41; Michaels, A. (1982) *A Practical Guide to Trade Marks*. Oxford: ESC Publishing.

4   For a brief discussion of counterfeiting in mediaeval times, see Rakoff, J.S. and Wolff, I.B. (1982) Commercial Counterfeiting and the Proposed Trademark Counterfeiting Act. *American Criminal Law Review*. Vol. 20, No. 2, pp 145-53.

5   Many other and more technical offences are listed in the Act, including the making of a false entry in the register of trade marks, and falsely representing that a mark is a registered trade mark (SS.94 and 95).

6   Further offences are specified in SS.198-202 and 229-235, including the fraudulent reception of transmissions (cable and satellite TV), frauds committed by trade mark or patent agents, and remedies for the use of groundless threats of infringement proceedings.

7   TRIPS, the Agreement on Trade Related Aspects of Intellectual Property Rights, is a World Trade Organisation agreement that obliges WTO Members to protect all the main categories of intellectual property (patents, trade marks and copyright). It sets out minimum standards of acceptable protection that should be contained in domestic laws, including standards pertaining to remedies against breaches and arrangements for law enforcement. TRIPS came into force on 1 January 1995 and should be progressively implemented with differing time scales for developed and developing countries. Further details are available on the following URLs: http://www.wto.org/intellec/11-over.htm and http://cerebalaw.com/gatttext.htm.

8   Counterfeiting Intelligence Bureau (1997) *Countering Counterfeiting*. Barking, Essex: ICC Counterfeiting Intelligence Bureau.

9   The former view is held by Weinburger, H.P. (1996) 50th Anniversary of the Lanham Act.

New York Law Journal. Vol. 2, December (available on-line at http://www.ljx.com/trademark/120254.html); and Wittenburg, M.B. and Overend, W.R. (1996) Counter Measures: Intellectual Property in the Information Age. *Daily Journal* (Intellectual Property Supplement). 25 April, Oakland, Ca. The latter is held by the Counterfeiting Intelligence Bureau (op cit).

10   Ibid.

11   Cordell, V., Wongtada N. and Kieschnick, R.Jr (1996) Counterfeit Purchase Intentions: Role of Lawfulness, Attitude and Product Traits as Determinants. *Journal of Business Research.* Vol. 35, No. 1, pp 41-53.

12   Weinburger, op cit.

13   Wittenburg and Overend, op cit.

14   Counterfeiting Intelligence Bureau, op cit.

15   Figure given on the National Law Center's Intellectual Property research project website, http://www.natlaw.com/intelpro.htm. No source is provided.

16   Counterfeiting Intelligence Bureau, op cit.

17   MORI: *Why Should I Care About Counterfeiting? A Public Opinion Survey.* Paper presented at the Anti-Counterfeiting Group Autumn Conference, York, October 1997.

18   In such cases, of course, there would be no pre-existing legitimate designs for packaging for the UK market. Some counterfeiters sold tapes without packaging; some used US designs; some invented their own.

19   A switch-head mark is a small white mark at the bottom of the picture, usually outside the screen area, that can be made visible using specially-designed television sets. Each re-recording of a tape results in one extra switch-head mark, so if two such marks are found on a tape it means that it is a first-generation copy from an original which will have only one mark.

20   Digital Video Disk: a recently-developed extension of the use of CDs capable of storing over 17 gigabytes of information, sufficient for the equivalent of 9 hours of high-resolution video. DVD is a 'crossover' product that can store not only video and audio images, but also computer software and games. Although readily available in the US, there are not as yet industry-wide standards for compatibility. The implications for counterfeiting at the moment include the ability of DVD to copy very large amounts of data without loss of quality, and problems in developing copy protection.

21   Cordell et al, op cit.

22   This point comes from a discussion about counterfeits held with several young people in Birmingham; we would like to thank the NACRO Birmingham office for arranging this.

23   Campbell, B. (1993) *Goliath: Britain's Dangerous Places.* London: Methuen, p 271.

24   However, one Trading Standards officer in the north of England suggested to us that this is not exclusively a strategy of youth, but a common feature of working-class self-presentation, at least in their own area.

25   One Trading Standards officer showed us some counterfeit shoes of comparatively poor quality that he had seized. Ironically, they came with swing-tags like those attached to the genuine product explaining how to detect fakes. Were a potential purchaser to have fol-

lowed the advice on these tags they would very quickly have concluded that the shoes were counterfeit.

26   In the course of our interviews we were shown several examples of genuine brand-name socks and hats where complaints had been made about the quality; in one case a manufacturer had explained that the poor quality goods had reached the UK market by mistake — they were manufactured for sale in Eastern Europe.

27   For a brief discussion of some of the enforcement strategies used by Trading Standards officers, see Vagg, J. (1995) The Policing of Signs: Trademark Infringement and Law Enforcement. *European Journal of Criminal Policy and Research*. Vol. 3, No. 2, pp 75-91.

28   Institute of Trading Standards Administration (1994) *National Counterfeiting Survey: Results in Full* (monograph). Hadleigh, Essex: Institute of Trading Standards Administration.

29   Clark, A. (1997) *Trends in Counterfeiting in the UK*. Paper presented at the Anti-Counterfeiting Group Autumn Conference Programme, York, October .

Chapter 14

Why Some Organisations Prefer Contract to In-house Security Staff

Mark Button and Bruce George MP[1]

This paper considers one of the main security strategies used by organisations to increase the risk to offenders: the employment of contract security officers. It explores briefly the structure of the contract guarding sector and then moves on to examine in depth the reasons for using contract security rather than in-house. It shows that some of the reasons for choosing contract include: the cost benefits of doing so, the ability to hire expertise, the greater flexibility offered, compulsion, to transfer liabilities, the higher standards offered, the prestige and image of the contractor, and problems with in-house security. The chapter then considers the potential impact of statutory regulation on this sector. Different forms of regulation may affect the decision to use contract and in-house security, which may ultimately have an effect on the overall standards of the sector and therefore the risk to offenders. Finally, the paper offers some views on related issues that require further research and a perspective on the model of regulation that should be introduced by the British government.

Introduction

The security professional, when assessing the security risks to his/her organisation has a wide range of strategies available to address them. The first option could be no action at all. It might be decided that the risks are minimal, that should they occur the costs would be negligible or the costs of addressing them are not economic. A second strategy that could be pursued by an organisation is to avoid the risk altogether. Thus a company that has been burgled repeatedly might decide to move elsewhere to avoid the risk entirely. A third strategy might be to transfer or contract out the risks to someone else. For instance, a company that is experiencing losses in its catering department through theft and fraud that cannot be seriously addressed, might decide to contract out the whole division, therefore transferring the problem. The use of insurance or self-insurance is another strategy that could be pursued by an organisation. The most common strategy for dealing with risks, however, is to seek to reduce the likelihood of them occurring by increasing the risk to offenders. To achieve this, a wide range of security strategies could be pursued, from the employment of security officers and investigators, to the installation of intruder alarms and other security equipment and the introduction of security procedures (to name a few).

Thus, if the aim is to increase the risk to offenders, the first decision that has to be made is whether to use security personnel, technology or a mixture of both. Technology is also increasingly being used to replace security personnel. Security products are becoming increasingly advanced: for instance, pictures from CCTV cameras can be transmitted down telephone lines to a remote site for surveillance to take place. Intruder alarms are becoming more sophisticated and reliable. And as one manager interviewed suggested, 'technology does not go on strike, sleep or set fire to the premises', although it does break down! Nevertheless, in many situations the security strategy that is used is a mixture of technology and security personnel. When the latter are used, the decision over whether to use contract or in-house security staff, or a mixture of both, needs to be made.

In the first volume of *Crime at Work* we considered why some organisations prefer in-house security staff.[2] In this volume the other side of the question is evaluated. The decision whether to use contract, in-house or a mixture of both, is one of the most frequent and important decisions a security manager has to make.[3] However, despite the importance of these decisions, there has been relatively little independent research into why this is the case.[4] This chapter will consider the rationale behind the use of contract security. The chapter will also move on to consider the possible impact of regulation on the contract guarding sector, as statutory regulation is now inevitable,[5] although it may only affect contract security;[6] and this, in turn, might affect the potential success of regulation. Before any of these issues are explored, however, it would be useful to describe the size and structure of the contract guarding sector in the UK after briefly discussing the methodology used.

Methodology

To assess the rationale for contracting out security a two-stage research strategy was pursued. First, as part of wider research into the private security industry, those with responsibility for this decision were interviewed as well as managers from contract security companies. The issues discussed were not restricted totally to the contract/in-house decision, but many other topics were included, such as regulation, risks faced and professional associations. Thus reasons for contracting out were extracted from these interviews. Additional information was also gained from literature from companies and trade associations promoting contract security. Secondly, a survey was conducted of the original organisations that replied to our survey of in-house security departments. Of the original 50 replies, 13 were anonymous, so it was only possible to write to 37; of those, 24 (65 per cent) replied. The questionnaire sought information on how their security arrangements had changed, if at all, the rationale for any changes, and views on statutory regulation. The number of replies received was not large enough to draw definitive conclusions on the issues explored. However, they do provide useful guides to views and trends in the in-house sector, especially given the lack of previous research.

The static manned guarding sector

The private security industry consists of an eclectic range of sectors offering services and products. We divide the industry into the manned guarding sector, private sector detention services (private prisons, escorts etc), professional security services (private investigators and security consultants), security storage and destruction services, security products (manufacturers, distributors, installers and maintainers), and marginal sectors (those activities that have security dimensions, but which are not unambiguously a part of the industry — couriers and gamekeepers for example). The static manned guarding sector is a sub-sector of the manned guarding sector comprising contract and in-house sections. The other sub-sectors are cash-in-transit services, door supervision and stewarding services, and close protection services. The focus of this chapter is the static manned guarding sector, which can be defined as organisations engaged in the provision of predominantly static security services — whether by an in-house organisation, contract company or combination of both — based upon guarding, patrolling, searching, surveillance and the enforcement of laws and organisational rules by predominantly full-time uniformed personnel.

The contract/in-house distinction is also in some instances blurred. This is particularly the case with some organisations using a facilities management company, such as the Bull Ring Shopping Centre in Birmingham. It directly employs its own in-house security force. The ultimate organisation that they provide security services to is the owner of the shopping centre, whom they are not directly employed by. Hence, are they contract or in-house? The answer would seem to suggest contract. However, a case could also be made for them being in-house.

The static manned security services is one of the largest sectors of the private security industry, with an estimated turnover of over £1.5 billion.[7] Recent research undertaken for the BSIA, illustrated in Table 1 below also shows the structure of the market, with a large number of small and medium-sized companies accounting for almost half the contract market turnover.

Table 1. Static manned security services sector size[8]

Section	Number of companies	Turnover £ million	Employees 000s
BSIA	40	530	40
IPSA	235	250	20
Non-affiliated	>1000	>250	>20
In-house		>500	38
Total	>1275	>1530	>118

The Table also illustrates the large number of personnel employed within this sector, with around 118,000, when in-house officers are included. However, any estimates of the size of this sector are open to criticism. There have been many attempts to gauge the size and they all seem to arrive at very different estimates. By contrast, for instance, recent research by the Policy Studies Institute (PSI) estimated there were 129,257 security officers.[9]

Estimating the respective sizes of in-house and contract is also difficult because of the problems of definition and the lack of empirical research. Such estimates are particularly difficult amongst in-house security, for where most contract companies seek to publicise themselves in order to gain business, most in-house do not. This makes it even more difficult to quantify as there may be in-house officers 'hidden' away in obscure organisations. Nevertheless, the Confederation of European Security Services (COESS)[10] estimated there were around 38,000 in-house officers and a ratio of 40 in-house to 60 contract. The BSIA[11] research recently estimated the ratio was 32.7% in-house officers to 67.3% contract officers, which would also mean there were approximately 38,000 in-house officers in a total of 118,000 security officers. A very different estimate of the size of the prospective sectors was found by Jones and Newburn,[12] who estimated there were 90,629 in-house guards and 38,628 contract guards. This totally contradicts most estimates that have so far been made on the size of the prospective sectors.

There are also a number of firms that mix their security provision, that is make use of both in-house and contract.[13] Some of the research that illustrates the extent of use of the different types of security provision is shown in Table 2.

Table 2. Estimates of the extent of use of contract, in-house and mixed security

Mode of use	BSIA research[14] per cent	Pinkerton research[15] per cent
Totally contract	56	69
Totally in-house	25	9
Mixed	19	22

The BSIA[16] research also estimated the in-house market to be worth around £500 million. Whatever the true size, in-house security is declining as a proportion of the manned sector. Indeed, South[17] estimated the ratio between in-house and contract was 60:40 respectively during the 1970s. Evidence from the BSIA would also suggest that the in-house sector has been declining in absolute terms. These different estimates illustrate the difficulties of calculating the size of this sector. Until there is statutory regulation it will be impossible to accurately gauge the size of this sector, and perhaps not even then.

In our own research of the original in-house security departments surveyed, of the 24 that responded only 17 still had the same security arrangements, five had moved to a new mix, one returned from mixed to totally in-house and only one had totally contracted out their security. Of the five that had changed the mixture of their security arrangements, four had moved towards functional mixing arrangements where contract night shifts were introduced to supplement in-house day shifts, to counter a specific threat such as theft of computers. Another respondent had replaced some in-house officers with technology.

Why contract security staff?

Before the reasons for choosing contract security over in-house are discussed it would be useful to briefly remind ourselves of the rationale for using in-house security. Previously we identified a number of reasons why organisations retain in-house security.[18] It was claimed in-house officers offered greater loyalty and reliability, they would stay with an organisation longer and offer more commitment to duties. The ability to recruit and train to the organisations' own standards was another issue cited. Some organisations had security roles that were very complex and took much time to learn; this, they argued, required a dedicated security unit committed to the organisation for the long term, and could only be achieved through in-house. The sensitivity of the organisation led some to retain in-house so as to minimise the number of individuals who have intimate knowledge of a site. Other organisations argued that more control could be exacted over in-house officers as there were clear lines of responsibility, compared to contract, where loyalties — they argued — were often divided. The cost of in-house was also claimed by some to be less and there were also legal barriers in the transfer of undertakings and protection of employment regulations (or TUPE as they are often called) to some organisations contracting out. Finally, most organisations had a very negative perception of contract security which precluded them from contracting out. Some of the reasons for choosing contract will now be considered.

Lower costs
The most salient reason for organisations using contract security staff is the cost benefits. Many argue that the total costs of using contract security are less than for in-house when the wider costs of the latter are taken into account. In-house security officers are generally paid more than their contract counterparts[19] and some have managed to secure extremely high remuneration packages because of the nature of their organisation. For instance, a leading car manufacturer's head of security who was interviewed claimed that when the security force was originally in-house there were some security staff earning as much as £30,000 per year. This could occur because their rates of pay were linked to shopfloor workers on the same rates of pay and overtime rates. The very high wage costs made it very attractive for the security to be contracted out. Not all in-house security officers earn salaries such as this, but their generally higher rates of pay do make it attractive in some organisations to reduce the costs overall by contracting them out.

Contract security firms can also provide security at lower costs by paying their own security staff lower rates of pay. For instance the BSIA minimum hourly rates of pay as of April 1997 were £2.75 for contracts outside London and £3.25 inside the M25.[20] These would be regarded by most as low rates of pay.[21] Many BSIA firms pay above these, but there are many firms outside the BSIA who pay less than these rates, and wages of £1 per hour are not unheard of. Invariably the costs of in-house security involve not only wages but also national insurance contributions; pensions contributions (if applicable); other remuneration costs (if applicable); security equipment costs; recruitment, vetting and training costs; and management costs. In addition, in-house security departments often have to be overstaffed to cover for holidays and sickness. A contract security company can lower some of these costs in total by simply not incurring some and by economies of scale. For instance, the management of a group of security officers at one organisation can be added to one manager's duties in combination with others, reducing the overall costs of supervision. Similarly, by having a pool of security staff for all contracts, holidays and sickness can be more economically covered. Thus, overall, contract security companies can often offer a security package at a lower cost for the reasons outlined above, while the purchaser faces just one fee with no other hidden costs. In the research the BSIA undertook, lower cost was the main reason for contracting out,[22] although in our previous research on the in-house sector some organisations did claim that in-house security was cheaper than contract.

Hiring expertise
Another common reason for using contract security staff was to hire expertise in specific security areas. Often this was linked to an organisation's desire to focus upon its core business, of which security was not a part. For instance, the specialist security skills required at airports and airlines made it more economical and rational for some organisations to contract out to a company specialising in aviation security. Some contract security companies have an expertise in retail security. This makes contracting out an attractive option to some retailers because of the specialist security packages such firms can put together. More generally, many security companies employ a large number of staff with varied security specialisms that can all be offered to a hiring organisation for a fee. For instance, some of the larger firms may employ staff with an expertise in intruder alarms, Electronic Article Surveillance (EAS) systems and safes. Linked to this, some security companies may have very good relations with the local police and other relevant organisations. These added services and links can all be drawn upon in the wider security package. Building together an in-house security team with such depth of knowledge for many small and medium-sized organisations would be very difficult and expensive to achieve.

Greater flexibility
Another popular reason for using a contract security company is the greater flexibility it can often bring. First, if the performance of a contractor is poor it can be replaced by another company. At another level, if a contract security officer's performance is unsatisfactory the client can ask for him/her to be removed. With an in-house officer the organisation would have to terminate their employment, which would require compliance with the relevant employment legislation, and this might be a lengthy and costly process. Second, the numbers of security staff can be more easily varied to deal with holidays, sickness and sudden increases in demand. An organisation can usually ask for additional security personnel to be provided when needed. For an in-house organisation, unless there was a very large pool of officers sudden increases in demand would require often lengthy procedures of recruitment, vetting and training. Third, in some large organisations the security requirements vary at different locations and times. Often the security officer required at different locations may need to be trained differently, and this may even warrant

a different rate of pay. This can be more easily achieved with a contract company, whereas with in-house staff they may, for industrial relations reasons, have to be paid the same rates and undergo the same initial training. Finally, many security companies employ a wide range of personnel, many with specialist skills and training. Thus, if an organisation suddenly required a specialist security officer or service, such as a dog handler, they can often provide it quickly, whereas with an in-house organisation they would have to recruit, vet and train such a person or contract him/her in, necessitating the additional burdens of finding a contract company that can provide those services at the right quality and most appropriate cost. An organisation already using a contract company would often simply have to ask for the additional service.

Compulsion

There are also a significant number of decision-makers on security in the public sector that have been forced to contract out their security services by various compulsory competitive tendering (CCT) regulations.[23] In many private sector organisations there has been a decision at corporate level to focus upon core business and this has meant that services such as security — which are generally not regarded as core — have been contracted out, often when those responsible for security do not wish it to be. Hence security decision-makers in these types of organisations have had little choice but to contract out their security provision.

Transfer of liabilities

In many situations where security staff are used there is a risk that their behaviour might lead to litigation against the organisation. For instance, if a security officer in a retail outlet arrested a suspected shoplifter and it transpired it was a mistake, they might sue for compensation. If the security officer was in-house, the organisation would be clearly responsible. However, if it was a contract firm the liability might be transferred to the contract company — unless for legal reasons it could be proved that the retailer was responsible. This transfer of liabilities makes it attractive to some organisations to contract out security provision. However, in *Photo Productions v Securicor* [1980] AC 827 the importance of attention to the finer details of the contract was illustrated. In this case the security officer had lit a fire which then got out of control, seriously damaging the factory he was guarding. Securicor were able to resist the suit by pointing to an exemption clause in the contract.[24]

Higher standards

Some of those interviewed also suggested that the standards of contract security were higher. Often this was linked to experience. In-house security when bad can be particularly so because of its cost, inflexibility and difficulties in changing the behaviour and standards of a group of static security personnel. However, without wider research into both in-house and contract security forces it would be difficult to assess which generally has the higher standards.

Prestige and image of contractor

There are some contract security companies that have a certain prestige or image that makes them attractive for an organisation to hire. One such example is the Corps of Commissionaires, which attracts attention because of its long history,[25] its association with ex-military personnel, and the attractive uniforms. They are often used for a special event such as a sporting occasion, VIP party or launch of a product where having Corps security is believed to add to the prestige. For instance, one leading car manufacturer uses the Corps for motorshows and the launch of new models, where their image is felt as appropriate for the occasion. There are also some organisations that use such personnel to control access to their organisation, again to convey a certain image to visitors. Indeed, there is even one prestigious manufacturer that pays the Corps for the privilege of some of their staff wearing their uniform when they are not even employed by the Corps!

Problems with in-house security
A number of disadvantages have also been identified with the in-house approach. The most common is the problem of generally higher costs, as was discussed earlier. The desire of some organisations to stick to their core business means that managing security interferes with the core management role of general managers. When they are managing security they could be managing the core business. Finally, some argue that in-house officers become too familiar with the workforce, which can compromise security. The argument is that if you have a permanent security force employed by the same organisation there is always a risk of them getting to know fellow employees and lowering security standards. At one level, this might be letting staff through without checking their identity cards; at another level, collusion between security staff and other staff in crimes. Nevertheless, this criticism could also be made of organisations that use the same contract company for a long period of time.

Problems with contract security
It might also be useful to briefly discuss some of the problems that have been identified with contract security staff. One of the most frequent criticisms is that companies do not vet their staff adequately and as a consequence many employ criminals or those of dubious character. The poor calibre of guards is another problem frequently identified. Often they are poorly paid, work long hours with inadequate training and as a consequence their motivation and standards are low. Some critics point to dubious practices such as the use of 'ghost' security officers. This is the practice where the organisation pays for x security officers, but is in fact supplied with fewer, but charged for x. Many of these and other types of problems have been identified in various publications.[26] It is also for some of these reasons that the issue of regulation of private security has become important. As this is likely to be finally achieved in the next few years, it is important to discuss this issue, as the type of regulation that is introduced may affect the decision to use contract and the quality of security, and thus ultimately the risk to offenders.

The regulation debate

The standards of private security, we believe, could be improved substantially by the introduction of comprehensive statutory regulation. Most private security strategies are directed at reducing the risk of crime by increasing the risks to offenders. Therefore the introduction of a regulatory system for the private security industry has implications for the risk to offenders because standards should be improved. Statutory regulation of the private security industry at last looks inevitable in Great Britain. However, the proposals that have been put forward by influential bodies such as the Home Affairs Committee (HAC) and the Home Office have excluded the in-house security sector.[27] The HAC recommended only regulation of the contract sector, although in terms of our classification of regulatory systems it was at least a form of comprehensive regulation. Elsewhere we have identified five models of regulation which start with non-interventionist, rising through minimal narrow, minimal wide, comprehensive narrow to comprehensive wide, the most effective model in our view.[28] Only the latter two models would address the quality of private security and thus ultimately have a significant impact on the risk to offending.

The watered-down proposals that eventually emerged from the Home Office, under the last Conservative Government, not surprisingly excluded in-house and also advocated a minimal form of regulation. At around the same time, however, the Police Foundation and Policy Studies Institute (PF/PSI) published a report that, *inter alia,* included recommendations on regulation of the private security industry.[29] They advocated regulation of both contract and in-house amongst other sectors, hence a form of comprehensive wide regulation. However, the impact of that report on the regulation debate has been limited.

The election of the Labour Government in May 1997 has made what seemed a Home Office impervious to reasoned arguments about the nature of a regulatory system more open. Indeed, one of the first actions of Alun Michael, the new Home Office Minister, was to announce a further consultation on the issue of regulation. Also, while in Opposition the Labour Party Home Affairs front bench presented the image of being more open to wider and comprehensive regulation. The in-house sector, however, was — as far as we are aware — never mentioned as a sector to be considered. If this were to be the case, it could cause a number of problems. First, it might cause confusion amongst the public, with, for instance, two shopping centres next to one another, one with contract security staff and regulated, and another with in-house staff and not. Second, there are also some firms who mix security by employing both in-house and contract staff working side by side. One could therefore have the even more bizarre situation of licensed and unlicensed staff working next to one another doing similar work. Finally, one would be excluding a significant sector from regulation — that might also grow — limiting the impact of regulation.

The type of regulation introduced could also affect the balance between contract and in-house, which in the context of this chapter would also raise a number of further questions. For if only the contract sector was subject to regulation which was comprehensive and therefore led to an increase in the costs of security to those organisations purchasing the services from companies currently operating with minimum standards, the increased costs which would arise might drive some organisations to set up their own cheaper in-house security departments, given that to many organisations security is a 'grudge' cost, with the cheapest to be bought. The lower costs might still be achieved because there would be no statutory minimum standards to be met. If this happened on a large scale, the overall standards of the sector would not rise, and thus the impact on increasing the risks to offenders would be limited.

On the other hand, might the improved standards of the contract sector as a consequence of comprehensive regulation lead some organisations currently using in-house to choose contract? After all, in our original research on in-house organisations one of the reasons for retaining in-house was the poor standards of contract security, which should be largely addressed with comprehensive regulation. This scenario might also arise if both sectors were comprehensively regulated, as the increased costs for some in-house security departments might lead to some decision makers choosing contract.

These are important questions that are very difficult to answer without further research into the two sectors. The consequences of not seriously addressing them could have important implications for the future success of any regulatory system. However, in the absence of more comprehensive research we did conduct a small survey of the original in-house respondents to the study reported in the first volume of *Crime at Work*. The results offer at best a guide to how some security professionals responsible for in-house departments might react to regulation. The following questions were posed.

Table 3. Attitudes of surveyed in-house sector to statutory regulation

---

Q1. If a statutory licensing system were introduced for only the contract guarding sector would it make you

a. Less likely to contract out?	13%
b. More likely to contract out?	-
c. No change?	87%
(n = 23)	

Q2. If a statutory licensing system were introduced for both the contract and in-house guarding sector would it make you

a. Less likely to contract out?	14%
b. More likely to contract out?	5%
c. No change?	82%
(n = 22)	

Note, percentages rounded to nearest whole number: hence they do not necessarily add up to 100 per cent.

If representative, the results suggest that for most of the organisations surveyed — who currently use in-house security — the decision on which form of security to use will be unaffected by whatever type of regulation is introduced. Those surveyed were also asked to identify whether there should be statutory regulation and if so whether it should be of only contract or in-house as well. All were in favour of regulation, with 62% favouring contract only and 38% both contract and in-house.

The above research does not consider the potential reaction of those organisations using contract security whose main priority is cost, and who might be tempted, if regulation increases costs and is applied only to the contract sector, to establish cheaper in-house departments. Research into their attitudes on this issue is crucial, as their decisions will be the most important for the overall raising of standards in this sector, should a comprehensive regulatory system be introduced only for the contract sector. However, we would suspect that their cost considerations will remain critical, and if contract security becomes more expensive and only it is subject to regulation, it seems likely that a significant element will move to cheaper forms of in-house security. This will lessen the impact of regulation and thus the overall impact in increasing the risks to offenders.

Conclusion

This chapter has considered the rationale for organisations using contract security services, which is a significant strategy used by organisations to increase the risk to offenders. It started by examining the structure of the static manned guarding sector and then moved on to consider the rationale for using contract security. Ultimately the decision on which security strategy to use is peculiar to an organisation. However, this chapter offered some of the many general reasons why some organisations choose contract security. These included the cost benefits of doing so, the ability to hire expertise, the greater flexibility offered, compulsion, to transfer liabilities, higher standards, the prestige and image of the contractor, and problems with in-house security. The chapter then went on to consider the potential impact of statutory regulation. Different forms of regulation are likely to have different impacts upon the standards of private security and therefore the risk to offenders. It identified some causes for concern should in-house security be excluded from any regulatory system and the impact a regulatory system might have on the decision to use in-house security.

Without further research, however, it is difficult to assess accurately what the impact of regulation might have on the balance between in-house and contract security. It should therefore be a priority for research to be conducted in this area so the most informed decisions about the nature of a regulatory system for this sector can be made. We believe that it is essential that regulation is applied to both contract and in-house security. Not to do so would risk the regulatory system being undermined by serious loopholes and ultimately reducing the risk to offenders. However, we would not want to create a system that significantly changed the balance between the two sectors. It is essential that the regulatory system that emerges should be flexible enough to address these challenges. This can only be achieved if there is a greater knowledge of what the impact of regulation might be. These findings at least represent the beginning of trying to find these answers.

Notes

1   Mark Button is a lecturer at the Institute of Police and Criminological Studies (IPCS), University of Portsmouth; and Bruce George is Member of Parliament for Walsall South.

All correspondence should be directed to IPCS, University of Portsmouth, Portsmouth PO1 2QQ (email: mark.button@port.ac.uk).

2   Button, M. and George, B. (1994) Why Some Organisations Prefer In-house to Contract Security Staff. In, Gill, M. (ed.) *Crime at Work*. Vol. I. Leicester: Perpetuity Press.

3   There are also many other professionals who have responsibility for making security decisions such as line managers, personnel managers, facilities managers, safety managers, to name a few. Many security managers may not have this responsibility but advise others with responsibility for the decision.

4   One of the few examples is Phillips, S. and Cochrane, R. (1988) *Crime and Nuisance in the Shopping Centre: A Case Study in Crime Prevention*. Crime Prevention Unit Paper 16. London: Home Office.

5   Speech by the Rt Hon Jack Straw MP to the 1997 Annual BSIA Lunch.

6   Home Office (1996) *Regulation of the Contract Guarding Sector of the Private Security Industry*. London: Home Office.

7   British Security Industry Association (BSIA) (1994a) *The UK Manned Guarding Market*. Worcester: BSIA.

8   Ibid.

9   Jones, T. and Newburn, T. (1995) How Big is the Private Security Sector? *Policing and Society*. Vol. 5, pp 221-232.

10   Confederation of European Security Services (COESS) (1991) *Private Security: An EC Market Analysis*. Holland: COESS.

11   BSIA (1994a), op cit.

12   Jones and Newburn, op cit.

13   Button and George, op cit.

14   BSIA (1994b) *Attitudes to the UK Manned Guarding Market*. Worcester: BSIA.

15   Pinkerton Security Services (1995) *Market Research Report 1995*. Richmond: Pinkerton Security Services.

16   BSIA (1994a), op cit.

17   South, N. (1988) *Policing for Profit*. London: Sage.

18   Button and George, op cit.

19   Ibid.

20   The M25 is the orbital motorway around London.

21   Cohen, L. and Reeve, T. (1997) Job Offers Fall Short of Industry Standards. *Security Management and Industry Today*. October.

22   BSIA (1994b), op cit.

23   Public Services Privatisation Research Unit (U.d) *Security Services - Unison CCT Sector Analysis*. London: UNISON.

24   Sarre, R. (1994) The Legal Powers of Private Police and Security Providers. In Moyle, P.

(ed.) *Private Prisons and Police*. Leichhardt: Pluto Press.

25   The Corps was founded in 1859 and is almost certainly the oldest contract security company in Great Britain.

26   See Home Affairs Committee (HAC) (1995) *The Private Security Industry*. Volume I and II. HC 17, I & II. London: HMSO.

27   George, B. and Button, M. (1998) Too Little Too Late? An Assessment of Recent Proposals for the Private Security Industry in the United Kingdom. *Security Journal*. Vol. 9, No. 1, pp 1-7.

28   For a discussion of the five different models of regulation see George, B. and Button, M. (1997) Private Security Regulation: Lessons from Abroad for the United Kingdom. *International Journal of Risk, Security and Crime Prevention*. Vol. 2, No. 3, pp 187-199.

29   Police Foundation and Policy Studies Institute (PF/PSI) (1996) *The Role and Responsibilities of the Police*. London: PF/PSI.

Index

Partners in Crime Prevention

Reliance is an established market leader in the provision of contract security management, manpower and electronic surveillance services. We employ over 6,500 people from a network of offices throughout Great Britain.

PARTNERSHIP

We place the highest value on partnership with our customers and on innovative management practices which promote employee involvement, skills enhancement and accountability. Our business culture has as its basis a fundamental commitment to continuous improvement in every aspect of our work.

Our constant priority is anticipating our customers' needs and meeting them speedily and effectively. Our success has been built on long term partnerships with our customers in which we provide services and products of the highest quality and value.

MULTI AGENCY APPROACH

We believe that as a leading supplier of contract security services we have an obligation to promote the work of fellow crime prevention agencies and work in partnership with them to reduce the effects of crime on business, to the benefit of the wider community.

Recently we have extended our efforts to make available our experience in best practice on a wide range of security and crime prevention topics. Working with local Police and other specialists, we have held a series of seminars around the country and produced a number of handbooks on key topics that have been welcomed by the business community.

For more information contact
Reliance Security Services Ltd
Marketing Department, Boundary House, Cricketfield Road, Uxbridge UB8 1QG
Telephone 01895 205000 or Email Ian.Dollimore@RelianceSecurity.co.uk